M
Themes in
Sociological
Theory

Major Themes in Sociological Theory

Second Edition

Calvin J. Larson

University of Massachusetts, Boston

DAVID McKAY COMPANY, INC.
NEW YORK

MAJOR THEMES IN SOCIOLOGICAL THEORY
Second Edition

Copyright © 1973 and 1977 by David McKay Company, Inc.

MANUFACTURED IN THE UNITED STATES OF AMERICA

Developmental Editor: Edward Artinian
Editorial and Design Supervisor: Nicole Benevento
Design: Pencils Portfolio, Inc.
Manufacturing and Production Supervisor: Donald W. Strauss
Composition: Fuller Typesetting of Lancaster
Printing and Binding: Haddon Craftsmen

Library of Congress Cataloging in Publication Data
Larson, Calvin J.
    Major themes in sociological theory.

    Bibliography: p.
    Includes index.
    1. Sociology—Addresses, essays, lectures.
I. Title.
HM24.L35 1977   301'.01   77-77775
ISBN 0-679-30348-0

For Edith, Erik, and Adam

Preface to the first edition

This volume is an outgrowth of experience gained in teaching courses in sociological theory. One impression acquired from this encounter is the lack of interest on the part of most students in anything written over one or two years ago. Soon, undoubtedly, along with the ever-quickening tempo of life in America, the period of relevance will be measured in days. Regardless of conditioning factors, the American student reveals a rather extreme sense of confidence in the originality of what he considers to be the present scene. Concomitantly, there is a tendency to neglect and underestimate not only the importance of so-called historical contributions per se, but also their manner of influence on and relevance for the present. This is unfortunate. Ideas have a way of fading out and reappearing in similar and different contexts, and it is important that the reasons for particular patterns be noted and analyzed. If they are not, continuity of experience is lost and the present lacks perspective.

Another impression obtained from teaching sociological theory is that often students (graduates and undergraduates) tend to approach the subject of theory much as one would expect seminarians to approach the study of theology: as an abstract truth system which enables them to obtain a meaningful orientation and guide to a complex range of thought. Students need to gain some personal (emotional as well as intellectual) perspective on the overall mission of science and the goals of the science of society. It is difficult to gauge the strength of this need, but I suspect that indifference to its existence and importance has discouraged many able students from continuing their sociological studies.

Furthermore, though there is some reticence on the part of students to express themselves on the subject (perhaps because of the hesitancy of many instructors to entertain certain historical and speculative hypotheses seriously), there is, nonetheless, considerable interest in interpretations of the nature of scientific progress. What, they would like to know, is the process of scientific development? Can one talk about scientific progress in the sense of movement toward a definite stage of knowledge; or must one be content merely to note movement from levels of ignorance?

Most students seek knowledge of methods, techniques, and strategies to integrate and structure particular kinds of data. Interest here revolves around such questions as: What varieties of sociological perspectives and frames of reference are available to shed light on which types of problems? What difference does it make if one looks at human behavior from one vantage point rather than another? Is the essence of a behavioral event in the eye of the beholder or in the phenomena observed? Are sociological phenomena different from other behavioral phenomena? What, in particular, is the relationship and difference between psychological facts and sociological facts? If all behavioral facts are unique to some degree, are there not, nevertheless, general laws of human behavior?

Although it is contrary to the traditional way of presenting initial exposure to sociological theory, the material in this book is presented with basic subjects accorded less attention than the orientations and strategies behind their interpretation. The effect of this approach is to produce combinations that may appear not only irregular but also meaningless. For example, customarily the works of Emile Durkheim and Karl Marx are presented as illustrative of opposite strands in the development of social theory. The one is said to be the apostle of order and harmony, the other of change and conflict. Nevertheless, the works of the two are presented here as having emanated from a common epistemological assumption, namely, that sociological phenomena are unique products of natural evolution and exist "outside" or independently of individual consciousness. Furthermore, both sought to identify the bearing of social variables on the activities of men who must relate to one another under the conditions of complex industrial society. It is this common orientation which enables us to refer to both as sociologists. However important this fact may be in itself, the point made here is that by examining the underpinnings of subjects studied, one is enabled not only to connect seemingly disparate theoretical efforts, but also to gauge the difference between what a group of practitioners is working toward and what individual investigators hope to accomplish.

Correlatively, some students search for the epistemological underpinnings of the discipline and science in general. Questions involving the sources, purposes, and functions of the basic scientific as well as the particular sociological perspective are of key concern. Recently students have begun to insist on answers to their questions and problems on a more personal and subjective level than has hitherto been overtly encouraged in academic training. Traditional conceptions of scientific objectivity based on value neutrality and ethical control have encouraged the stance of the distant, detached, and aloof observer. It is being asserted that this position may be more a convenient rationalization for status protection than a meaningful concession to the canons of science. The aloof approach, it is said, fosters an unnatural distance between respondent and social scientist which may protect and insulate the latter from getting involved in controversial situations but which hinders rather than facilitates accurate awareness of the social condition of people variously situated in the social structure. The point is being made that to know is to become involved. To become involved is to assume personal and ethical responsibility for doing something about alleviating arbitrary social constraint.

In one form or another, the humanistic, ethical, and scientific concerns of contemporary students have always been present to some degree in sociological thought. It is one of the main purposes of this volume to identify their presence and meaning in the works of sociologists past and present.

I would like to acknowledge the assistance of my wife Edith in the preparation of this book. Her astute sense of syntax has enabled me to overcome many an apparent impasse. I am also indebted to Edward Artinian of David McKay. Through the "ups and downs" of this effort Ed maintained an encouraging attitude. And finally, I wish to pay homage to all those whose contributions I have had the great pleasure of working with. I have endeavored to remain faithful to their intentions. Any sins of commission are mine, not theirs.

Preface to the second edition

For the second edition of this book, new material has been added in chapters 2, 3, and 5, and some additions have been made to the Glossary. The chapter alterations more fully develop or clarify the ideas and contributions of Dahrendorf, Marx, Merton, Sumner, Ward, and Weber while leaving intact the basic structure of the book.

The goal of the book remains the same: to introduce the undergraduate to the structure and content of sociological theory. The first chapter identifies basic components of social theory—for example, concepts, constructed types, and propositions—and their interrelationship, in order to provide the student with a framework for locating and comparing the contributions of the scholars discussed in chapters 2 through 6. The last chapter examines philosophical problems and issues in contemporary sociology in terms of the goals of the discipline, the moral and ethical dilemmas that confront the social scientist, and the uses to be made of sociological data. This chapter seeks to provide the student with questions to consider in deciding what stand to take on controversial subjects.

I recommend the use of this book with primary sources. To become intimately aware of the theoretical foundations of the discipline, students should be introduced to original work of the writers discussed as soon as possible. Without a guidebook such as this one, however, initial attempts to comprehend the translated works of Durkheim, Marx, Weber, and other innovators can be an overwhelming if not a totally discouraging experience.

Preface to the second edition

Contents

Major Themes in Sociological Theory

ONE · The components
of sociological theory
and their interrelationship

"Today," says George Homans, "we should stop talking to our students about sociological theory until we have taught them what a theory is." [1] This statement suggests that the substance of sociological theory should be discussed *after* the structure of scientific theory has been identified. It is the main purpose of this chapter to identify the various structural forms and components of scientific theory.

Theory and Research

Before getting into the structural character of scientific theory, some remarks are in order concerning the relationship between theory and research. Today, most sociologists matter-of-factly assume the interdependence of theory and research, but they would be hard pressed if asked to specify where one leaves off and the other begins. As far as that revered archetype, "the working scientist," is concerned, all the essential phases of his work, including the selection and application of technological apparatus, involve theoretical analysis. Indeed, his business is theory building by means of the application of the scientific method to a relevant problem. In order to accomplish his task, he can, and often does, make certain theoretical distinctions according to data-collection stages. Thus, a working scientist may distinguish between pre-data-collection, during-data-collection, and post-data-

1

collection strategy. Before undertaking an investigation, a scientist customarily states his theory and specifies the hypothesis(es) to be studied. After initiating research, he may encounter experiences that suggest a need to modify or revise his initial design. Finally, after completing an experiment, he may choose to examine his findings from different theoretical perspectives. The crux of the matter is that the working scientist is so constantly engaged in relating theory to observation, and vice versa, that it is somewhat foreign for him to think of theory and research as meaningfully separable scientific tasks. How, he sometimes asks in an exasperated tone, can one talk about scientific theory apart from a particular body of data?

Because people do write about theory apart from specific research, the working social scientist is inclined to distinguish between "grounded theory" and "grand theory," although in this case the natural antonym, and probably the more preferred term, would be "ungrounded theory." To Glaser and Strauss, for example, grounded theory means "the discovery of theory from data systematically obtained from social research." [2] Furthermore, they say, "Our basic position is that generating grounded theory is a way of arriving at theory, suited to its supposed uses. We shall contrast this position with theory generated by logical deduction from a priori assumptions." [3] To put it briefly, the working scientist requires that theory be anchored solidly in the empirical world. Too often the working scientist's position has not been appreciated as much as it should be, but there is another side in the matter.

In sociology, as in all the sciences, some individuals have assumed the role of theorist apart from conducting research of their own—at least in the usual scientific sense. Such persons may take upon themselves the task of synthesizing the diverse findings of investigators involved in a wide variety of studies, perhaps from a number of disciplines. The role has deep historical roots in sociology and is a valuable one. Even though his work is much maligned or ignored by contemporary sociologists, Herbert Spencer's fanciful notions as to the similarity between an organism and a society contributed to the rationale behind the current systems approach to the study of human groups. One should not, therefore, say that the strictly theoretically oriented have nothing valuable to contribute to scientific work.

The problem is that those who have formulated general or grand theory have frequently revealed a tendency to avoid an important responsibility of the scientifically oriented. They have shown a penchant for presenting their analyses without adequately explaining how it was that they were able to arrive at certain conclusions rather than others. If an author does not take it upon himself to specify the sources and contexts of his ideas, it is virtually impossible to appraise the validity and utility of his work logically. It should not be surprising, therefore, that general or grand theorists have frequently been accused of believing that their powers of reason are unique, so original as to preclude explanation. Hence, more often than not, the personal style of the grand theorist rather than the content of his work comes to be the focal point not only of his detractors but also his admirers. As C. Wright Mills has pointed out: "To those who do not claim to understand [grand theory], but who like it very much—and there are many of these—it is a wondrous maze, fascinating precisely because of its often splendid lack of intelligibility." [4] The whole effect is to remove from consideration the objectivity essential to the scientific method.

While grand theory may be the most blatant example of an abstract impressionistic approach to the study of social phenomena, sociology as a whole is rife with lesser examples. Sociology, perhaps more than any other social science, has been criticized for its excessive jargon. Some of the most severe critics of the prevalance of confusing terminology in sociology have been sociologists themselves. Here are the words of one perturbed sociologist: "Our field of study is plagued by loose thinking concealed in technical terms that are ill defined." [5] The reasons for the omnipresence of jargon in sociology are many, but often they can be traced to attempts to compensate for poor methodological technique by means of hopefully effective rhetoric. Other reasons frequently cited range from lack of observational experience to lack of immersion in an authentic empirical problem.

The upshot of this discussion is that sociologists are not in firm agreement as to the proper methods of originating and developing scientific theory. While all seem to agree that theory should initially be based on something scientifically verifiable, they disagree as to what the inductive procedure entails. To some, induction is accomplished solely by means of the naked eye in combination with an ability to grasp intuitively the essence of what is observed. For others, establishing a scientifically valid premise is a problem of measurement. This entails step-by-step analysis by means of reliable instruments such as a carefully constructed questionnaire. As C. Wright Mills saw the issue,

> Serious differences among social scientists occur not between those who would observe without thinking and those who would think without observing; the differences have rather to do with what kinds of thinking, what kinds of observing, and what kinds of links, if any, there are between the two.[6]

The Components of Sociological Theory

If sociologists differ in important ways about what constitutes basic scientific procedure, we should expect their conceptions of theory to reflect this difference. In point of fact, it must be emphasized at the outset that theory is one of the most amorphous terms in science. To one writer, it is also "one of the most misused and misleading terms in the vocabulary of the social scientist."[7] In scope, it may be as broad as all thought or as narrow as a single thought. The word may be applied to the thinking process per se or only to its results and conclusions. In form it may vary from complete conjecture to solid confirmation, from unarticulated impression to precisely defined prediction.

Probably, one most often thinks of theory in the sense of speculative reasoning, that is, as a possible interpretation or explanation for the behavior, character, form, or whatever it may be that we wish to understand about something. While scientists, too, think of theory as something tentative, they also view it as having more substance than a mere hunch. To some, a "theory is an explanation of the relationships between phenomena which is not as solidly established as a law, but is more than a mere hypothesis." [8] To others, however, a theory is "a hypothesis which has undergone verification and which is applicable to a large number of related phenomena." [9]

On the one hand theory is thought of as something that connects the results of tested hypotheses toward the aim of becoming law. At some point, in other words, tentative reasoning (theory) is viewed as giving way to accepted fact (law). On the other hand, all of science is interpreted as theoretical in that its ideas and findings never can be said to transcend entirely the realm of tentativeness. All science is hypothetical; some interpretations of findings simply have greater generalizability and are felt to be more valid than others. While these two views may be held in a complementary fashion, they may also form the basis of quite different interpretations of the way to generate theory in terms of interrelating the elements of its different stages. The following are representative of the components or subtypes of theory and how they may be organized in stages or levels of complexity:

1. Concept–construct–constructed type
2. Frame of reference–conceptual scheme
3. Hunch–hypothesis–theorem–postulate
4. Proposition–axiom–law
5. Model—paradigm

Several points must be noted about this list. First of all, any one of the terms may be referred to as theory. The term *theory*, however, is most applicable to the totality. Second, some of the listed combinations (such as model and paradigm) may or may not be used synonymously. Sometimes a stronger, more impressive term is used than may be called for; for example, the use of the word *model* instead of the less impressive sounding *hypothesis*. Nevertheless, each term may be interpreted as conveying a distinctive meaning.

Third, regardless of their diverse manner of interpretation, terms such as the above may refer to both the means and the ends of scientific work. For example, to some the discovery of laws is the goal of science. To others laws are useful insofar as they describe the limits of existing knowledge and suggest explanations for new and different subjects.

Finally, while the sequence is subject to considerable variation, the ordered listing may be interpreted as describing a continuum which moves from the least to the most advanced level of explanation. What, then, is the relationship of terms within and between the five categories?

1. Concept–Construct–Constructed Type A concept, says Ely Chinoy, "is a general term that refers to all members of a particular class of objects, events, persons, relationships, processes, ideas—of any kind of unit or entity." [10] Concepts describe the objects of everyday human discourse and the particular phenomena of sociological analysis. They are used to label and categorize abstract ideas as well as physically observable entities. Regardless of what they describe, they serve to facilitate communication by focusing language and making it more accurate. Thus, the word *chair* identifies a seating device that can appear in numerous sizes and shapes. Lacking the concept *chair*, we would have to have a separate word for all the objects which we now subsume under a single label. Furthermore, each time a new object was identified or created, or the shape or function of an existing object happened to be altered, new words would have to be coined to describe these "different" things. The result, no doubt, would be the existence of literally thousands of words known only to a few individuals. In such a situation, each individual would effectively come to speak his own language. Although not to such an extreme degree, this is similar to what happens in the case of any scientific discipline.

One of the major tasks of science is the discovery of patterns of relationship in nature. Discovery in science often involves knowledge of syntheses which require unique designation in order to portray their differentiating character. In metallurgy, for example, the word *pewter* identifies an alloy produced by a combination of tin and lead. And in sociology, the term *institution* is used to describe a particular clustering of roles and norms. Since more than one combination is possible between most elements, a separate nomenclature must be developed.

Furthermore, in order to discover something original it has often been found useful to vary the conceptual manner of interpretation. For example, by viewing authority as a property of subordinates rather than an attribute of superiors, Chester Barnard was able to uncover a number of factors not previously appreciated or recognized.[11] It is certain that language patterns influence to the point of restricting the individual's possible interpretations of the world. As one observer put it: "Whatever cannot be named cannot be observed." [12] Thus, in order to see something new and different, one may very well have first to change one's linguistic habits. The technique of free association in psychoanalysis is a method of gaining insight into one's character by deliberately altering customary patterns of verbal expression. We become so subtly but nonetheless firmly committed to certain symbolic habits that we must at times literally force ourselves to try different frames of reference within which to observe and interpret phenomena. Since the young are least likely to be rigidly committed to certain behavioral habits, it is not surprising that they rank high among the discoverers in science.

To discover something, then, is to an important degree a matter of original conceptualization. Not only must one hit upon a relevant perceptual context, but also one must be able to accurately and symbolically interpret what is seen. Interpretation occurs in several symbolic ways. Maps, diagrams, pictures, models, and for that matter, practically any visual aid known to man can be used by a scientist to communicate an impression. John Greenway has described the plight of Erasmus Darwin in the early part of the nineteenth century. Lacking a prescribed notational system, Darwin found it necessary to describe a chemical process by means of a poem. Today, says Greenway, a chemist would illustrate the natural formation of potassium nitrate as follows:

$$N_2 + O_2 \rightarrow 2NO$$
$$2NO + O_2 \rightarrow 2NO_2$$
$$4NO_2 + O_2 \rightarrow 2N_2O_5$$

$$N_2O_5 \begin{bmatrix} water \\ rain \end{bmatrix} + KOH = KNO_3$$

$$\downarrow \begin{array}{c} + \\ H_2O \end{array}$$

crystallization

Here is the way Erasmus Darwin described the same process:

> Hence orient nitre owes its sparkling birth
> And with prismatic crystals gems the earth,
> O'er tottering domes the filmy folliage crawls,
> Or frosts with branching plumes the mould'ring walls,
> As woos Azotic Gas the virgins Air
> And veils in crimson clouds the yielding fair.[13]

To conceive something new and to convey one's meaning of it adequately to others often requires innovative procedures. The situations in which innovation may be necessary are not as uncomplicated and obvious as they might appear to be. There are times when an individual must conceptually innovate in order to develop his own knowledge. But it must be kept in mind that the problems of the individual scientist may not be the fault of his particular discipline. An individual may, for example, alter or add to language for no other reason than his own vocabulary deficiencies. The words exist, he simply is not aware of them. This phenomenon is readily apparent in the vocabulary patterns of young children. There is also the embarrassing possibility that one's own conceptual breakthrough may turn out to be little more than commonplace knowledge described in different words. By way of illustration, here is the way the philosopher Max Black interpreted the basic working assumptions of social theorist Talcott Parsons: [14]

Talcott Parsons' Basic Assumptions	Translated
1. All human action is directed toward goals.	1. "Whenever you do anything, you're trying to get something done."
2. All human action is relational, in the sense of being a function of the actor's innate needs (or "viscerogenic needs"), his acquired orientations, and the particular situation in which he finds himself.	2. "What you do depends upon what you want, how you look at things, and the position you find yourself in."
3. All human response to stimuli has two distinct dimensions—is simultaneously cognitive and cathectic.	3. "You can't do anything without thinking and having feelings at the same time."
4. All human action involves selection between alternative orientations and responses.	4. "Human life is one long set of choices."
5. Selection (or evaluation) involves the use of standards.	5. "Choosing means taking what seems best for you or what others say is the right thing."
6. All interaction between actors involves complementarity of expectation, in the sense "that the action of each is oriented to the expectations of the other."	6. "When you deal with other people, you always have to take account of what they expect you to do."
7. Orientations and actions are organized in systems.	7. "There's a lasting pattern to the way people behave."
8. All the above principles apply to social systems of all levels of complexity, up to and including the total society, as well as to individuals.	8. "Families, business firms, and other groups of persons often behave surprisingly like persons."

"On the whole," says Black, "it seems to me, the component concepts of Parsons' scheme are laymen's concepts in the thin disguise of a technical-sounding terminology." [15] Interestingly enough, Parsons' response to Black, though quite elaborate, did not include reference to the alleged triteness of his concepts. The point, however, is quite important in this case, as Parsons' goal is the construction of a general frame of reference for the study of human society. As the issue now stands, there is some doubt as to the generalizability of his terms for they may not transcend a particular cultural and ideological milieu. In developing a scientific concept, one must take considerable pains to assess its interpretive range within the context of concern. In Parsons' case, interdisciplinary and cross-cultural examination of his concepts is clearly in order.

In order to appreciate the problems of conceptualizers such as Parsons, however, it is necessary to consider the fact that their task entails combining proper amounts of creative imagination and descriptive accuracy. They are expected to synthesize disparate detail and point the way to new perspectives on data; at the same time their readers often insist that their product remain firmly grounded in what they consider relevant.

Creative synthesis, in other words, is likely to be more welcome in some contexts than others. It is probably most appreciated when it paves the way for a solution to a riddle that has perplexed a number of investigators for some time. When a conceptualizer delves into an area not particularly problematic at the moment, his ideas are as likely as not to be either rejected or ignored. He may even be chided to the point of ridicule for "utopian" speculation.[16] Scientists, therefore, have the problem of reconciling how much of their conceptual work is to be recognized for its individual creativity as opposed to its group relatedness; that is, how different from or closely related it is to the contributions of their colleagues.

The role of creativity in conceptualization has been the subject of debates among philosophers for a number of years. The points of view of William Whewell and John Stuart Mill are classic and clearly reveal the two major positions on the subject. This is Whewell's point of view:

> When the Greeks, after long observing the motions of the planets, saw that these motions might be rightly considered as produced by the motion of one wheel revolving in the inside of another wheel, these Wheels were Creations of their minds, added to the Facts which they perceived by sense. And even if the wheels were no longer supposed to be material, but were reduced to mere geometrical spheres or circles, they were not the less products of the mind alone—something additional to the facts observed. The same is the case in all other discoveries. The facts are known, but they are insulated and unconnected, till the discoverer supplies from his own stores a Principle of Connexion. The pearls are there, but they will not hang together till someone provides the String. The distances and periods of the planets were all so many separate facts; by Kepler's Third Law they are connected into a single truth: but the Conceptions which this law involves were supplied by Kepler's mind, and without these, the facts were of no avail.[17]

Here is Mill's reaction to Whewell:

> Dr. Whewell maintains that the general proposition which binds together the particular facts and makes them, as it were, one fact, is not the mere sum of those facts, but something more, since there is introduced a conception of the mind, which did not exist in the facts themselves. . . .
>
> According to Dr. Whewell [Kepler's conception of an ellipse] was something added to the facts. He expresses himself as if Kepler had put something into the facts by his mode of conceiving them. But Kepler did no such thing. The ellipse was in the facts before Kepler recognized it, just as the island was an island before it had been sailed around. Kepler did not put what he had conceived into the facts, but saw it in them. A conception implies and corresponds to something conceived; and though the conception itself is not in the facts but in our mind, yet if it is to convey any knowledge relating to them, it must be a conception of something which really is in the facts, some property which they actually possess, and which they would manifest to our senses if our senses were able to take cognizance of it.[18]

To Whewell, conceptual discovery involves a creative addition of the mind of the observer to the facts observed. To Mill, conceptualization is strictly a process of conceiving or recognizing something that is in the facts themselves. We shall examine these ideas in more than one context in this volume. The task at hand now is to examine their impact on the relationship between a concept and a construct.

According to John C. McKinney, "All concepts are constructs that have been developed out of experience." [19] Furthermore, ". . . all concepts are generalizations and all generalization implies abstraction." [20] The claim here is that concepts are constructs because both are abstractions from observable phenomena. Few would dispute the notion that all human perception is imperfect in the sense that no one perceives phenomena distortion-free. It is generally accepted that human symbolic techniques derive from selective perception of objects. Going one step further, it may be said that objects are not only seen from limited vantage points, but also are ascribed characteristics that go beyond their substance. For example, in human history the element *gold* has undoubtedly been more often perceived in terms of its use as wealth than in terms of its physical qualities per se. If, then, McKinney means to say only that all human symbolization involves abstraction, we should most certainly agree with him that all concepts are constructs. However, abstraction from observables can also be viewed in terms of degree in which case all concepts are not constructs to the same extent.

An often cited and cogent distinction between levels of perception has been made by Hans Reichenbach. In his words,

When we attempt to construct a consistent system of laws for physical things, we are often compelled to introduce the assumption that there are certain other physical things that cannot be observed directly. For instance, in order to account for electrical phenomena we introduce the assumption that there is a physical entity, called electricity, which flows through wires or travels as waves through open space. What we observe are phenomena such as the deflection of a magnetic needle or the music coming from a radio receiver; electricity is never observed directly. For such physical entities I use the name *illata*, meaning "inferred things." They are distinguished from the concreta that make up the world of observable things. They are also distinguished from abstracta, which are combinations of concreta and are not directly observable because they are comprehensive totalities. For instance, the term "prosperity" refers to a totality of observable phenomena, of concreta, and is used as an abbreviation which sums up all these observables in their interrelationship. The illata are not combinations of concreta, but separate entities inferred from concreta, whose existence is merely made probable by the concreta.[21]

As William Catton has noted, while one has little difficulty in distinguishing between concreta and abstracta, the distinction between abstracta and illata may be troublesome.[22] It is important to keep in mind that both abstracta and illata derive from concreta. Concreta are those phenomena that are capable of being directly sensed by human faculties. Abstracta identify common properties among concreta. Illata are inferred from concreta.

Durkheim's approach to the study of suicide (to be outlined in the next chapter) may be used to illustrate how these terms might be applied in sociology. Thus, the act of suicide would constitute an *observable*, but mostly, of course, in the sense of being a potentially verifiable incident (concreta). Suicides manifest uniform rates of occurrence (abstracta). Suicide rates may be interpretable as effects of anomie, i.e., tears in the social fabric which wrench from people important social anchors (illata).

Suicide, suicide rates, and anomie are all concepts and human constructs. Yet, the construct which defines an observable is not intended to function in the same way as that which relates observables. The latter involves, or is a consequence of, a certain imaginative flexibility that goes beyond what is intended and given in the former. To be sure, and as John Stuart Mill pointed out, a unifying construct must describe something that is in the relationship between observable subjects. The mind, while potentially a creative and imaginative component, does not in the scientific world create something out of nothing.

In sociology, type constructs represent the extreme in terms of imaginative input. But even these originate from something observable. McKinney defines the constructed type "as a purposive, planned selection, abstraction, combination, and (sometimes) accentuation of a set of criteria with empirical referents that serves as a basis for comparison of empirical cases." [23] The main purpose of constructed types, says Mc-Kinney, "is to furnish a means by which concrete occurrences can be compared, potentially measured, and comprehended within a system of general categories that may be developed to comprise the types." [24] A constructed type furnishes a baseline from which to gauge the range of comparable phenomena.

Undoubtedly the most employed variety of constructed type in sociology is the *ideal type*. As conceived by Max Weber, an ideal type is an imagined extreme example of something which in fact does not exist, has never existed, may never exist, but could conceivably exist. It is, simply put, "a one-sided exaggeration or accentuation of the elements of a phenomenon." [25] It is a method of magnifying phenomena in order to make their shape and composition more readily apparent.

Perhaps the best-known example of an ideal type was proposed by Weber some years ago. Around the turn of the century, Weber noted that bureaucratic organization was to become a major concomitant of advanced industrialization. In order to gain perspective on existing bureaucracies, and to acquire knowledge of the dynamics of this type of social organization, Weber identified what he thought to be the key characteristics of bureaucracy and conceptualized them as they might exist in "ideal" form. These were delineated as follows:

I. There is the principle of fixed and official jurisdictional areas, which are generally ordered by rules, that is, by laws or administrative regulations.

1. The regular activities required for the purposes of the bureaucratically governed structure are distributed in a fixed way as official duties.

2. The authority to give the commands required for the discharge of these duties is distributed in a stable way and is strictly delimited by rules concerning the coercive means, physical, sacerdotal, or otherwise, which may be placed at the disposal of officials.

3. Methodical provision is made for the regular and continuous fulfillment of these duties and for the execution of the corresponding rights; only persons who have the generally regulated qualifications to serve are employed.

II. The principles of office hierarchy and of levels of graded authority mean a firmly ordered system of super- and subordination in which there is a supervision of the lower offices by the higher ones. . . .

III. The management of the modern office is based upon written documents ("the files"), which are preserved in their original or draught form. . . .

IV. Office management, at least all specialized office management—and such management is distinctly modern—usually presupposes thorough and expert training. . . .

V. When the office is fully developed, official activity demands the full working capacity of the official, irrespective of the fact that his obligatory time in the bureau may be firmly delimited. . . .

VI. The management of the office follows general rules, which are more or less stable, more or less exhaustive, and which can be learned.[26]

Span of control, chain of command, professionalization of work, fixed hours, rules—these are the elements of bureaucratic organization. The question for Weber was: by what means are they realized and what ends are served by their implementation?

It was not Weber's intention that the ideal type should be interpreted to be a theory or a hypothesis to be tested. Some have regarded it as a model or a paradigm, but we shall see that this, too, would not be an entirely correct interpretation. Most Weberian scholars tell us that the functions of the ideal type as conceived by Weber were heuristic in nature. That is, and in Weber's words, "The more sharply and precisely the ideal type has been constructed, thus the more abstract and unrealistic in this sense it is, the better it is able to perform its methodological functions in formulating the clarification of terminology, and in the formulation of classifications, and of hypotheses." [27]

Although based on observables, then, the ideal type does not have an empirical existence. Hence, it cannot be refuted because it is not subject to empirical confirmation. It contains no built-in safeguard against being misused in a stereotypical fashion. A stereotype has been defined as "a belief which is not held as an hypothesis buttressed by evidence but is rather mistaken in whole or in part for an established fact." [28] The same interpretation may apply to the ideal type. Generally speaking, a stereotype is thought of as something which limits one's perspective and an ideal type as something which broadens it. But, if a construct cannot be interpreted so as to be examined and rejected or confirmed by objective criteria, its continual and timeless presence may very well be conducive to its creeping into thought patterns as a stereotype.

In summary, and in Reichenbach's terminology, it may be said that concepts basically refer to *concreta*, constructs to *abstracta*, and constructed types to *illata*. That is, concepts fundamentally identify observables; constructs describe common properties among observables; and constructed types are inferences from concreta. The student must be aware, however, that sociologists are not always mindful of such distinctions and frequently use the terms interchangeably.

2. *Frame of Reference—Conceptual Scheme*   Basically, a frame of reference is a manner of focusing attention on certain concepts and constructs. It has been described as "the most general framework of categories in terms of which empirical work 'makes sense.'" [29] Since it is not possible, at least at present, to look at everything at once and from all possible

angles, one must decide what is important to observe, where it can most profitably be observed, and how it is to be observed. A frame of reference not only delimits a field of vision, but also conveys, either implicitly or explicitly, "a set of basic assumptions necessary to determine the subject matter to be studied and orientation toward such study." [30]

In a very real sense, a frame of reference is to sociology what a microscope is to biology or a telescope is to astronomy. All three are intended to function as neutral instruments that facilitate observation. Hopefully, a frame of reference will serve to permit a better understanding of the behavior patterns of units of analysis so that plausible interpretations of their activity can be introduced and examined.

A conceptual scheme describes an interrelated group of concepts that provide base points within a frame of reference. For example, the key conceptual components of the Parsonian action frame of reference are actors, situations, goals, normative standards, orientations, decision making, and "action." Parsons describes the frame of reference within which these concepts are applied as follows:

> The theory of action is a conceptual scheme for the analysis of the behavior of living organisms. It conceives of this behavior as oriented to the attainment of ends in situations, by means of the normatively regulated expenditure of energy. There are four points to be noted in this conceptualization of behavior: (1) Behavior is oriented to the attainment of ends or goals or their anticipated states of affairs. (2) It takes place in situations. (3) It is normatively regulated. (4) It involves expenditure of energy or effort or "motivation." [31]

Quite obviously, even though a conceptual scheme may serve to pinpoint analytical categories, it certainly may not thereby simplify the application of a frame of reference. Theoretically, for example, the content of a situation in the action scheme may vary from one man in a controlled milieu to all the people on earth in their natural habitat. One may be concerned with explaining an act of a single individual or the millions of acts of millions of people.

A distinguishing feature of a frame of reference, regardless of its degree of conceptualization, is that while it orients one toward certain phenomena in a certain way, it, nevertheless, allows great flexibility in terms of substantive input. In the case of the action frame of reference, for example, one may analyze the impact of situational objects (both human and nonhuman) on the behavior of an individual; the effect of individual actions on situational objects; or, the interaction patterns of people in a given social situation. Parsons, of course, would consider it necessary to undertake a complete inventory. In any case, a frame of reference is not unlike a roadside viewpoint overlooking a vast panoramic scene. It gives you something worth looking at but, depending on your stance, lets you put into it and take from it pretty much what you will.

In addition, though, a frame of reference should direct the perception of phenomena in such a way as to include the quality of dimension. A perspective that merely guides one into an intersection from a single direction may not be of much use when approaching it from another route. Ideally, the social field should be narrow enough to permit concentrated attention to important detail, but broad enough not to omit a slant on the shape and magnitude of relevant phenomena. It is by means of such methods that scientists acquire an idea as to how and why certain phenomena are interrelated, and frames of reference are useful insofar as they stimulate thought about patterns in nature and generate testable hypotheses.

3. *Hunch–Hypothesis–Theorem–Postulate* The difference between these four terms is basically one of degree. A hunch is little more than a strong intuitive impression. It is probably best described as an explanatory feeling about why something happens the way it does. The basis, that is, the logical justification of the intuition, is not usually immediately susceptible to accurate and logical articulation.

A hypothesis may be nothing more than a hunch; that is, a mere inkling of a connection between the behavior of conceptualized phenomena. It may also, however, take the form of a highly rationalized and empirically verifiable proposition.

Thus, to some social scientists a hypothesis is "any conjecture or surmise that states a relationship among variables." [32] The elementary type is referred to as a working hypothesis and frequently interpreted as "a preliminary assumption based on few, uncertain or obscure elements, which is used provisionally as a guiding norm in the investigation of certain phenomena." [33]

From another point of view, a hypothesis is a deduction from a verified proposition. In the words of Goode and Hatt:

> . . . a theory states a logical relationship between facts. From this theory other propositions can be deduced that should be true, if the first relationship holds. These deduced propositions are hypotheses.[34]

To them, and to many others as well, a hypothesis is a minor theory. It "states what we are looking for" and "leads to an empirical test." It is a proposition capable of empirical verification but not yet verified.

It is apparent that there is more than a semblance of circularity in the reasoning of those who discuss the relationship between a theory and a hypothesis. It is commonly claimed that all "scientific" hypotheses are derivations from empirically supportable theory. It is also typically asserted that every theory had its beginnings in an hypothesis. Hence, one man's hypothesis may be another's theory. It all depends on the aim and ingenuity of the investigator.

A theorem is generally defined as "any proposition which is demonstrated in terms of other more basic propositions." To Hans Zetterberg, theorems are hypotheses derived from basic postulates. The first step in developing deductive theory, he says, is to identify basic concepts. After concepts have been adequately delineated and defined, hypotheses may be formulated. Next, and in his words:

> We will select from among the hypotheses formulated a certain number to be the postulates of our theory. The postulates should be chosen so that all other hypotheses, *the theorems*, should be capable of derivation from these postulates.[35]

Zetterberg, then, considers all his propositions hypotheses. Postulates and theorems are hypotheses with different theoretical functions. The systematic or logical combination of postulates and theorems results in an axiomatic theory. Formalization of sociological theory along axiomatic lines is of major contemporary interest and will be discussed below.

4. *Proposition–Axiom–Law* A basic aim of structural work, such as conceptualization, the precise articulation of hypotheses, and the derivation of theorems from postulates, is objectively to wed thought to observation with one's goal, the uncovering of lawful relations among phenomena. Many scientists assume the search for laws to be the raison d'être of science and the foundation of scientific procedure. To Norman Campbell, for example, ". . . nothing can be admitted to the domain of science at all unless it is a law, for it is only the relations expressed by laws that are capable of universal agreement." [36] More directly, Campbell suggests that science "begins" when a number of practitioners agree that a relationship among verifiable phenomena has been established and forms the basis of all their individual efforts. What, then, is a scientific law?

According to R. B. Braithwaite, "While there is general agreement that a scientific law includes generalization, there is no agreement as to whether or not it includes anything else." [37] A common definition is the following: "A statement of an order or relation of phenomena which so far as known is invariable under the given conditions." [38] For example, Newton's law of gravitation states that the force of attraction between two bodies is proportional to the product of the masses of the two bodies, and inversely proportional to the square of the distance between them, and independent of their chemical nature or physical state and of intervening matter. Succinctly put, a scientific law is an accepted statement of relationship between empirically observable phenomena. Just why and how it is that certain kinds of explanations are accepted as scientific law is not readily apparent. The state of knowledge of a discipline, timing, context, and a host of other factors are always involved. Whatever the details of the case may be, it is important to recognize that a law is more than an observable uniformity in nature. Above all, it is an explanation of the relationship among variables which accounts for an observable pattern.

To constitute an acceptable explanation, a law must usually satisfy some kind of procedural rule or rules. Social scientists, in particular, would be loath to accept a statement of law that did not meet the canons of formal logic. There is some disagreement, however, as to the merits and validity of beginning the logical process with an untested and hypothetical proposition as opposed to one that has been empirically validated. These two positions are akin to what Albert Einstein referred to as "the eternal antithesis between the two inseparable components of our knowledge, the empirical and the rational. . . ." [39] In the case of sociology, the problem is one of reconciling abstract and ideal logical procedure with the limitations of existing empirical method. Most contemporary sociologists seem to feel that their techniques of observation and experimentation are not presently adequate for the task of discovering invariant relationships among complex social variables.

Instead of seeking the discovery of laws of human behavior, sociologists are more engaged in searching for statistical relationships among specifically sociological variables. For example, many studies have been made to examine the relationship between voting behavior and socioeconomic factors such as income, education, and occupation. Logical truths in the order of laws or principles are avoided in favor of the less pretentious-sounding propositions and postulates.

A proposition is the most general statement of relationship between variables. It is a flexible term whose variable components can be stated in a number of ways. For example, a proposition may take the form, if X, then Y, regardless of anything else; or if X, and only if X, then Y. The first proposition describes a "sufficient" relationship (an X is sufficient, or enough, to produce a Y), and the second a "necessary" relationship (X is necessarily required to produce Y).[40]

Some sociologists see the goal of the discipline to be the isolation of necessary and sufficient relationships which can be treated as axioms. An axiom may be defined as an established proposition which "though not necessarily true, is universally received." [41]

Isolation of axioms makes possible the construction of axiomatic theory. To Hans Zetterberg, axiomatic theory refers to "systematically organized, lawlike propositions about society that can be supported by evidence." [42] The following example, taken from George Homans' interpretation of the work of Emile Durkheim, is an illustration of the basic form of axiomatic theory:

(Postulate-Axiom)   1. In any social grouping, the *suicide rate* varies directly with the *degree of individualism* (egoism).

(Hypothesis-Theorem)   2. The *degree of individualism* varies with the *incidence of Protestantism.*

3. Therefore, the *suicide rate* varies with the *incidence of Protestantism.*

4. The *incidence of Protestantism* in Spain is low.

5. Therefore, *the suicide rate* in Spain is low.[43]

The italicized terms in the propositions are concepts or variables. Statements of relationship between variables should be capable of symbolic representation by signs such as x, y, and $=$. Using A to represent suicide rate, B for degree of individualism, C for incidence of Protestantism, and by accepting the rule that things equal to the same thing are equal to each other, the following logical structure can be seen to be behind the organization of that particular content:

$$\text{If } A = B$$
$$\text{and } B = C,$$
$$\text{then } A = C.$$

Hence, if C is low, then A also must be low.

According to Zetterberg, there is no such thing as scientific theory apart from that which follows a deductive format. Other so-called theoretical types are categorized as sociological classics, sociological criticism, and sociological taxonomy. In reference to the relationship between sociological theory and sociological classics, Zetterberg has written:

> . . . there is a habit of designating all the better sociological writings of older vintage as "social theory." Statistical studies of suicide, historical studies of the effect of religion on the economy, informal observations of the role of secrets in social life, and anything else written at least a generation ago is likely to be called "social theory." . . . An alternative and better term than "theory" for this material would be "sociological classics." [44]

While quite appealing for its neatness and because of its definiteness, axiomatic theory has not been much employed by sociologists, largely because of certain compelling methodological considerations. Costner and Leik have pointed out that basic deductive rules may or may not yield logically valid sociological theorems and axioms. Since most sociologists study relationships between variables by means of correlation coefficients, it must be decided, they suggest, how strong a statistical relationship must be arrived at before one can justify the identification of an axiom. That is, Costner and Leik pose the crucial question: under what statistical conditions is it valid to assume that $A = B$? [45]

Some argue that statistical analyses are too incomplete and imperfect to permit the kind of exact measurement necessary to arrive at valid axiomatic conclusions. Others claim that the use of statistics is an implicit if not explicit acknowledgment of an inability to isolate all relevant variables and establish precise links between those that can be identified. This is the way May Brodbeck states the position:

> The social scientist, striving to merit the honorific half of that title, settles for something less than perfection. Completeness being far beyond his grasp, he renounces it as a goal. The renunciation has its price and its rewards. Which face will turn up when a die is cast is determined by numerous

causes, the center of gravity of the die, the force with which it is thrown, and so on. An attempt to calculate the results of each throw by means of the laws of mechanics is practically hopeless, because of the difficulty in precisely measuring all the initial conditions. Instead, we represent, as it were, this multiplicity of causes by a probability distribution for the attribute in question. The use of the statistical concept marks our ignorance of all the influencing factors, a failure in either completeness or closure or, usually, both.[46]

Schwirian and Prehn have identified yet another point of detraction in the use of axiomatic theory. As they point out,

Unfortunately, the axiomatic model provides no criteria for decisions concerning the inclusion or exclusion of individual variables. Such a rationale is dependent upon the investigator's arguments.[47]

Put another way, the authors suggest that even though the structure of axiomatic theory may be set, its content is fundamentally subject to the ingenuity of the individual scientist. They feel that there is a need to develop explicit criteria for the determination of the susceptibility of variables to axiomatic interpretation.

To some, the Schwirian and Prehn criticism is merely simple validation for the overriding contribution of subjective and inherently unobjectifiable human creativity. To others, and apparently the majority of sociologists, the message is that much more needs to be known about axiomatic theory before it can give us with validity an objective interpretation of the empirical world.

One inference that may be drawn from this situation is that sociologists make little distinction between an empirical axiom and a scientific law. The standards of verification applied to each make them equally difficult to establish. In effect, the axiomatic theorist has been told that he cannot legitimately apply his scheme until he can demonstrate to his colleagues that his major premise has attained the status of confirmed law. The irony here is that axiomatic theory was proposed as a vehicle for the discovery of laws.

There is little doubt that theory building in sociology has reached something of an impasse with the methodological critique of axiomatic theory. Several alternative responses to the current predicament are possible: (1) wait for a methodological breakthrough; (2) accept ad hoc generalizations as the bases for theory building; or (3) treat axioms as hypotheses, i.e., hunches with at least some logical plausibility and empirical support. None of these is entirely satisfactory, although each has its adherents. Over all, the current situation resembles what Thomas Kuhn refers to as "the pre-paradigm" stage of scientific development.

5. *Model–Paradigm* Model and paradigm are most often thought of as synonymous terms. Standard dictionaries invariably define a paradigm as a model. In spite of their apparent equivalence, social scientists have managed to use them in such varying contexts that they cannot be assumed to be different ways of describing the same thing. After surveying a number of publications, one observer concluded that ". . . the terms 'model' and 'paradigm' are used with divergent meanings and . . . often it is not clear which meaning is intended." [48]

Of the two terms, social scientists reveal a preference for *model*. Perhaps this is mainly due to the fact that the term is frequently associated with mathematics—a subject of considerable interest to contemporary social scientists. Currently, the word *paradigm* seems to be interpreted as having a more general and abstract meaning than model.

The following are common dictionary definitions of *model*: a copy; a miniature representation of something; a pattern; a design; an archetype; anything that may serve as an imitative example; a preliminary outline; a detailed plan.[49] In all these, "one thing is regarded as the pattern or example of another." [50] Typically, then, a model is thought of as a "known" or a "given" which serves as a constant reference point. In science, however, nature is the point of reference and models are something devised to replicate some of its patterns. Model building in science is an attempt physically to describe the unknown and partially understood by a trial and error process. Watson and Crick, for example, "solved" the structure of the DNA molecule by means of model building.[51] Their goal, it must be emphasized, was to reproduce a pattern in nature exactly. A physical model enabled them to see more clearly qualities and relations of objects only dimly perceived by other available instruments. By moving back and forth from model to nature they were able eventually to arrive at an acceptable reconstruction of their subject.

An interesting question is: did Watson and Crick have a model before they arrived at their final success? It is certain that their answer to the query would be a resounding negative. Interestingly enough, some social scientists would give an affirmative response because it is their opinion that a model is something untested or unconfirmed—that is, a working hypothesis. Still others equate model with scientific law. According to Robert Nordberg: " 'Model' is sometimes a completely arbitrary construct; sometimes it is synonymous with 'hypothesis'; sometimes, with 'theory'; sometimes, even with 'law.' "[52] Laws may be models. As May Brodbeck points out, "If the laws of one theory have the same form as the laws of another theory, then one may be said to be a model for the other."[53] The essential requirement is that the model be isomorphic with its referent. That is, that the model have the same form as its subject. This does not necessarily mean that a model must be an exact copy of something. It may be a miniature replica. So long as the basic elements of an original are contained in the same relationship to one another in the model, isomorphism may be attained.

Some social scientists do not accept isomorphism as necessary to define a model. To the psychologist Melvin Marx, for example,

> A model is an conceptual analogue, generally of a physical or mathematical nature, which is used to suggest empirical research. Once a particular model has been selected, the researcher is not concerned at all about modifying the model itself on the basis of data obtained by means of it; this insensitivity to data is a major difference between the model and other forms of theory.[54]

From this definition we are led to believe that model is a generic term used to describe any heuristic theoretical construct—particularly an "ideal type." In effect, there are those who interpret a model as something "analytical" and those who view it as something "empirical." [55] Of course, an empirical model invariably has analytical functions. In their initial stages, empirical models are inclined to deflect and rechannel observation by leading to the discovery of previously unrecognized data. An analytical or heuristic model, however, does not have built-in features which enable it to become empirical fact. Thus, we must ask the inevitable question: is the same term being used to describe different things; or is the same thing being described from different perspectives? The answer contains a little of both and considerable ambiguity. As Brodbeck summarizes the point:

> The same term applied to . . . different kinds of things is of course confusing. Moreover, the resulting ambiguity is quite unnecessary, since other terms are at hand which adequately characterize these further uses. "One thing, one word" is still a good idea.[56]

The term *model* not only may have more than one meaning, but also it has a synonym which may be used to refer to something not of the same form and function. For the most part, the word *paradigm* is used interchangeably with model. However, the scientist of science, Thomas S. Kuhn, has interpreted the term in a decidedly unique way with significant effects.

To Kuhn, a paradigm is a universally recognized scientific achievement that for a time provides model problems and solutions for a community of scientists. Examples include Einstein's general theory of relativity, Copernican astronomy, Kepler's laws of planetary motion, and so on. The essential quality of all these achievements is that they come to generate a consensus among scientists as to their validity. As John Ziman points out, "Science is unique in striving for, and insisting on, a consensus." Furthermore, he says,

Science is not merely *published* knowledge or information. Anyone may make an observation, or conceive a hypothesis, and, if he has the financial means, get it printed and distributed for other persons to read. Scientific knowledge is more than this. Its facts and theories must survive a period of critical study and testing by other competent and disinterested individuals, and must have been found so persuasive that they are almost universally accepted. The objective of Science is not just to acquire information nor to utter all non-contradictory notions; its goal is a *consensus* of rational opinion over the widest possible field.[57]

A paradigm, then, has more general and fundamental scientific functions than a model. Here is the way Kuhn attempts to differentiate the two:

In its established usage, a paradigm is an accepted model or pattern, and that aspect of its meaning has enabled me, lacking a better word, to appropriate "paradigm" here. But it will shortly be clear, that the sense of "model" and "pattern" that permits the appropriation is not quite the one usual in defining "paradigm." In grammar, for example, amo, amas, amat is a paradigm because it displays the pattern to be used in conjugating a large number of other Latin verbs. . . . In this standard application, the paradigm functions by permitting the replication of examples any one of which could in principle serve to replace it. In science, on the other hand, a paradigm is rarely an object of replication. Instead, like an accepted judicial decision in the common law, it is an object for further articulation and speculation under new or more stringent conditions.[58]

In Kuhn's perspective, a scientific model is meant to be an exact copy of something with a definite form. A scientific paradigm, he says, while certainly empirically relevant, is seldom so exact a structure as to permit empirical replication. In fact, it is the suggestiveness of its incompleteness rather than the exactness of its completeness that is the distinguishing feature of a paradigm. The paradigm, by demonstrating promising applicability, acts as a catalyst in that it induces a group of scientists to study particular problems from a certain interpretive and experimental standpoint. "Paradigms," explains Kuhn, "are the source of the methods, problem-field and standards of solution accepted by any mature scientific community at any given time." [59]

In Kuhn's scheme, there are three crucial phases in the evolution of a scientific discipline: the pre-paradigm phase, the paradigm phase, and the post-paradigm phase. The pre-paradigm phase is "characterized by continual competition between a number of distinct views of nature." Several schools of thought vie with each other in hopes of converting all to their particular point of view. Each feels that if its perspective were accepted and practiced, the discipline would concern itself with the most relevant subjects and pursue the most promising line of development. Eventually, one or another wins out and the paradigm phase begins.

It is from the point of the establishment and acceptance of a paradigm that a science marks its progress. Kuhn offers the idea that scientific knowledge accumulates *from* a certain level of ignorance rather than toward some definite goal. As he says,

> The developmental process [described in his book] has been a process of evolution from primitive beginnings—a process whose successive stages are characterized by an increasingly detailed and refined understanding of nature. But nothing that has been or will be said makes it a process of evolution toward anything. Inevitably that lacuna will have disturbed many readers. We are all deeply accustomed to seeing science as the one enterprise that draws constantly nearer to some goal set by nature in advance. [60]

Paradigms do not last forever. Sooner or later, they fail to provide adequate explanations for observed events and recognized problems. Loss of confidence in a paradigm may become so severe as to provoke a state of crisis. This is a period of insecurity and discouragement due to the absence of solid direction for investigation. Debates occur among those who defend the paradigm, those who wish to reform it, those who wish it to be abandoned, and those who present new paradigms for consideration. In time the situation may eventuate in a revolution. To Kuhn, scientific revolutions are "those non-cumulative developmental episodes in which an older paradigm is replaced in whole or in part by an incompatible new one." [61] The use of the modifier "non-cumulative" is consistent with Kuhn's interpretation of the nature of scientific progress. That is, he wishes to emphasize that scientific revolutions do not denote qualitative advances in the sense of movement toward a fixed point of knowledge. However, he most certainly views them as the expression of accumulated difficulties.

A question that comes to mind is, how does a paradigm differ from a theory? According to Kuhn, ". . . not all theories are paradigm theories. . . . Only as experiment and tentative theory are together articulated to a match does the discovery emerge and the theory become a paradigm." [62] As he carefully emphasizes, "By choosing [the term paradigm] I mean to suggest that some accepted examples of actual scientific practice—examples which include, law, theory, application, and instrumentation together—provide models from which spring particular coherent traditions of scientific research." [63]

Summary

The listed combinations of theoretical structures presented earlier in this chapter describe one possible evolutionary sequence in theory building. That is, theory building may be interpreted as moving from a stage of primitive conceptualization to the evolution of complex networks of interrelated conceptualizations in the form of paradigms.

To Kuhn, the distinguishing characteristic of a mature science is paradigm-guided research. According to him, it is not yet known which parts of social science have evolved to the paradigm stage of development. It is doubtful that sociology has reached Kuhn's level of scientific maturity. Mostly because, and as Ziman has noted,

The "methodological problem" has not been surmounted; there is not yet a reliable procedure for building up interesting hypotheses that can be made sufficiently plausible to a sufficient number of . . . scholars by well devised observations, experiments or rational deductions. It was the sort of problem facing Physics before Galileo began seriously to apply mathematical reasoning and numerical measurement to the subject. The ideal of a consensus is there, but the intellectual techniques by which it might be created and enlarged seem elusive.[64]

The methodological problems of sociology can be traced as much to factors beyond the control of sociologists as to the nature of their own limitations. That is, even if sociologists could devise impeccably efficient instrumentation there is no assurance that they would permit themselves or be permitted by society to apply them without restriction. The ethical and moral implications of experiments involving human subjects present problems to both social scientists and society that have not been given the consideration they deserve. It is the purpose of chapter 7 to explore the implications of these problems.

For more than one reason, then, methodological limitations have retarded the development of sociological theory. It is painfully evident that the phenomena of the discipline have yet to be satisfactorily identified, let alone categorized. Whether or not presumed social facts are stable entities or kaleidoscopic manifestations is still debatable. Nevertheless, this is not to suggest that sociological research has been unguided by accepted theoretical and methodological procedures. It is to say that the discipline has yet to reach a stage where it has uncovered behavioral laws by means of a paradigm or a specific synthesis which has been the generally accepted common source of theory, method, and problem for a group of practitioners. In Kuhn's sense of the term, the paradigm stage of development must be regarded as an ideal yet to be attained.

For the most part, sociological investigation has been guided by very general frames of reference. In order to justify the need for a separate science of society, early social thinkers were confronted with the task of devising a theoretical perspective that could be used to identify and differentiate social facts from other behavioral facts. Furthermore, they had to demonstrate convincingly that this perspective contributed something vital to the understanding of human behavior. Though major credit for a breakthrough in this direction goes to Karl Marx, the work of Emile Durkheim must be regarded as of nearly equal importance. Though their subjects varied, there is little doubt that their common sociologistic orientation has provided a unique and compelling point of departure for the study of human behavior. In good measure, sociological investigation may still be described as heavily oriented around expanding the ideas of Marx and Durkheim. The contributions of these two men are the subject of the next chapter.

Few contemporary sociologists would disagree with the observation that sociological theory is at a rudimentary stage of development because of the sociologist's inability to pinpoint precisely the phenomena of the discipline. Most sociologists remain inclined toward the Durkheimian tenet that social facts are not directly observable. They believe one can study only the presumed effects of social phenomena by means of certain constructed "indicators." As Durkheim reasoned,

> . . . social solidarity is a . . . phenomenon which, taken by itself, does not lend itself to exact observation nor indeed to measurement. . . . We must substitute for this [social fact] which escapes us an external index which symbolizes it and study the former in the light of the latter.[65]

Essentially, Durkheim found that his unit of analysis, social solidarity (or what keeps people living together in some sort of orderly pattern), had to be broken down into its essential components and their manner of interaction observed before an overall configuration could be discerned and understood. Durkheim's goal was to identify the various ways social solidarity was and could be structured and to analyze its effects on human social behavior.

Because social phenomena may not be readily apparent, considerable effort in sociology has been and continues to be devoted to the task of conceptualization. In a recent appraisal of trends in the development of sociological thought, William Catton observed that twentieth-century sociologists are in large measure engaged in "attempts to invent concepts and formulas that would serve as ad hoc descriptions of more or less recurrent aspects of interhuman behavior." [66]

Furthermore, sociologists, particularly in America, continue to be preoccupied with identifying the roots of social solidarity. Though Marx, too, had this interest, his analytical powers were focused on the dynamics of social change. For him, the problem was how to create rather than maintain social order.

In spite of this different substantive concern, Marx shared Durkheim's epistemological viewpoint. From his perspective, social facts are unobservable abstract symbols called *ideas* whose shape and origin are to be traced to observable economic indicators, that is, to the technological elements—machinery, tools, raw materials, and so on—of existing economic systems.

Even though the theoretical interests of Marx and Durkheim are much in evidence in contemporary sociology, American sociologists in particular have traditionally found it troublesome to accept without question the "sociologistic" tenet espoused by both Marx and Durkheim that as emergent phenomena, social facts can only be explained in terms of other social facts. To those who adhere to this position it is illegitimate to trace, or "reduce," the causes of social customs to, say, their biological or psychological origins. Raised in an ideological milieu which emphasizes the possibility and desirability of the autonomous individual and inclined toward the view that all matter is interrelated and has a common "natural" source, American social scientists have found it difficult to devise a theory that would adequately differentiate man from, but at the same time accurately locate his place among, all other phenomena. In contemporary sociology these two concerns are evident in the contrast between "field theory" and "exchange theory"—the subjects of chapter 6. The germ of both perspectives can be discerned in the contrasting ideas of Lester F. Ward and William G. Sumner; their contributions are the subject of chapter 3.

In many ways Ward and Sumner can be viewed as the

American counterparts of Marx and Durkheim. Marx and Ward shared an optimistic conviction that men could and should use scientifically acquired social knowledge to construct a society faithful to the highest ethical and moral ideas of mankind.

Durkheim and Sumner shared a much less confident, a somewhat fatalistic interpretation of man's ability to implement his social knowledge. For them, the problem was not so much adjusting society to suit the interests of men as vice versa. Their common concern was how to maintain the strength of certain "naturally" rooted and "extra somatic" social phenomena (norms, folkways, mores, institutions, customs, beliefs, values) which enable basically egocentric men to act altruistically and behave peacefully. In contrast to Marx and Ward, Durkheim and Sumner subscribed to a theory based on a view of social change as an inevitably slow, continuous, adaptive growth process not subject to rapid acceleration by means of human intervention. They did not believe that men could or should attempt to rationally construct a just order out of whole cloth. According to them,

> What keeps ordinary men on the decent road . . . is in part at least habit, and a kind of emotional identification the individual makes with the society of which he feels himself part. This feeling is not something that can be produced to order; it has to grow, slowly and naturally.[67]

The relationship between individual autonomy and social responsibility was a key topic of interest to all four men. Were these two independent subjects or merely different sides of an inseparable whole? Must the path to one inevitably lie through the territory of the other? Accepting this, are there not times when one of these variables is a prior condition for the other? As will be seen in chapter 4, the contributions of the first American sociologists to concern themselves with constructing social-psychological perspectives reflect differences of opinion as to when, and even if, one side of the question should be accorded priority over the other. Gradually, however, sociologists began to dwell on social facts to the virtual neglect of the range of individual facts.

For instance, a common, if not the primary, subject of investigation among American social psychologists has been the process of socialization. That is, how one acquires the ability to become an accepted participant in the social world in which he must function. Although fully aware that the socialization process is rife with complications because of ambiguities in the social sphere, social-psychologically-oriented sociologists have been inclined to interpret socialization as a series of stages by which the individual gradually adjusts, or perhaps more accurately, succumbs, to social demands. How society could and can be molded to suit the needs of unique individuals has not been given equal attention. The sociological subordination of the individual can be traced to a number of factors, including the ascendancy of Durkheimian social theory in American sociology.

Along with the rise of Durkheimian sociology in America came interest in developing the methodological side of the discipline. Having considered ways to define and study social facts, the next order of business was seen by many to entail the identification of a basic set of scientifically defensible procedures by which valid knowledge could be obtained. For George Lundberg (whose ideas as well as those of his arch rival, Robert MacIver, are discussed in chapter 4), this meant adherence to the principles of physical mechanics as interpreted in the doctrine of behaviorism. He stressed the need to acquire data tied to observables and capable of verification by any trained investigator, that is, behavioral events whose occurrence could be independently corroborated by anyone capable of using reliable instruments and following precisely identified procedures under specified conditions. Thus, to Lundberg, interpretations of human behavior, particularly those based on impressions of the subjective motivation of individuals, which had not been interpreted by reference to something observable could only be regarded as scientifically meaningless. Whatever his intentions, Lundberg provided many with an additional rationalization for neglecting the study of unique individual behavior.

From the late 1930s, one can detect a growing rift between those who would initiate their social research by following accepted methodological procedure and those who stressed the need, regardless of the methodological state of the discipline, to be initially and primarily concerned with what C. Wright Mills later referred to as the relationship between "the personal troubles of milieux" and "the public issues of social structure." [68] Fundamentally, the debate concerned a difference of opinion—based on ideological predilections—as to the relative emphasis to be placed on pure vs. applied social research. The more applied-oriented insisted that sociological knowledge must be continually and immediately useful for the solution of insistent social problems. For those of this view, a disjunction between the source of research problems and methods posed no great difficulty for either the long-term improvement of society or the advancement of sociology as a science.

Those who emphasized the pure side of the question felt just the opposite to be true. To them, for sociology to advance as a science and for its acquired data to be socially useful, the discipline had to evolve within itself a common source not only of problem and method, but also of theory. The debate has not been resolved. If anything, the current scene reveals an intensification of the dispute. [69]

Nevertheless, attempts have been made to construct theoretical syntheses. Nurtured during the Great Depression and expanded, if not brought to maturity, during the "quiet" 1950s, the social theory of Talcott Parsons (the subject of chapter 5) is the outstanding example in recent American sociology. His work represents an attempt to unite the behavioral sciences under a common theoretical frame of reference. There is little doubt that his goal is to isolate a paradigm that will be the common source of theory and problem—but not method—for a body of practitioners. Though far from being satisfactorily complete to himself or anyone else, Parsons' voluminous effort has furnished a basis for interdisciplinary cooperation and thought about the subject.

A major criticism of Parsons' approach is that it is couched at too high a level of abstraction to attain scientifically precise knowledge about human behavior. Primarily because he wants behavioral knowledge to be cumulative and believes this possible only if the data of the several behavioral sciences are collected from a common theoretical orientation, Parsons sees it necessary to begin with broad general theory which can be gradually broken down into its particulars. Some of his critics, Robert K. Merton and George C. Homans in particular, disagree. For them, general theory must come after the acquisition of detailed knowledge of particular types of human behavior.

Merton recommends the identification of theories of the "middle range," that is, theories midway between everyday working hypotheses and all-inclusive general theories, for example, a theory of suicidal behavior. Presumably, at some point, middle-range theories will provide their own impetus for combination and synthesis in the form of general theory.

Homans sees it necessary to "bring men back" into the sociological perspective by building up a wealth of knowledge of their elementary behavior. In his view, sociologists should be working toward the isolation of behavioral laws which can be done only by means of the direct analysis of "actual" human behavior. To him, American sociologists, by largely following the lead of structuralists such as Durkheim and Parsons, have been overly preoccupied with the analysis of certain results of human behavior, i.e., norms and roles, and only minimally concerned with the study of the basic behavioral processes which produce them. To correct this deficiency (as detailed in chapter 6), Homans has proposed the adoption of an "exchange theory" of human behavior; that is, the analysis of the process by which two or more individuals, by means of mutual give-and-take, establish patterned ways of responding to one another.

As currently developed, exchange theory is a limited sociological perspective. A host of potentially important behavioral variables (e.g., psychological facts of an idiosyncratic nature, biological facts, climatic facts, and so on) have not been included in the analyses of those who espouse it. Thus, at present the exchange perspective is not up to the standard that Homans requires of acceptable scientific theory, namely, the "explanation" of some type of human behavior.

To explain exchange behavior, or any other category of

human activity, something along the lines of a "field" perspective (also discussed in chapter 6) is required. As interpreted by Kurt Lewin, field theory described a frame of reference concerned with the identification of the precise linkages among all the variables involved in effecting human activity as it occurs at a particular point in time and space. As he saw it, accomplishment of this task would permit the isolation of laws and explanations of human behavior.

Though field theory is not presently a widely adopted perspective, behavioral scientists in increasing numbers are expressing an interest in the discovery of behavioral laws and subscribing to the view that this can be accomplished only by means of an inclusive behavioral science theoretical approach. The proliferation of world physical and social problems has had much to do with the current multidisciplinary mood among behavioral scientists. Only time will tell how much benefit such efforts will have for the paradigmatic development of behavioral science.

In short, the chapters to follow chart the development of major themes—concepts, frames of reference, and other elements—in recent sociological theory. The contributions of those examined were organized by interpreting them as dialectically generated. As Robert A. Nisbet reminds us,

> Ideas are dialectical responses caught up in the logic of circumstances of antithesis. This is, no doubt, as true in the physical sciences, philosophy, and art as it is in the social sciences; but it is more immediately evident and dramatic in the latter. To a striking extent, every major social idea begins as an attack on, a criticism of, or a response to, some other idea.[70]

TWO · The sociologistic perspective and the works of Marx and Durkheim*

Karl Marx

Karl Marx (1818–83) was born in Treves, Germany. At the age of eighteen he entered the University of Berlin. He chose jurisprudence as his major field of study, but he also "devoted himself with the utmost zeal to the most diversified domains of science and literature, trying all things by turns." [1] In 1841, Marx was awarded in absentia a doctorate in philosophy by the University of Jena.

For a number of reasons Marx became a revolutionary intellectual rather than a professor of philosophy. [2] Among other things, he was appalled at the working conditions that men, women, and children endured at the hands of the owners of what he referred to as the "means of production." Early in *Das Kapital* Marx detailed what the working day was like in the factories and firms of the British Isles during the latter half of the nineteenth century. Typically people worked at least twelve hours a day, six days a week. But it was not unusual for an employee to work longer hours and seven days a week. Marx described Mary Anne Walkley, a twenty-year-old employee of a London dressmaking firm whose average working day was 16.5 hours. During the height of the fashion

* The sociologistic connection between the works of Marx and Durkheim is not an original idea of the author's. It was initially put forth by Pitirim A. Sorokin. See his *Contemporary Sociological Theories* (New York: Harper & Bros., 1926), pp. 433–599.

season, Mary Anne might work thirty hours without a break. In June 1863 she died, according to one newspaper report, from "simple over-work." As Marx summarized the story,

> Mary Anne Walkley had worked without intermission for 26.5 hours, with 60 other girls, 30 in one room, that only afforded [one-third] of the cubic feet of air required for them. At night, they slept in pairs in one of the stifling holes into which the bedroom was divided by partitions of board. And this was one of the best millinery establishments in London. Mary Anne Walkley fell ill on the Friday, died on Sunday, without, to the astonishment [of the proprietress], having previously completed the work in hand.[3]

There was widespread employment of children in nineteenth-century British industry, and their work could be as demanding as that of adults. Marx told of nine- and ten-year-old boys routinely working twelve hours a day, seven days a week. He cited a government study which reported that

> at a rolling-mill where the proper hours were from 6 A.M. to 5:30 P.M., a boy worked about four nights every week till 8:30 P.M. at least . . . and for six months. Another, at 9 years old, sometimes made three 12-hour shifts running, and, when 10, has made two days and two nights running. A third, now 10 . . . worked from 6 A.M. till 12 P.M. three nights, and till 9 P.M. the other nights. Another, now 13, . . . worked from 6 P.M. till 12 noon next day, for a week together, and sometimes for three shifts together, e.g., from Monday morning till Tuesday night.[4]

As much as the workers' physical health was abused, Marx thought that the abuse of their psychological well-being was the most demeaning quality of employment. He believed that the laborer in capitalistic societies was inevitably made to feel *alienated* from himself, his work, and his fellow men. Marx put it this way:

> The worker is related to the product of his labour as to an alien object. For on this premise it is clear that the more the worker spends himself, the more powerful the alien objective

world becomes which he creates over-against himself, the poorer he himself—his inner world—becomes, the less belongs to him as his own. It is the same in religion. The more man puts into God, the less he retains in himself. . . .

Just as in religion the spontaneous activity of the human imagination, of the human brain and the human heart, operates independently of the individual—that is, operates on him as an alien, divine or diabolical activity—in the same way the workers's activity is not his spontaneous activity. It belongs to another; it is the loss of self.

As a result, therefore, man (the worker) no longer feels himself to be freely active in any but his animal functions—eating, drinking, procreating, or at most in his dwelling and in dressing-up, etc.; and in his human functions he no longer feels himself to be anything but an animal. What is animal becomes human and what is human becomes animal.[5]

For Marx the solution to the exploiting and alienating effects of capitalism could be found through the application of *dialectical materialism*. The "dialectic," from the Greek *dialego*, "to debate," described a tripartite process of change. The first phase, the *thesis*, describes a state of affirmation and unity; the second, the *antithesis*, is a process of negation; and the third phase, the *synthesis*, is the process by which the antagonism between thesis and antithesis is resolved. These phases were not conceived of as mere repetitive cycles; the synthesis was described as a qualitative advance. "The dialectical method . . . holds that the process of development should be understood not as movement in a circle, not as a simple repetition of what has already occurred, but as an onward and upward movement, as a transition from an old qualitative state to a new qualitative state, from the lower to the higher." [6]

Marx borrowed the dialectical notion from G. W. F. Hegel who used it to explain the manner in which God (sometimes referred to as the "Absolute Spirit" or the "Absolute Idea") works through men to give shape to the material world. For Hegel the Absolute Spirit is the precondition of all nature. Man, however, is something special, for he was created in God's image. He was endowed by the Creator with the potential for self-consciousness that could, when rationally cultivated, lead to the realization of the essence of the Absolute Spirit. Though it would seem to follow that man is therefore capable of transcending the immediate world, Hegel adhered to the view that man is always the son of his times. Hegel regarded the human will as in a continuous state of evolution. Self-awareness, the rational ability to realize the meaning of the creative spirit, had to be developed—it was not an inherent certainly. As a process, self-awareness follows a dialectical pattern in which thought leads to action, reaction, and their eventual unity. For example, possessive thoughts may lead to the appropriation of objects coveted by another (thesis-antithesis). The two reconcile their differences by the formation of a conception of "our" or common property and this synthesis represents a qualitative advance. Because action is always performed at a specific point in time and within a particular physical and cultural milieu, man's ability to approach self-awareness is always limited by the nature of the conditions during his life span.

Those, like Hegel, who assert the primacy of mind over matter are called *idealists*. *Materialists*, such as Marx, hold to just the opposite point of view. To Marx, matter is not a product of mind; on the contrary, mind is simply the most advanced product of matter. Though Marx rejected Hegel's content orientation, he retained his dialectical structure. As Marx described the differences between the two perspectives,

> My dialectic method is not only different from the Hegelian, but is its direct opposite. To Hegel, the life-process of the human brain, i.e., the process of thinking, which, under the name of "the Idea," he even transforms into an independent subject, is the demiurgos of the real world, and the real world is only the external, phenomenal form of "the Idea." With me, on the contrary, the ideal is nothing else than the material world reflected by the human mind, and translated into forms of thought.[7]

Where Hegel was concerned with developing a philosophy to foster the attainment of the Absolute Idea, Marx's primary concern was with the construction of a theoretical perspective that would account for the dynamics of human social organization. Once the laws of societal evolution were uncovered, they were to be rationally manipulated to permit individual self-determination. As one student of Marx emphasized, "Instead of the Absolute Idea, Marx held that it was human society that develops in history, in a dialectical pattern and in accord with laws that can be discovered by its students—the social scientists." [8]

The basic postulates of the Marxian dialectical method are the following: (1) all the phenomena of nature are part of an integrated whole; (2) nature is in a continuous state of movement and change; (3) the developmental process is a product of quantitative advances which culminate in abrupt qualitative changes; and (4) contradictions are inherent in all realms of nature—but particularly human society.[9] For example, capitalism is an organized system for effecting the production, distribution, and consumption of the necessary means of existence. It is based on the principle of increasing profit, and, therefore, is characterized by inherently continuous change. Capitalism is the product of two interrelated and antagonistic groups: the owners of the productive enterprise (the bourgeoisie) and their workers (the proletariat). Eventually, the antagonism between the two groups leads to a revolution in which the working class overthrows the employing class. When this occurs, communist society is at hand and, according to Marx, this form of social organization is a qualitative advance because it will reconcile the interests of all men.

The basic premise, or the axiomatic base, of the Marxist philosophy of materialism has been described by Lenin as follows: "Materialism in general recognizes objectively real being (matter) as independent of consciousness, sensation, experience. . . . Consciousness is only the reflection of being, at best, an approximately true (adequate, ideally exact) reflection of it." [10] To Stalin, "Marx's philosophical materialism holds the world is by its very nature *material*, that the multifold phenomena of the world constitute different forms of matter in motion, that interconnection and interdependence of phenomena, as established by the dialectical method, are a law of the development of moving matter, and that the world develops in accordance with the laws of movement in matter and stands in no need of a 'universal spirit.' " [11] Crudely translated, this means that God is dead and science is king.

Applied to human society, Marxian dialectical materialism has been popularly interpreted as meaning *economic determinism*. The label is not without justification. Marx and his close collaborator, Frederick Engels, purposely, but not naively, emphasized the dominating influence of the economic facts of life. For example, to Engels, ". . . the production of the immediate material means of subsistence and, consequently, the degree of economic development attained by a given people or during a given epoch, form the foundation upon which the state institutions, the legal conceptions, the ideas on art, and even on religion, of the people concerned have been evolved." [12] And here are the words of Marx,

> In the social production of their life, men enter into definite relations that are indispensable and independent of their will, relations of production which correspond to a definite stage of development of their material productive forces. The sum total of these relations of production constitutes the economic structure of society, the real foundation, on which rises a legal and political superstructure and to which correspond definite forms of social consciousness. The mode of production of material life conditions the social, political and intellectual life process in general. It is not the consciousness of men that determines their being, but, on the contrary, their social being that determines their consciousness. [13]

Key concepts in the Marxian vocabulary include the mode of production; forces of production; relations of production; and means of production. The mode of production refers to the general economic institution, that is, the particular manner in which people produce and distribute the means to sustain life. The forces of production and the relations of production together define the mode of production. The forces of production include the instruments of production—tools, machinery, and people. The relations of production describe the organization of the division of labor by which production is carried out by people. The means of production refer to something more than the instruments of production. The means of production include all the elements (land, raw materials, and work plant, and so on) that enter into the manufacture of the final product. The essentials of the Marxism conceptual scheme may be diagramed as shown on page 46.

In the capitalistic mode of production, the means of production are privately owned. The owners of the means of production in capitalistic society, said Marx, always represent a small minority, the capitalists, who are motivated to appropriate the fruits of production at minimum expense to themselves and, hence, at the expense of the workers, who comprise the proletariat. In the words of a noted British Marxist,

> It follows that in every mode of production which involves the exploitation of man by man, the social product is so distributed that the majority of people, the people who labour, are condemned to toil for no more than the barest necessities of life. Sometimes favourable circumstances arise when they can win more, but more often they get the barest minimum— and at times not even that. On the other hand, a minority, the owners of means of production, the property owners, enjoy leisure and luxury. Society is divided into rich and poor.[14]

The mode of production determines the particular form of the relations of production. In complex societies the relations of production take the form of a division of labor which places people into categories or groups according to their role in the productive enterprise. These groups constitute social classes. In Lenin's words, "Social classes are large groups of people which differ from each other by the place they occupy in a historically definite system of social production, by their relation (in most cases fixed and formulated in laws) to the means of production, by their role in the social organization

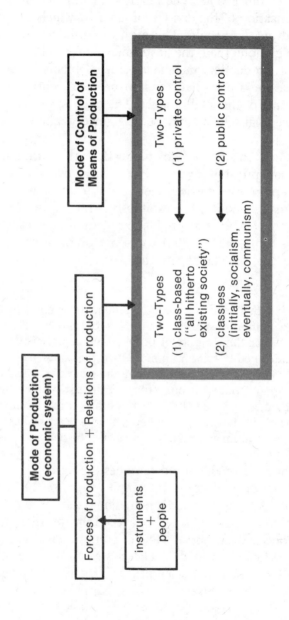

of labor, and consequently by the dimensions of the social wealth that they obtain and their method of acquiring their share of it." [15]

Classes are antagonistic toward each other when their positions in production are such that one thrives at the expense of the other. Because all complex societies known to Marx and Engels were hierarchically organized, they declared that "the history of all hitherto existing society is the history of class struggles." [16] The termination of class conflict will occur when the source of conflict, private property, has been eliminated. The process will be violent because no ruling class has ever voluntarily given up its power or has failed to fight to regain its lost power. It is the task of the working class, the proletariat, to overthrow and eradicate by any and all available means capitalistic relations of production and replace them with socialistic relations of production. In order to ensure the victory of socialism and the inevitable evolution of communism, it will be necessary, for a time, to establish the dictatorship of the proletariat, an all powerful, coercive authority. In the *Manifesto of the Communist Party*, Marx and Engels listed the following as the immediate goals of the dictatorship of the proletariat:

1. Abolition of property in land and application of all rents of land to public purposes.
2. A heavy progressive or graduated income tax.
3. Abolition of all right of inheritance.
4. Confiscation of the property of all emigrants and rebels.
5. Centralisation of credit in the hands of the State, by means of a national bank with State capital and an exclusive monopoly.
6. Centralisation of the means of communication and transport in the hands of the State.
7. Extension of factories and instruments of production owned by the state; the bringing into cultivation of waste-lands, and the improvement of the soil generally in accordance with a common plan.

8. Equal liability of all to labour. Establishment of industrial armies, especially for agriculture.

9. Combination of agriculture with manufacturing industries; gradual abolition of the distinction between town and country, by a more equable distribution of the population over the country.

10. Free education for all children in public schools. Abolition of children's factory labour in its present form. Combination of education with industrial production, etc.[17]

When these and other measures have eliminated class distinctions, the centralized authority will "wither away."

The period between the establishment of the dictatorship of the proletariat and its withering away was not extensively analyzed by Marx. He emphasized, however, that strong leadership would be necessary in the interim to eliminate the vestiges of capitalistic exploitation, to prevent a successful counterrevolution, and most of all, to effect the following necessary economic changes: (1) to increase production to the point where the needs of all could be completely satisfied; (2) to relocate the production and distribution of goods in the hands of a single organization representative of all the people; and (3) to eliminate all subordination to the division of labor by the elevation of work to a self-selected desirable and satisfying activity.

Marx was not specific as to when these goals could be observed to have been attained. Nor was he concerned over the fact that the dictators—a minority institution of the proletariat—would have complete authority to decide when they had been reached. The immediate tasks of bringing about the revolution and the institution of the dictatorship of the proletariat were sufficiently problematic to Marx to command his complete attention. The following terse comment is Marx's last word on the post-revolutionary phase in the evolution of communist society:

The question then arises: what transformation will the state undergo in communist society? In other words, what social functions will remain in existence there that are analogous to present functions of the state? The question can only be answered scientifically, and one does not get a flea-hop nearer to the problem by a thousandfold combination of the word people with the word state.

Between capitalist and communist society lies the period of the revolutionary transformation of the one into the other. There corresponds to this also a political transition period in which the state can be nothing but the revolutionary dictatorship of the proletariat.

Now the programme does not deal with this nor with the future state of communist society.[18]

In the final analysis, it is not surprising that the Marxist message was received by many as meaning the total and permanent subordination of mankind to economic facts. Ideas, morality, ethics, religion, rationality—distinguishing human traits—were said to be reflections of phenomena whose existence and evolution were governed by natural laws. Yet Marx's intention was decidedly not to convey to man the helplessness of his condition. On the contrary, the Marxian goal was clearly the establishment of a rationally organized society in which men would be released from the tyranny of economics. As Edmund Wilson has observed: "What is important and inspiring in [dialectical materialism] is the idea that the human spirit will be able to master its animal nature through reason; but they [Marx and Engels] managed to make a great many people think they meant something the opposite of this: that mankind was hopelessly the victim of its appetites." [19] Engels once wrote,

According to the materialist conception of history, the ultimately determining element in history is the production and reproduction of real life. More than that neither Marx nor I have ever asserted. Hence if somebody twists this into saying that the economic element is the *only* determining one, he transforms that proposition into a meaningless, abstract, senseless phrase. The economic situation is the basis, but the various elements of the superstructure . . . also exercise their influence on the course of the historical struggle, and in many cases preponderate in determining their *form*.[20]

Marx and Sociology

In spite of his importance, Marx's impact on American sociological thought has yet to be appraised in scholarly depth.[21] That it has been significant and far-ranging is apparent even to those of casual acquaintance with the subject matter, literature, and orientation of the discipline. Unfortunately, too many of those who have dealt seriously with the Marxian perspective seem to have been more motivated out of reactionary patriotic zeal than neutral scholarly interest. There is a vast literature on the inapplicability of Marxian theory to the American context.

Nevertheless, the epistemological basis of sociology reveals much that is consistent with (regardless of whether or not the source has been direct) Marxian theory. American sociological research can be seen to be centered around the idea that human behavior is patterned considerably (to some contemporary sociologists, *determined*) by the impact of phenomena external to man and which he cannot identify and comprehend in depth without the benefit of an empirically oriented science of society. Furthermore, more sociologists than ever are manifesting a concern for the collection of information useful for the betterment of the human condition. There is considerable doubt among sociologists that mankind will be able to maintain a civilized existence in the absence of thoroughgoing social planning based on substantial empirical knowledge of human behavior. Contrary to Marx, and for many obvious reasons, serious attention is yet to be given by sociologists to the problem of whether or not a "power elite" (a totalitarian few) will be necessary eventually to prevent the devolution if not demise of mankind.

In a recent statement, T. B. Bottomore observed that Marx contributed two important ideas to the sociological perspective:

One was to adopt, and to maintain consistently in his work, a view of human societies as wholes or systems in which social groups, institutions, beliefs, and doctrines are interrelated and have to be studied in their interrelations rather than treated in isolation, as in the conventional separate histories of politics, law, religion, or thought. The second contribution was the view of societies as inherently mutable systems, in which changes are produced largely by internal contradictions and conflicts, and the assumption that such changes, if observed in a large number of instances, will show a sufficient degree of regularity to allow the formulation of general statements about their causes and consequences.[22]

The first contribution is quite prominent in contemporary sociology and may be subsumed under the label either of social systems theory or the structural-functional frame of reference. As for the second, it is frequently observed that American sociology has been much more concerned with the problem of social order than the problem of social change.[23] A variety of reasons have been offered to account for this tendency. Some, for example, refer to the fact that sociology in America is primarily a post-World War II development and that the period since 1945 has been marked by the omnipresent challenge to American-style democracy engendered by the spread of communism throughout the world. Hence, American sociological concern with the problem if social order is to be viewed as a defensive reaction to not only the threat but also the actuality of conflict with the Communist world.

In addition to external factors, certain internal circumstances are also said to account for the American sociological interest in social order. It is often stated that because of the newness of the discipline, its practitioners have sought legitimacy and power by demonstrating the usefulness of their science to the heads of business, industry, and government; and that in fact, sociologists have been so successful in their quest for recognition that they have been coopted, or bought out, by the conservative powers that be. For whatever reasons, and even though since the mid-1960s there has been considerable interest in Marxian-type conflict theory, it is obviously the case that American sociology has been and continues to be heavily influenced by the study of the nature of social order. Whether because of their persuasiveness and/or their compatibility with prevailing currents of thought, the sociologistic contributions of Emile Durkheim have been more congenial to American sociologists than those of Marx.

Emile Durkheim

Emile Durkheim (1858–1917) was born in Épinal, France. In 1882 he graduated from the illustrious academy, the École Normale Supérieure. He received his doctorate in philosophy from the University of Paris in 1893. In 1896, a special chair was created for him at the University of Bordeaux, and he became the first professor of social science in France.

For Durkheim, the units of sociological analysis were "social facts." A social fact, he said, is "every way of acting, fixed or not, capable of exercising on the individual an external constraint; or again, every way of acting which is general throughout a given society, while at the same time existing in its own right independent of its individual manifestations." [24] In keeping with his working assumption that social facts are not directly observable and, therefore, must be studied indirectly by means of constructed indicators designed to gauge their presumed effects, Durkheim postulated their two basic identifying qualities to be their "exteriority" to the individual and their "coercive" or constraining effect on his behavior.

He illustrated the extraindividual nature of social facts in the following way: ". . . when I fulfill my obligations as brother, husband, or citizen, when I execute my contracts, I perform duties which are defined, externally to myself and my acts, in law and in custom." Furthermore, "Even if they conform to my own sentiments and I feel their reality subjectively, such reality is still objective, for I did not create them; I merely inherited them through my education." [25] The constraining effect of social facts is mostly a function of the fact that they are imposed on the individual regardless of his wishes. But of course, said Durkheim, ". . . when I fully consent and conform to them, this constraint is felt only slightly, if at all, and is therefore unnecessary. But it is nonetheless," Durkheim insisted, "an intrinsic characteristic of these facts, the proof thereof being that it asserts itself as soon as I attempt to resist it." [26]

To Durkheim, social facts were reflections or manifestations of group morality. He described his doctoral dissertation, *The Division of Labor in Society*, as primarily an attempt to treat the moral facts of life according to the method of the positive sciences. For him, morality covered the entire normative range—from the minor rules of social etiquette to the most reverentially regarded custom.

The relationship between morality, its institutional sources and forms, and the nature of the social bond was the primary problem of concern in all of Durkheim's works. In *The Division of Labor in Society*, Durkheim interpreted the evolution of social organization to be from a state of mechanical solidarity to a state of organic solidarity. Neither type of social bond could be observed directly. Both were discernible, however, in terms of certain indicators—the kind of sanctions applied to violations of morality.

Sanctions were viewed as emanations of the "collective conscience," or the "totality of beliefs and sentiments common to average citizens of the same society." [27] An act is criminal, said Durkheim, "when it offends strong and defined states of the collective conscience."

Mechanical solidarity describes the condition of a society with a strong and pervasive sense of collective conscience. An offense against one person is an offense against all. In such a society, primarily the small "primitive" type, sanctions are applied automatically or mechanically in that they tend to be "nonreflective" in character. A preponderance of "repressive law" indicates the existence of mechanical solidarity. As Durkheim explained:

> It is this solidarity which repressive law expresses, at least whatever there is vital to it. The acts that it prohibits and qualifies as crimes are of two sorts. Either they directly manifest very violent dissemblance between the agent who accomplishes them and the collective type, or else they offend the organ of the common conscience. In one case as in the other, the force that is offended by the crime and which

suppresses it is thus the same. It is a product of the most essential social likeness, and it has for its effect the maintenance of the social cohesion which results from these likenesses. It is this force which penal law protects against all enfeeblement, both in demanding from each of us a minimum of resemblances without which the individual would be a menace to the unity of the social body, and in imposing upon us the respect for the symbol which expresses and summarizes these resemblances at the same time that it guarantees them.[28]

Organic solidarity was viewed as a concomitant of the complex division of labor characteristic of industrial societies. What holds people together in complex industrial societies is not so much their commonality as their interdependence. A man can become a specialist only insofar as others specialize in the production of goods and the provision of the services that he must neglect to produce for himself in order to concentrate his efforts. Durkheim defined organic solidarity in the following manner:

This solidarity resembles that which we observe among the higher animals. Each organ, in effect, has its special physiognomy, its autonomy. And, moreover, the unity of the organism is as great as the individuation of the parts is more marked. Because of this analogy, we propose to call this solidarity which is due to the division of labor, organic.[29]

Organic solidarity, then, is the product of advanced division of labor which in turn is the effect of "dynamic or moral density." Dynamic or moral density refers to the heightened or intensified interaction among people engendered by the increase in the number of individuals "sufficiently in contact to be able to act and react upon one another. . . . If we agree to call this relation and the active commerce resulting from it dynamic or moral density, we can say that the progress of the division of labor is in direct ratio to the moral or dynamic density of society." [30]

Population density does not necessarily produce dynamic density and the complex division of labor. It does so only if it increases the struggle for existence. "If work becomes divided more as societies become more voluminous and denser, it is not because external circumstances are more varied, but because struggle for existence is more acute." [31] The intensification of the struggle for existence itself is not an inevitable concomitant of population density. Also possible are "emigration, colonization, resignation to a precarious, disputed existence, and, finally the total elimination of the weakest by suicide or some other means." [32]

The source of advanced division of labor must be sought among the cultural values of the collective conscience of the "members of an already constituted society." Unfortunately, Durkheim did not pursue the matter much beyond this point. He felt, apparently, that he had uncovered the "efficient" causes of the division of labor in society and that further analysis was not necessary for purposes of examining the fact of organic solidarity.

The existence of organic solidarity is indicated by a preponderance of "restitutive law" in society. "What distinguishes this sanction," said Durkheim, "is that it is not expiatory, but consists of a simple *return in state.*" Furthermore,

> Sufferance proportionate to the misdeed is not inflicted on the one who has violated the law or who disregards it; he is simply sentenced to comply with it. If certain things were done, the judge reinstates them as they would have been. He speaks of law; he says nothing of punishment. Damage-interests have no penal character; they are only a means of reviewing the past in order to reinstate it, as far as possible, to its normal form.[33]

Durkheim does not suggest that societies which manifest organic solidarity do not have repressive law or penal codes. His point is that as the division of labor advances, the application of sanctions (whether they be penal or civil in character) comes to be more of a specialized task than a general responsibility.

To summarize the foregoing, it may be said that Durkheim's sociologistic perspective was derived from two essential postulates: (1) social facts are not directly observable and can only be discerned by means of identified empirical

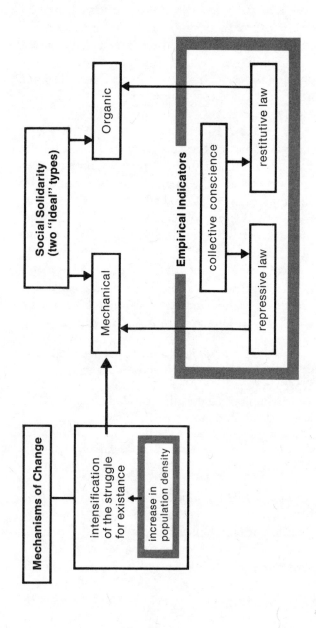

indicators; and (2) social facts must be accounted for by reference to antecedent social facts. The conceptual scheme developed by Durkheim in *The Division of Labor in Society* can be diagrammatically represented as on page 56.

The subject of primary concern was the nature of social solidarity, that is, what keeps people living together in some sort of orderly pattern. Early, Durkheim discerned two "ideal" types of social solidarity—mechanical and organic. Neither type was thought to be exactly represented by examples in the "real" world. They were to be used to chart the poles of a continuum which in turn could be used to order the variation possible among actual instances. Location on the continuum would provide a basis for the comparative study of two or more societies. The type of social solidarity prevalent in a given society was indicated by the character of its negative sanctions. Societies tending toward the mechanical pole manifested a preponderance of repressive law. Those tending toward the organic pole were dominated by restitutive law. Both type of solidarity were conceived of as emanations of collective conscience, or the totality of beliefs and sentiments common to the average members of the same society. Finally, the antecedent social fact which generated the initial shift from the mechanical to the organic side of the continuum was traced to an intensification of the struggle for existence which may or may not have been the effect of an increase in population density.

Types of social solidarity and types of negative sanctions were, then, the social facts of Durkheim's initial sociological treatise. Regardless of their particular type, said Durkheim, social facts should be viewed as "things." As he reasoned, "All that is given, all that is subject to observation, has thereby the character of a thing." Hence, "To treat phenomena as things is to treat them as data, and these constitute the point of departure of science." [34] Durkheim demonstrated the impact of social facts on human behavior in his study of suicide. This demonstration case came to be a model for sociological analysis.

The selection of suicide as a subject of study was not fortuitous. What other form of behavior would be less thought to be the consequence of the effect of social facts? What other behavioral act was more thought of as the result of the idiosyncratic experiences of unique individuals? In effect, Durkheim in large measure selected suicide as a demonstration case because he wished to be as convincing as possible in regard to the importance of social facts as behavior affecting phenomena. He wished to establish a firm basis for the existence of sociology as an independent scientific discipline by performing a crucial experiment.

In *Suicide*, Durkheim sought to implement his major methodological postulate: "The determining cause of a social fact should be sought among the social facts preceding it and not among the states of the individual consciousness." [35] Thus, to carry out this prescription, his job was to conceptualize suicide in peculiarly sociological terms and then account for it by means of uniquely sociological variables.

Durkheim's solution to the conceptual problem—the problem of specifying his unit of analysis—is conveyed in the following statement:

> If instead of seeing in [individual acts of suicide] only separate occurrences, unrelated and to be separately studied, the suicides committed in a given society during a given period of time are taken as a whole, it appears that this total is not simply a sum of independent units, a collective total, but is itself a new fact *sui generis*, with its own unity, individuality and consequently its own nature—a nature, furthermore, dominantly social. [36]

That is, if suicide was strictly a random individual act, there should not be a consistent trend in the number of suicides per year over a given time period in a given society. However, since societal suicide rates tended to be very stable over time, Durkheim concluded that suicide must to a very considerable degree be considered as a social fact to be accounted for by means of other social facts. The fact to be accounted for, it must be understood, is not why individual A at such and such a time and place took his own life, but why a certain number of individuals over a specified time period in a certain society committed suicide.

To analyze the great number of cases necessary to validate his case, Durkheim used the typological method. "A satisfactory method must above all, aim at facilitating scientific work by substituting a limited number of types for the indefinite multiplicity of individuals." [37] The first type of suicide he identified was ascertained from the inference that "suicide varies inversely with the degree of integration of the social groups of which the individual forms a part." [38] An absence of stable group bonds was found to be associated with susceptibility to commit suicide. Essentially, people who lack obligations to others and/or who do not have others obligated to them are more prone to suicide than their opposites. Durkheim referred to this type as "egoistic" suicide.

Another type of suicide was accounted for by appeal to the opposite line of reasoning. That is, strong group bonds may promote the willingness of the individual to sacrifice his life on its behalf. "It often happens, in primitive as well as other societies, that suicide becomes a duty, an obligation, a satisfaction of a social demand or a religious requirement, and in these circumstances men tend to commit it precisely because they recognize their obligations to the group." [39] This type was obviously "altruistic" suicide.

A third type of suicide was found to be associated with societal crises. Abrupt tears in the social fabric, such as those brought about by economic depressions, which result in the elimination of societal regulation are conducive to "anomic" suicide. "In anomic suicide, society's influence is lacking in the basically individual passions, thus leaving them without a check-rein." [40] As Robert Bierstedt elaborated on the type,

> . . . it cannot be emphasized too strongly that [for example, in the case of economic depression] it is not poverty . . . that conduces to suicide but rather sudden changes in the economic situations of people. Poverty itself . . . is almost a protection against the temptation to commit suicide. . . . It is rather rapid changes in the economic equilibrium . . . that exert a positive influence upon the suicide rate.[41]

Hence, economic prosperity may also engender anomie and proneness to commit suicide. ". . . [E]ven fortunate crises, the effect of which is abruptly to enhance a country's prosperity, affect suicide like economic disasters."[42] As Durkheim concluded,

> Every disturbance of equilibrium, even though it achieves greater comfort and a heightening of general vitality, is an impulse to voluntary death. Whenever serious readjustments take place in the social order, whether or not due to a sudden growth or to an unexpected catastrophe, men are more inclined to self-destruction.[43]

To Durkheim, then, social order, though typically taken for granted and generally assumed to be a simple extension of individual qualities, had, nonetheless, powerful and transcendent consequences for human mortality.

An important question here has to do with whether or not social regulation comes from social facts such as norms and roles, or social facts such as particular human beings. Thus, some cases of anomic suicide, according to Durkheim, result from the sudden loss of an important role or status, as may occur, for example, during an economic depression. Still others apparently result from the loss of a cherished other, as in the case of widowhood. A widow, suggested Durkheim, may commit suicide because she has lost a highly depended-upon functional role complement or/and a presumed irreplaceable human relationship. Thus, one may be naturally led to ask: Of those widows who remarry, which seek and obtain in a new partner comparability to the former partner in terms of expressive or emotional qualities, and which place greater emphasis on instrumental or practical capabilities? Why do some widows with plenty of opportunity choose not to remarry? The question we wish to explore here is quite obviously: why do specific individuals behave one way rather than another?

Unfortunately or fortunately, depending upon the point of view, Durkheim, though well aware of behavioral options to anomic stimuli, deliberately opted in favor of limiting the direction and depth of his analyses. The rationale for restricting the scope of the sociological perspective was in good measure a consequence of his conception of valid causal analysis.

To seek the cause of something in science was to look for its "efficient" causes.[44] The efficient cause of something was thought of as what could be empirically determined as having occurred "immediately" prior to an observed effect. One need not "reduce" his analysis to the point of uncovering the only possible originating source of an event before presuming to identify the cause. Hence, and since any science worth the title should demonstrate that its subject matter is the source of both its problems and solutions, sociology must seek the cause of social facts in other social facts. Besides being perfunctory in his treatment of the problems involved in identifying an efficient cause,[45] Durkheim was not at all clear as to where social facts came from and how the sociologist might weigh their importance vis-à-vis other behavioral facts.

Durkheim resolved the problem of the origin of social facts to his own satisfaction by defining them as emergent phenomena—the effects of "creative synthesis"—of individuals in association. In his words, ". . . society is not a mere sum of individuals. Rather, the system formed by their association represents a specific reality which has its own characteristics." [46] Although empirically inclined, Durkheim did not treat emergence as an empirical problem. To do so might well have been to admit the necessity of bringing the observation of individuals into the sociological realm. As Brodbeck observed,

> Philosophically, the . . . assumption that there are group properties over and above the individuals making up the groups, their properties, and the relations among them is counter to empiricism. For the latter holds that all terms must ultimately refer to what is observable, directly or indirectly, and that what we observe are people and their characteristics not supraindividual groups and their characteristics.[47]

"What is important," emphasizes George Homans, "is not the fact of emergence but the question of how the emergence

is to be explained." [48] He thinks that sociological propositions are most likely psychologically rooted. Here is the way
he puts it:

> . . . reduction implies that there are general sociological prop-
> ositions that can then be reduced to psychological ones. I
> now suspect that there are no general sociological proposi-
> tions, propositions that hold good of all societies or social
> groups as such, and that the only general propositions of
> sociology are in fact psychological. [49]

Some have thought that ideological conservatism—an
aversion toward social conflict and a preference for social order—lay behind Durkheim's neglect of such subjects as the details of emergence. To Irving Zeitlin, for example, "Taken as a
whole, Durkheim's system bears an overwhelmingly conservative bias." [50] There is much to support this point of view. As
Zeitlin noted, comments such as the following are not uncommon in Durkheim's writings:

> What is needed if social order is to reign is that the mass of
> men be content with their lot. But what is needed for them
> to be content, is not that they have more or less but that
> they be convinced they have no right to more. And for this,
> it is absolutely essential that there be an authority whose
> superiority they acknowledge and which tells them what is
> right. [51]

Zeitlin acknowledges that Durkheim believed that the past
could not be meaningfully reconstructed in the present, but
he says that his basic theme was "social order at all costs."
This is an overstatement that belies the importance of the
problem that Durkheim chose to study, namely, the complex
relationship between individual autonomy and social responsibility. As Nisbet puts it, it seemed to Durkheim that "It is
only through the practice of moral rules that man develops the
capacity to govern himself—that is, to be free." [52] Without a
certain amount of faith in the predictability of the behavior of others, one is not "free" to pursue the round of
activities possible. The basic theme running throughout Durk-

heim's work, then, was not "social order at all costs," but the human cost in the absence of social order.

Most likely, the appropriate label for Durkheim's ideological position is *pluralistic*. As Nisbet has stated,

> Durkheim must be placed among the pluralists. . . . Of Durkheim's dedication to society, order, and authority, there can be no doubt whatsoever. But to make this dedication synonymous [with any number of monistic ideologies] is to miss the very essence of a theory of man's relation to society that culminates in pluralism of authority. . . .[53]

Durkheim was concerned with discovering ways of liberalizing authority without diminishing its hold on people. Freedom entailed working out a balanced relationship between two omnipresent entities—the individual and society. Both had autonomous needs and mutual obligations. The question was: what combination of the two would allow them to live together without one attempting to eliminate or dominate the other? As he saw it, the answer to the question lay in strengthening individual attachment to the "diverse spheres of kinship, local community, profession, church, school, guild, and labor union, as well as political government."[54]

According to Zeitlin, "To understand the sociology of Emile Durkheim one must, in his case as in so many of his contemporaries, examine his relation to socialist thought and to the socialist movement of his time."[55] What, then, are the similarities and differences in the Durkheimian and socialistic perspectives?

Durkheim and Socialism

According to Joseph Neyer, "From the beginning Durkheim was aware that the unhealthy state of the moral conscience of Western man would continue until the anarchy of economic life had been moderated by some measure of control."[56] There is little doubt that he accepted some form of socialism as part of the evolution of human social organization. "Far from being a turning back," he said, "socialism . . . appears, on the contrary, to be implied in the very nature of the higher societies." [57] By socialist, "We denote . . . every doctrine which demands the connection of all economic functions, or of certain among them, which are at the present time diffuse, to the directing and conscious centers of society." [58]

Durkheim was entirely sympathetic with the plight of the working class in industrial society. In the style of Marx, he referred to the evils of the "forced division of labor"—a condition in which the worker feels his job to be an arbitrary constraint rather than a self-satisfying role-task. "Doubtless," he said, "we are not, from birth, predestined to some special position; but we do have tastes and aptitudes which limit our choice." Furthermore,

> If no care is taken of them, if they are ceaselessly disturbed by our daily occupations, we shall suffer and seek a way of putting an end to our suffering. But there is no other way out than to change the established order and to set up a new one. For the division of labor to produce solidarity, it is not sufficient, then, that each have his task; it is still necessary that this task be fitting to him.[59]

Having said this, he felt, nevertheless, that the overthrow of the ruling class in favor of the dictatorship of the proletariat would most likely amount to little more than the substitution of one form of tyranny for another. The immediate socialistic goal was not for him the elimination of the capitalist as much as the "rearrangement of the social structure, by relocating the industrial set-up [the mode of production] in the totality of the social organism, drawing it out of the shadow where it was functioning automatically, summoning it to the light and the control of conscience." [60] Durkheim's basic premise, the line of thought followed throughout his studies of social organization, was that "the economic functions can co-operate harmoniously and maintain themselves in a state of equilibrium only if they are submitted to moral forces which go beyond them, which contain and govern them." [61] Thus, as Gouldner has pointed out, Durkheim viewed society as "requiring moral rearmament rather than economic reconstruction." [62]

Revolution, then, was not out of the question for Durkheim.

He simply did not see the socialistic control of the means of production as the necessary or sufficient means to the realization of a more gratifying social order. His goal, however, was quite compatible with that of the Marxian socialists. He, as they, hoped for a social milieu which would produce solidarity spontaneously by allowing each individual the freedom to pursue "the free unfolding of the social force that each carries in himself."

Contrary to Marx, however, Durkheim did not feel that his analytical powers enabled him to uncover the essence of institutional structure and the inevitable course of social evolution. He saw his perspective as providing a framework for the beginning of empirically oriented social research. He did not claim to have developed a conclusive interpretation of the nature of social organization.

Unlike Marx, who presumed to have identified the third and future state of a dialectical pattern (that is, the synthesis that he labeled *communism*), Durkheim identified only two types of solidarity (mechanical solidarity may be likened to a dialectical thesis and organic solidarity to its antithesis) and modestly suggested that a viable industrial society would require a combination of the two. He did not speculate about how his two types of solidarity might give rise to a qualitatively advanced synthesis.

An essential part of the reason behind Durkheim's reluctance to speculate into the future can be traced to doubts about the ability of man to implement his acquired knowledge rationally. He did not foresee a time when men could do without the constraining effects of traditional social facts.

In opposition to Herbert Spencer and other laissez faire apologists, Durkheim did not believe that social order in advanced societies is "automatically produced through the pursuit of each individual of his own interests." He accepted the Hobbesian interpretation of "natural" man and argued,

. . . where interest is the only ruling force each individual finds himself in a state of war with every other since nothing comes to mollify the egos, and any truce in this eternal antagonism would not be of long duration. There is nothing less constant than interest. Today, it unites me to you; tomorrow, it will make me your enemy. Such a cause can only give rise to transient relations and passing associations.[63]

To Durkheim, spontaneous and trusting relationships are possible only within an accepted normative context. Thus, he argued, the binding nature of a contract between two individuals cannot be accounted for by reference to mutual self interest, for it may be to the interests of one or the other to violate the terms of the past at the expense of the other. The binding force must come from a higher source, namely, society. In his words, ". . . wherever a contract exists, it is submitted to regulation which is the work of society and not that of individuals, and which becomes ever more voluminous and more complicated."[64] It is obvious, noted Gouldner, that Durkheim was "saying something quite consistent with the Marxian formula that 'social being determines social consciousness.' "[65]

The question is, how is this higher morality created and what precisely is it? Durkheim did not resolve either part of this question, but he began the attempt. In regard to the origin of social norms, it has been noted that:

> . . . there is one theme that recurs in his studies. It is, above all, that moral norms grow up around sustained patterns of social interaction. It is clear, even in *The Division of Labor*, that he was beginning to focus on patterns of social interaction, as providing the focus around which moral beliefs emerge and develop.[66]

As to the nature of the higher morality, Durkheim recommended the creation of a science of ethics to isolate its essence. He planned to write a treatise on the subject but death prevented its fruition.

Durkheim and Sociology

The impact of Durkheim's work on sociology has been variously interpreted. In a 1928 publication, Pitirim Sorokin wrote,

We may say . . . that Durkheim's monographic studies have shown clearly that purely social factors in the form of social interaction . . . cannot be ignored in an explanation of social and psychical phenomena. Durkheim's works made this especially clear. But recognizing this value of the sociologistic interpretation, shall we follow Durkheim as far as to exclude all other interpretations? I think we shall not. . . .[67]

In point of fact, American reaction to the analyses of Durkheim remained largely skeptical and negative up to the 1930s. "During the period 1890–1917," observed Roscoe Hinkle, "few European sociologists were more generally disregarded and less enthusiastically received by American sociology than Durkheim." [68] The prevailing point of view in American sociological circles was heavily oriented around (1) an individualistic and voluntaristic conception of human behavior, and (2) belief in an inherent and progressively evolving human rationality. Thus, a line of reasoning which attributed the source of human civility to the constraint exercised by extra-somatic forces, and which predicted the course of social change to be toward collectivism, seemed to the American scholar the epitome of misguided thought. As Nisbet stated,

Durkheim's impress upon the American mind was made only slowly; much more slowly than that upon the European mind. Between American sociological thought and the acceptance of Durkheimian perspectives lay the wilderness of homespun individualism, pragmatism, and general suspicion of theory that Europeans, starting with Tocqueville, were so struck by. In retrospect it can be seen that early suspicion and incomprehension of Durkheim in the American scholarly mind were predictable and inevitable. Individualism, as an analytical perspective, was common enough in Europe in the nineteenth century; in America it was a part of the very air men breathed.[69]

It was not until after the occurrence of a major economic depression (Durkheim's penetrating discussions of the disorganizing consequences of social disruptions such as economic depressions undoubtedly contributed heavily to his "rediscovery" by American scholars) and two world wars that

American social scientists began to seriously consider the importance of the Durkheimian perspective. In 1960, Hinkle wrote,

> The interest in Durkheim in the 1940's and 1950's, which apparently originated in the 1930's has become so extensive and diversified—especially since 1945—that it warrants a separate study. Durkheim has become a central figure in a number of specialized fields. It seems likely that his impact could be observed in such specialities as the sociologies of values, knowledge, law, religion, industry, communications, crime, small groups, formal organization, social change, and, perhaps, collective behavior.[70]

Nisbet judges Durkheim's impact on social thought to be on a level with that of Marx, Darwin, and Freud. In his view,

> More than any other figure in the history of sociology, Emile Durkheim seems to embody what has proved to be conceptually most distinctive in the field and most fertile in its contribution to other modern disciplines. Durkheim, it might be said, is the complete sociologist.[71]

Marx and Durkheim: A Summary

The contributions of Durkheim—his methodology and theoretical orientation—are solidly entrenched in sociological thought and they influence significantly the working activities of contemporary American sociologists. The same cannot so easily be claimed in the case of the contributions of Marx. The subjects of conflict, revolution, and social change are outstanding lacunae in the literature of American sociology. In recent years, however, there has been a concerted effort on the part of some (mostly European scholars closely acquainted with American sociology) to integrate Marxian thought into mainstream American sociology. (This subject is touched upon in chapter 5.) Up to the late 1960s, Marx's impact on American sociology could be observed mostly in terms of his sociologistic perspective. It is difficult to say, though, how much of Marx's contributions were and are acknowledged by American sociologists because of or in spite of their acceptance of similar Durkheimian tenets.

Sociologism describes a frame of reference based on the assumption that society is a reality sui generis. That is, that social facts are different from and cannot be reduced to psychological or other behavioral facts. Hence, the Durkheimian postulate: "The determining cause of a social fact should be sought among the social facts preceding and not among the states of the individual consciousness"; and the Marxian postulate: "It is not the consciousness of men that determines their being, but, on the contrary, their social being that determines their consciousness." For both, social behavior was determined, or caused, by certain "extrasomatic" forces which can be discerned—that is, objectively studied—in their coercive effects. To Durkheim, society in general, but eventually the religious institution in particular, was the locus of these coercive facts. Hence, in his words, ". . . the individual is dominated by a moral reality greater than himself: namely, collective reality." [72] To Marx, the economic institution was primary. In his words, for example, "The union [of wage laborers] into one single productive body and the establishment of a connexion between their individual functions, are matters foreign and external to them, are not their own act, but the act of the capital that brings and keeps them together." [73]

There is much to support the interpretation of the sociologistic frame of reference as a paradigm. It can be said with confidence that it has provided sociologists with subject matter, theory, and method. Yet it has not done so in the rigorous way that Kuhn would demand of a full-fledged scientific paradigm. Accurate prediction of complex behavior is still beyond the grasp of social scientists. Perhaps, however, facts such as this have more to do with basic differences between the social and the physical sciences than to the nature of a paradigm.

In any event, it is time now to turn to an examination of the initial attempts to develop a unique sociological perspective by American scholars. The next chapter is devoted to a discussion of the theoretical work of the two men most responsible for establishing sociology in America: Lester Frank Ward and William Graham Sumner. Much of Marx and Durkheim is alive in their words, but in a distinctly American form.

THREE · The Ward-Sumner controversy

A good deal of the motivational force behind the initiation of sociology in late-nineteenth-century America can be traced to the nature of the times. The period was characterized by great social change engendered by rapid industrialization and urbanization. It was also the century of Darwin and Marx. While Darwinian evolutionary theory and Marxian revolutionary theory have their points of divergence, they also have much in common. The mechanism of change in both cases is *conflict* which is postulated to be an omnipresent fact of life on earth. The two theories also parallel each other in that both contain a conception of the behavior of living things as being significantly influenced, if not determined, by extrasomatic factors such as geographical location and sociocultural variables. They differ in their orientation to change. For the most part, change in Darwinian evolutionary theory is a slow and continuous process. In Marxian theory, evolutionary change often gives rise to radical and abrupt alteration. Revolutionary change comes about through the gradual unfolding of events, but it is not explainable by a simple summation of its precipitating ingredients. It is a progressive leap which is greater than the sum of its parts.

The essential point for Marx was that the laws of evolutionary and revolutionary change could be discovered and applied by men to improve their lives. He felt that his theory enabled him to identify these laws and that they should be used to construct a socialistic state—a society in which men would maintain orderly and just relations free from the turmoil produced by competition and strife.

Most nineteenth-century evolutionists maintained an idea of progress in their formulations, but many doubted that men could rationally foresee what would be in their best interests in the future on the basis of present conditions. They thought that nature, if let alone, would evolve in the most beneficial direction for mankind. Man could chart the course of evolution and upon occasion interfere with its flow, but in the long run he and all else would be pulled along by the force of its current. The two opposing strands of thought—the one rather anthropocentric and optimistic and the other more oriented to nature and fatalistic—were exemplified by the writings of Lester Frank Ward and William Graham Sumner.[1]

Lester Frank Ward

Lester Frank Ward (1841–1913) has sometimes been referred to as the father of American sociology because of his *Dynamic Sociology* (initially published in 1883 at his own expense), the first sociological treatise by an American.[2] To Harold W. Pfautz, "Ward's life history represents one version of the American success story: from farm to city, from hand work to head work." [3] Ward was born and raised on a farm in Joliet, Illinois (on the site of a rock quarry where today a state prison stands), the youngest of ten children. Not blessed with the financial resources to obtain much formal education, Ward taught himself the rudiments of Latin, Greek, French, and German while working at odd jobs as a teen-ager.

Upon being discharged from the Union Army in 1865, Ward took a job as a clerk in the Treasury Department in Washington, D.C. By attending night school at what is now George Washington (then Columbian) University, he earned an A.B. in 1869 and an LL.B. in 1871. In 1872, he was admitted to the bar, received an M.A. in botany and a diploma in medicine. In 1881 he was promoted to geologist and in 1883, the year he published *Dynamic Sociology*, he became the chief paleontologist for the United States Geological Survey. After retiring from government service, Ward, in 1906, went to Brown University to occupy a newly created chair of sociology.

In developing a rationale for the raison d'être of a science of society, Ward chose to identify its subject matter as an evolutionary product of nature. He set out to demonstrate that human association was just as much a product of natural law as were geological formations. Everything, he said, must be viewed as emanations of matter, motion, and energy. Matter was posited as the ultimate reality and presumed to be infinitely divisible. Matter was to be observed by its motion or actions and by its effects or energy transformations. All matter was attributed with innate irritability and constant motion or activity. Particles of matter in motion came into contact and exerted force and pressure on each other. Certain chance meetings of particles produced combinations or aggregates which were syntheses and sui generis phenomena. According to Ward there are three types of aggregation and these are stages in the evolution of the cosmos: (1) primary aggregation (the evolution of inorganic matter), (2) secondary aggregation (the evolution of organic matter), and (3) tertiary aggregation (the evolution of superorganic matter or society).

As Pfautz observes, "Ward was primarily concerned with the elaboration of this evolutionary scheme." Furthermore,

In spelling out the sequence, Ward introduced the concept of "synergy"—a combination of the ideas of energy and mutuality. Synergy is a process that operates among the antithetical forces of nature and leads to the development of increasingly complex structures. Successive levels of complexity consist of more than the sum of the preceding elements, and this emergence of new levels he called creative synthesis (borrowing the term from [Wilhelm] Wundt).[4]

Ward did not grant nature a teleological motive for its creativity. Nature, he said, "must be regarded as *unconscious*." In addition,

Throughout all the changes which have resulted in the evolution of man, the process has been purely automatic. No thought, no ideas, no plan, nor purpose has entered into the great cosmic movement.[5]

Mind, the necessary resource for contrived and rational organization, is found only in man and he represents the end rather than the beginning of the evolutionary process. "[Mind] is the distinctive attribute of the creature, and not of the creator." [6] Therefore, man should attempt to understand nature and control it.

To those who urged adaptation to nature and the acceptance of the principle of survival of the fittest in support of a laissez faire economic system, Ward addressed the following statement:

. . . an entirely different set of principles must be applied to man from those which can be applied to irrational life. There competition is free, or rather it is pure. It continues as long as the weaker can survive it, and when these at last go to the wall and the better adapted structures survive and triumph, it is the triumph of a real superiority, and the strong and robust alone are left to recruit the earth. But when mind enters into the context the character of competition is at first completely changed, and later competition itself is altogether crushed out, and while it is still the strong that survive it is a strength which comes from indirection, from deception, artfulness, cunning, and shrewdness, necessarily coupled with stunted moral qualities, and largely aided by the accident of position. In no proper sense is it true that the fittest survive. If this were their only function it is evident that brains would be a positive detriment to society. Pure animal competition would be far better. It is probably contemplation of the hopelessness of this state of things which has given the gloomy cast to Oriental philosophy, and it is no wonder that those moderns who consider the present order unalterable should maintain that we live in the worst possible universe. Those who can see a surplus of good in things as they are, or can hope for their improvement under the laws of evolution unaided by social intelligence must be set down as hopelessly blinded by the great optimistic illusion of all life.[7]

In Ward's sociological perspective, societal institutions—religion, government, law, marriage, and so on—were means rather than ends. They were means devised by men (not, for the most part, in the deliberate and calculative sense) to improve their adaptive capacities. The problem is that one generation's institutions and adaptive problems are not necessarily the next's. "This results," he said, "from the constant changes that are going on in every direction through the activities of individuals seeking their ends, and from time to time causing the needs of the mass to outgrow the restrictions which society under very different previous circumstances was obliged to impose." Hence,

> ... if a state of perfect adaptation of the individual society could be at any given moment conceived to exist it would soon again throw the individual units out of harmony with the social aggregate. It is this inertia of society and its inability to keep pace with the growth of the living mass within it that gives rise to social reformers who are legitimate and necessary, nay, natural products of every country and age, and the ignoring of this fact by conservative writers who lay so great stress on the word natural, is one of the amusing absurdities of the present period.[8]

Thus, he concludes,

> So long, therefore, as society remains the unconscious product of the individual demands of each age, so will the organized social state continue to be found out of accord with and lagging behind the real spirit of the age, often so intolerably so as to require more or less violent convulsions and social revolution. But if ever an ideal social organization shall come to be a clearly defined conscious individual want, it will be possible to establish one that will have elements of flexibility sufficient to render it more or less permanent.[9]

Ward believed the direction of evolution of human society was toward the increasing efficiency of its institutions in satisfying the individual and collective needs of mankind. For the most part, he viewed social institutions as the unconscious products of men attempting to devise means to pursue their diverse interests in the most orderly and effective manner. He thought the institutions of society should be the focus of deliberate study, not only to increase awareness of their structure and function, but also to bring about when necessary their conscious and rational reorganization. Toward these ends, Ward envisioned a sociology with two branches—pure and applied—and two major subject areas—statics and dynamics.

Pure sociology was to be oriented toward the pursuit of knowledge for its own sake, and applied sociology was to be concerned with the application of obtained knowledge for the betterment of society. Social statics was the study of social organization, its structure and functioning. As Ward emphasized, "The investigation of structures is anatomy, that of functions is physiology, and in all sciences, including sociology, the study of both anatomy and physiology belongs to the department of statics." [10] Dynamics is the study of changes in structure and function. In his words,

> Both the organization of structures out of the structureless condition and the modification of the type of structures already formed are dynamic phenomena. All nature is plastic and this incessant pressure of the social forces for the betterment of types of structure has resulted in an almost universal but exceedingly gradual change in these structures. The sociologist has before him the task of explaining the precise *modus operandi* of these changes.[11]

Ward's conception of the active element behind social change requires some explanation. His primary concern, it must be emphasized, was to specify and rationalize the "social factor" as a unique variable in need of independent study. For him, as well as other members of his generation, the social factor was viewed as the consequence of association among essentially autonomous individuals. It was thought that man was led to seek out his kind because of inherent needs which could only be satisfied with the assistance of others. The problem was to identify the various forms of association and account for them by means of certain compelling "forces" within the individual. The dynamic agent (that is, the general motive force behind human behavior leading to social organization and social change), said Ward, "resides in the feelings or affective forms of appetitive desire constituting impulses, or impelling forces, and motives, or moving forces, all of which may be embodied under the general term will, and regarded as making up the true soul of nature; of man, and of society." [12] The social forces, or innate desires and emotions which compel endless "gratification and expansion," were classified as follows:

I PHYSICAL OR ESSENTIAL FORCES [13]
(function bodily)

1. *Preservative Forces*	2. *Reproductive Forces*
They form the basis of all action and desire and preserve and maintain individual life.	They form the basis of all efforts of nature to continue the race.
The chief force is hunger, which gives rise to property, slavery, labor, and industry.	The chief force is love, the influence of which is internal and molding, not creative.
(A) Positive or attractive, seeking pleasure.	(A) Direct. The sexual desire.
(B) Negative or protective, avoiding pain.	(B) Indirect. Affections for parents or kin.

II THE SPIRITUAL OR NONESSENTIAL FORCES
(function psychically)

3. *Socializing Forces*

They are the basis of race elevation, and the chief civilizing impulses.

(A) Emotional or moral, seek the safe and the good.

(B) Esthetic, seek the beautiful.

(C) Intellectual, seek the true and the useful.

Practically every sociologist of Ward's generation felt the necessity of presenting a similar list of social forces in the articulation of his own theoretical system.[14] Today, the social forces are often interpreted as a misguided effort to conceptualize human behavior as the effect of biological instincts. While accurate as far as it goes, this view, if taken by itself, would minimize the main point, i.e., the goal that Ward set for the sciences and sociology. Ward believed that the goal of sociology was the explanation of all forms, rather than a particular form, of human behavior, or, in his words, "human achievement." The rationale for this seemingly pretentious goal for the infant science of society was Ward's acceptance of the Comteian notion of a hierarchical ranking of the sciences. Comte held that sociology represented an evolutionary advancement over its predecessors, which included in rank order: biology, chemistry, physics, astronomy, and mathematics. Ward assumed, as was not uncommon at the time, that scientific knowledge evolved toward increasing levels of complexity and abstraction, and that each science had the job of synthesizing the knowledge of all those lower in rank. So he claimed that "The more specific data of sociology consist in the facts contributed by the various branches or sciences that fall directly under it. . . ." [15] Ward's classification scheme, which is an abbreviated "tabular view of all knowledge in the order in which it has been evolved." [16] appears on pages 80–81.

To Ward, then, sociology was not given a narrowly conceived subject matter and a highly specific field of vision. The general unit of analysis was human society (its statics and dynamics) conceived of as an emergent product of the association of individuals. The sociological task was to construct theories and explanations of society by synthesizing the data collected by the "subordinate sciences." The goal was to uncover laws of *human behavior*.

In searching for behavioral laws, sociologists should never, said Ward, lose sight of the fact that ". . . the true test of a science is the application of its principles to some useful purpose." [17] Sociological knowledge should be used to organize society in such a way as to enable each individual to attempt the realization of his full potential. In order to achieve this goal he thought that a new form of government would be required. To Ward, America was a plutocracy, a tool used by men of wealth to protect and extend their operations. In an article published in 1895 he put it this way,

> The very possession of wealth is only made possible by government. The safe conduct of all business depends upon the certain protection of law. The most powerful business combinations take place under legal forms. Even dishonest and swindling schemes, so long as they violate no penal statute, are protected by law. Speculation in the necessaries of life is legitimate business, and is upheld by the officers of the law though it result in famine; and even the bread riots are put down by the armed force of the state. Thus has society become the victim of its own system, against the natural effects of which it is powerless to protect itself. It has devised the best possible scheme for satisfying the rapacity of human nature.[18]

The proposed alternative to plutocracy was *sociocracy*. For Ward,

> The term designed to note a state of society or form of government in advance of any hitherto attained, was sociocracy, meaning a government by society, or the art which corresponds to the science of sociology. The great social problem must be solved by society itself, when it shall have become conscious of itself, conscious of its power and sufficiently intelligent to exercise that power, in the execution of its own will. This presupposes a wider acquaintance on the part of the individual member of society of the true principles of social science, and a fearless application of those principles by the collective mind of society as embraced in its form of government, in the interest of the whole social organism.[19]

It was claimed by some that *sociocracy* was a euphemism for socialism. Ward denied this and attempted to differentiate the two terms in the following manner:

1. Individualism [read, *laissez-faire* capitalism] has created artificial inequalities.

| Kinds of Knowledge | | Subjects of the Sciences |
SCIENCES	SUBSCIENCES	PRODUCTS OF EVOLUTION COSMIC STRUCTURES
Sociology		Human Society
	Pedagogy	Knowledge
	Pathology	Disease
	Esthetology	The Fine Arts
	Nomology (jurisprudence)	Justice
	Politology, Civiology (politics)	The State
	Ecology (economics)	Wealth, Property
	Theology	God, Religion
	Ethology (ethics)	Customs, Conduct
	Philology	Language
	Gamology (sex relations)	The Family
	Ethnology	Human Races
	Anthropology	Man
Psychology		
	Objective Psychology	Man
	Subjective Psychology	Animals
Biology		Organisms
	Zoology	Animals
	Botany	Plants
	Plasmatology	Protoplasm
Chemistry	Organic Chemistry	Organic Compounds
	Inorganic Chemistry	Inorganic Compounds
Physics		
	Barology	Matter
	Radiology	Electrons
	Etherology	Ether
	Thermology	

| Kinds of Knowledge | | Subjects of the Sciences PRODUCTS OF EVOLUTION |
SCIENCES	SUBSCIENCES	COSMIC STRUCTURES
	Photology	
	Electrology	
Astronomy		Celestial Bodies
	Solar Astronomy	The Solar System
	Sidereal Astronomy	Stars
	Cosmical Astronomy	Nebulae

2. Socialism seeks to create artificial equalities.

3. Sociocracy recognizes natural inequalities and aims to abolish artificial inequalities.

4. Individualism confers benefits on those only who have the ability to obtain them, by superior power, cunning, intelligence, or the accident of position.

5. Socialism would confer the same benefits on all alike, and aims to secure equality of fruition.

6. Sociocracy would confer benefits in strict proportion to merit, but insists upon *equality of opportunity* as the only means of determining the degree of merit.[20]

About the details of his conception of sociocratic government, its structure, powers, and responsibilities, Ward was remarkably laconic. He did, however, recommend the establishment of a national academy of social science, the purpose of which would be to train prospective decision makers. Ward felt that intelligent and informed leadership was an acquired not an inherited trait. Thus, as historian Henry Steele Commager has pointed out, Ward believed that "the major task of society [was] to provide education for all, to discover talent and develop it and enlist it in the attack on social problems."[21]

Ward did not think that violence and revolution were necessary to produce the changes he advocated. Sociocracy would be a natural outgrowth of democracy, and he saw both as parts of an inherently progressive evolutionary pattern. As he stated,

> Sociocracy will differ from all other forms of government that have been devised, and yet that difference will not be so radical as to require a revolution. Just as absolute monarchy passed imperceptibly into limited monarchy, and this, in many states without even a change of name has passed into more or less pure democracy, so democracy is capable of passing as smoothly into sociocracy, and without taking on this unfamiliar name or changing that by which it is now known.[22]

Although Ward diverged from Marx in denying the necessity of revolution, he was equally committed to the idea that the path to greater individual freedom led through collective organization. As Ward's biographer put it,

> In 1883, the year of Marx's death, Ward came upon the American scene with his *Dynamic Sociology*. . . . He pointed out the widening crack in the existing individualistic system, and the necessity of building a collectivist order in which human life would be above dollars, and the interest of society above that of any of its members. His argument has the simplicity of all great truths. We cannot live alone, any more than by chance or drift. . . . By himself, the individual is a letter in a vast alphabet. In co-operation with his fellows, he spells words and expresses ideas which rock the world.[23]

Starting with the same basic problem—how to lay the foundation of the sociological enterprise—Ward's arch rival, William Graham Sumner, developed a different emphasis in his study of society.

William Graham Sumner

Sumner (1840–1910) was born in Paterson, New Jersey, the son of an immigrant mechanic from Lancashire, England. He attended Yale University and graduated in 1863 destined for the ministry. The following year, however, was spent abroad. This was made possible because a friend's brother was persuaded to grant him the necessary funds to continue his education. However, before he could leave he was drafted by the Union Army. According to this biographer, Sumner's benefactor again supplied him with the funds to purchase exemption. Sumner left the task of finding a substitute to his father, but, as Harris Starr noted, it is doubtful that anyone actually served in his stead. Be this as it may, the authorities were apparently sufficiently satisfied with his behavior not to interfere with his leaving the country and studying at Geneva, Göttingen, and Oxford.

In 1867 Sumner was ordained deacon in the Protestant Episcopal Church. In 1872, he was appointed professor of political and social science at Yale and three years later taught the first course in sociology ever offered in the United States. He held his position at Yale until retiring in 1909. Concerning his reasons for leaving the ministry, it has been written that,

> . . . at the root of his uneasiness in the ministry, was the fact that the topics in which he was becoming increasingly interested he could not discuss from the pulpit, nor could he battle there for the principles which at that time, he felt, called imperatively for bold and intelligent support. Currency and the tariff he considered matters of most urgent importance, threatening all the interests of the nation, moral, social, and economic. About these it was impossible to preach, "But I got so near to it," he confesses, "that I was detected sometimes, as, for instance, when a New York banker came to me, as I came down from the pulpit, and said, 'There was a good deal of political economy in that sermon.'" Moreover, he had recently read the essays of Herbert Spencer, which were afterwards collected in the volume, *The Study of Sociology*. The conception of society, of social forces, and of the science of society there offered were just what he had long been groping after. "It rescued social science from the dominion of the cranks, and offered a definite and magnificent field of work, from which we might hope at last to derive definite results for the solution of social problems." This was the field to which Sumner felt himself most loudly called. An academical career would offer him the opportunity

to enter it and at the same time teach, preach, and fight for righteousness and truth. He left the ministry because he was persuaded that he could best employ his capabilities elsewhere.[24]

Sumner did not build his sociological thought on the principle of the natural sociability of mankind. "We do not believe," he said, "that man was outfitted with any innate quality of sociability implanted in his germ-plasm, but that the tendency to associate is acquired rather than inherited, and that man's association with his kind is a product of societal rather than organic evolution." [25] For him *sociability* was one of those terms that are referred to nature because their origin is unknown.

Even though men are not "naturally" social, social organization is natural in that it has been created primarily in a spontaneous and automatic fashion. Society, he said,

> is not, in its origin, artificial or designedly disciplinary, like that of an army or an orchestra. Historically it has been produced by the process of trial and failure, the organization which grew up was the one that gave most satisfaction with the least pain. From time to time the elements of the situation changed, and then the organization had to adapt itself anew. It did so without rationally conceived and visualized purpose, without reflection and analysis.[26]

To Sumner, man was by nature, if anything, a self-centered creature whose actions were largely the effect of nonintellectual forces. As Starr put it, ". . . he had learned that human beings in general are not controlled in their actions by cold logic, and that the reasonableness of a policy, however vividly demonstrated, does not in itself impel them to adopt it." [27] While he agreed with those, such as Ward, who viewed the human intellect as an evolutionary advancement, he was not of the opinion that its application was generally the most gratifying human experience. He regarded the intellect primarily as a means for the attainment of ends, and he felt that the most numerous and most important of these sprang from animal urges. He was inclined to emphasize the limitations as much as, if not more than, the assets of intellectual activity. He referred, for example, to "the superstitution of education," and observed that:

> Our faith in the power of book learning is excessive and unfounded. It is a superstition of the age. The education which forms character and produces faith in sound principles of life comes through personal influence and example. . . . It is taken in from the habits and atmosphere of a school, not from the school textbooks. School work opens an opportunity that a thing may be, but the probability that it will be depends on the person, and it may be nil or contrary to what is desired. High attainments in school enhance the power obtained, but the ethical value of it all depends on how it is used. These facts are often misused or exaggerated in modern educational controversies, but their reality cannot be denied. Book learning is addressed to the intellect, not the feelings, but *the feelings are the spring of action*.[28]

Sumner believed in the policy of laissez faire, and particularly for education. To be educated was to become better able to direct oneself, not to become aware of how better to be directed by others. In a curiously modern tone, he wrote:

> School education, unless it is regulated by the best knowledge and good sense, will produce men and women who are all of one pattern, as if turned in a lathe. When priests managed school it was their intention to reach just this result. They carried in their heads ideas of the Christian man and woman, and they wanted to educate all to this model. Public schools in a democracy may work in the same way. Any institution which runs for years in the same hands will produce a type.[29]

Furthermore, he pointed out,

> If a teacher is to be displaced by a board of trustees because he is a free-trader, or a gold man, or a silver man, or disapproves of a war in which the ruling clique has involved the country, or because he thinks that Hamilton was a great statesman and Jefferson an insignificant one, or because he

says that he has found some proof that alcohol is not always bad for the system, we might as well go back to the dominion in education of the theologians.[30]

The point he stressed was that we can teach only what we know up to the present time. He thought that this notion was contrary to that disseminated by school boards and boards of trustees. "They teach," he said, "that there are absolute and universal facts of knowledge, whereas we ought to teach that all our knowledge is subject to unlimited verification and revision." [31]

Sumner's views on education were, of course, a reflection of certain basic assumptions regarding man and society. He thought of human behavior as being motivated by a combination of psychobiological and socioenvironmental forces. The intraindividual forces were hunger, love, vanity, and fear. These were described as "psycho-physical traits, instincts, and dexterities, or at least 'predispositions' inherited by men from their 'beast ancestors.'" In the beginning, the individual forces stimulated association, or "currents of similarity, concurrence, and mutual contribution." Association led to the origination of the "folkways," or the extraindividual forces. As he described them,

> The folkways are unconscious, spontaneous, uncoordinated. It is never known who led in devising them, although we must believe that talent exerted its leadership at all times. Folkways come into existence now all the time. The folkways are habits of the individual and customs of the society which arise from efforts to satisfy needs. In time, the folkways become the "right" way to do all things. They extend over the whole of life.[32]

Thus, concluded Sumner,

> In the present work [Folkways] the proposition to be maintained is that the folkways are the widest, most fundamental and most important operation by which the interests of men in groups are served, and the process by which folkways are made is the chief one which elementary societal or

group phenomena are due. The life of society consists in making folkways and applying them. The science of society must be construed as the study of them.[33]

Folkways take more than one form. Some, such as styles of dress and certain forms of social etiquette, may not be terribly binding nor provoke strong negative sanctions if violated or ignored. Others, particularly those relating to sexual conduct, may require literal compliance, and if transgressed, carry the most severe forms of societal punishment. Sumner referred to this latter group of folkways as *mores*.

From the mores are derived other essential structural components of society. In his words,

Institutions and laws are produced out of mores. An institution consists of a concept (idea, notion, doctrine, interest) and a structure. The structure is a framework, or apparatus, or perhaps only a number of functionaries set to cooperate in prescribed ways at a certain conjuncture. The structure holds the concept and furnishes instrumentalities for bringing it into the world of facts and action in a way to serve the interests of men in society. Institutions are either crescive or enacted. They are crescive when they take shape in the mores, growing by the instinctive efforts by which the mores are produced. Then the efforts, through long use, become definite and specific. Property, marriage, and religion are the most primary institutions. They began in folkways. They became customs. They developed into mores by the addition of some philosophy of welfare, however crude. Then they were made more definite and specific as regards the rules, the prescribed acts, and the apparatus to be employed. This produced a structure and the institution was complete.[34]

The folkways are not so independent a force that they cannot be altered. It was Sumner's view that in the usual case they were gradually modified as conditions changed and new interests arose. Calculated change was possible, but only if the mores were ready for it. "That is why," he said, "the agitator, reformer, prophet, reorganizer of society, who has found out 'the truth' and wants to 'get a law passed' to realize it right away, is only a mischief-maker." If reformers are successful it is because they have taken up something which the mores have made vulnerable to change. Here is the same idea expressed in more eloquent terms:

> If this poor old world is as bad as they say, one more reflection may check the zeal of the headlong reformer. It is at any rate a rough old world. It has taken its trend and curvature and all its twists and tangles from a long course of formation. All its wry and crooked gnarls and knobs are therefore stiff and stubborn. If we puny men by our arts can do anything at all to straighten them, it will only be by modifying the tendencies of some of the forces at work, so that, after a sufficient time, their action may be modified. This effort, however, can at most be only slight, and it will take a long time. In the mean time spontaneous forces will be at work, compared with which our efforts are like those of a man trying to deflect a river, and these forces will have changed the whole problem before our interferences have time to make themselves felt. . . . Everyone of us is a child of his age and cannot get out of it. He is in the stream and is swept along with it. . . . The men will be carried along with it and be made by it. The utmost they can do by their cleverness will be to note and record their course as they are carried along, which is what we do now, and is that which leads us to the vain fancy that we can make or guide the movement. That is why it is the greatest folly of which a man can be capable, to sit down with a slate and pencil to plan out a new social world.[35]

What particularly annoyed Sumner about social reformers was what he perceived to be their tendency to focus attention on the problems of "the poor and the weak" and to ignore the plight of the middle classes. He expressed his views on this subject in "The Forgotten Man," an article that has influenced the past and recent campaign strategies of the Republican party. As Sumner saw it,

> The philanthropists and humanitarians have their minds all full of the wretched and miserable whose case appeals to compassion, attacks the sympathies, takes possession of the

imagination, and excites the emotions. They push on towards the quickest and easiest remedies and they forget the real victim [the Forgotten Man].[36]

Who is the Forgotten Man? "He is the simple, honest laborer, ready to earn his living by productive work. . . . He does not appeal to the emotions or excite the sentiments. . . . Every particle of capital which is wasted on the vicious, the idle, and the shiftless is so much taken from the capital available to reward the independent and productive laborer. . . . We do not remember him because he makes no clamor; but I appeal to you whether he is not the man who ought to be remembered first of all, and whether, on any sound social theory, we ought not to protect him against the burdens of the good-for-nothing."[37]

Actually, Sumner was more opposed to idealistic notions of reform than he was to reform per se. He felt, for example, that many reform doctrines were based on "a poetical and metaphysical notion of liberty," namely, "that a man may do as he has a mind to do." As far as he was concerned,

If there were any such liberty as that of doing as you have a mind to, the human race would be condemned to everlasting anarchy and war as these erratic wills crossed and clashed against each other. True liberty lies in the equilibrium of rights and duties, producing peace, order, and harmony. As I have defined it, it means that a man's right to take power and wealth out of the social product is measured by the energy and wisdom which he has contributed to the social effort.[38]

Having said this, one might be led to believe that Sumner would not object to plutocracy. In fact he was as opposed to "the greed and arrogance of plutocrats" as he was to "the venality of the humbler sets of people." In an article published in 1899, "The Conquest of the United States by Spain," which stuns the reader because it contains so much that is relevant to the recent Vietnam war, Sumner bluntly stated his position on plutocracy.

The great foe of democracy now and in the near future is plutocracy. Every year that passes brings out this antagonism more distinctly. It is to be the social war of the twentieth century. In that war militarism, expansion, and imperialism will all favor plutocracy. In the first place, war and expansion will favor jobbery, both in the dependencies and at home. In the second place, they will take away the attention of the people from what the plutocrats are doing. In the third place, they will cause large expenditures of the people's money, the return for which will not go into the treasury, but into the hands of a few schemers. In the fourth place, they will call for a large public debt and taxes, and these things especially tend to make men unequal, because any social burdens bear more heavily on the weak than on the strong, and so make the weak weaker and the strong stronger.[39]

Sumner ended his days pessimistic about the future of America and the ability of social reformers to do much about it. His doubts regarding efforts to reconstruct society rationally were the product of more than an arbitrary ideological inclination. A perusal of the ethnological record convinced him that folkways and their structural derivatives played a much more complicated role in human affairs than was generally appreciated.

To Sumner, men and social institutions were so intimately interwoven that it was difficult, if not impossible, to disentangle one from the other. He was certain that most people were not consciously aware of how much their identity was a result of exposure to a particular social milieu. Doubtless, social customs were largely the unconscious products of generations of men. Their existence, however, was not made less important because of this fact. Out of all those possible, some customs rather than others were adopted. It was a fundamental task of the science of society to account for the origin of continually evolving folkways and mores and analyze their effects on human organization.

It seemed to Sumner that social order and rational human behavior were possible because of, not in spite of, the presence of folkways and mores.[40] Certain arbitrary but accepted notions of ideal conduct—of values that transcend the idiosyncratic and fleeting interests of each individual—were deemed necessary if human relations were to be more than contests of animal cunning and guile. In Sumner's hands, social institutions took on the aura of sacred objects. They were not to be regarded as simple human artifacts to be manipulated at will. Hardly, for until their place in men's lives was understood and their own interrelationships charted, it was probable that their deliberate alteration, replacement, or rejection would yield more negative than positive results.

Comparison and Summary

Though they exhibited basic disagreement, Ward and Sumner shared a major basic premise: both interpreted human sociability as the outgrowth of individual behavior activated by psychobiological drives. Society was conceived of as the product of the chance meetings of acting individuals. They agreed that orderly social behavior was an acquired rather than an inherited human trait. It is from this point that they went their separate ways.

Ward postulated that the evolution of the human mind enabled men to become rationally aware of the essence of their own condition in society. Men can deliberately work toward and effect the construction of a social milieu within which each individual will be able to seek the realization of his intellectual promise. Ward emphasized that the liberating social structure he had in mind should not be devised so as to impose artificial constraint upon individual creativity. Conformity to tradition was accorded secondary importance to innovation and change. Social organization was a means to an end rather than an end in itself.

Sumner also emphasized the importance of individual freedom and creativity in social life. However, his belief was that change and innovation had to be balanced by a considerable degree of normative constraint. He did not think that men were more rational than irrational. The relationship between the two human attributes was extremely complex and, thus, he urged the acquisition of more knowledge about their mixture lest the manipulation of one at the expense of the other provoke more harm than good. It seemed doubtful to Sumner that men could ever rationally formulate a plan to guarantee themselves satisfying amounts of individual freedom and social order without an accurate measure of the origins and state of their own rational and irrational composition. The problem was that neither rationality nor irrationality existed in fixed form in an individual or a society. Today's rational attitude was yesterday's irrational motive. Furthermore, it appeared to Sumner that men could be rationally aware of their own irrationality without necessarily being able to do much about it. Often we can recognize our own mental illness without being able to cure it, either by ourselves or with the help of trained "experts." Also, men can think rationally about something while behaving irrationally toward it. For example, one can unconsciously act in racist ways while maintaining an antiracist rationale. All this seemed readily apparent to Sumner. Thus he declared that to sit down with pad and pencil with every confidence of rationally constructing a proper social organization is the greatest folly of which a man is capable.

Eventually, the development of sociological theory proceeded more along the lines prescribed by Sumner than by Ward. Ward's efforts to establish an applied sociology came to be interpreted as premature. His pure sociology apparently was too general in design to have inspired followers to elaborate on it in a long-term and concerted sense.

Neither Ward nor Sumner was able to develop a unique and compellingly attractive sociological paradigm. Both envisioned the goal of sociology, no less than that of any other science, to be the discovery of laws in nature. General laws of human behavior were sought and these were to be grasped by means of the intuitive powers of superior minds in possession of encyclopedic knowledge. Summarily put, ". . . sociology had no boundaries, and failed to offer interested students the means of covering its uncharted scope." [41]

Many "second-generation" sociologists maintained the view that the aim of the discipline should be the discovery of laws of human behavior. However, there was an ever-growing recognition of the need to conceptualize types and forms of human behavior within a restricted analytical frame of reference. Something approximating the experimental method had to be devised if scientifically meaningful generalizations were to be obtained.

The individual continued to be the focus of attention, but his behavior came to be viewed as the consequence of the interaction of his psychobiological potential and socioenvironmental situation. It is toward the emerging social-psychological perspective that the discussion will now turn.

FOUR · The social-psychological perspective

The Sumner-Ward controversy pointed to the complexity of the relationship between social and psychological facts. To many sociologists, it became increasingly evident that the study of interaction between individual and society should be the central concern of the discipline. The question was: to what extent was psychological disposition influenced by social milieu; and, to what extent was social milieu influenced by the individual? In the words of E. A. Ross, one of the first American social psychologists, "Social psychology falls into two very unequal divisions. viz., *Social Ascendency* and *Individual Ascendency*, the determination of the one by the many and the determination of the many by the one; the moulding of the ordinary person by his social environment, and the moulding of the social environment by the extraordinary person." [1]

The Organic Interpretation: Charles Horton Cooley

The initial attempts to deal with the subject stressed the need to take both sides of the issue into account simultaneously. For example, in discussing the development of personality in the child, James Mark Baldwin wrote:

> I do not see, in short, how the personality of this child can be expressed in any but social terms; nor how, on the other hand, social terms can get any content or value but from the understanding of the developing individual. This is a circle

in the process of growth; and that is just my point. On the one hand, we can get no doctrine of society but by getting the psychology of the "socius" with all his natural history; and on the other hand, we can get no true view of the "socius" at any time without describing the social conditions under which he normally lives, with the history of their action and reaction upon him.[2]

From this point of view, referred to as the *organic perspective,* dualisms, such as "heredity and environment," "ego and alter," and "the individual and society," misrepresent their actual interrelatedness. Each pair merely describes different aspects of a single whole. One of the more articulate advocates of the organic interpretation of human behavior was Charles Horton Cooley (1864–1929) whose viewpoint is well expressed in the following statement:

> Mind is an organic whole made up of cooperating individualities, in somewhat the same way that the music of an orchestra is made up of divergent but related sounds. No one would think it necessary or reasonable to divide the music into two kinds, that made by the whole and that of particular instruments, and no more are there two kinds of mind, the social mind and the individual mind.[3]

To be aware of oneself was to be aware of society. Social consciousness and self-consciousness are inseparable because we cannot conceive of ourselves without reference to some group, or some group without reference to ourselves. Self and society are concomitants; that is, neither is accorded temporal priority over the other. "Self and society are twin-born, we know one as immediately as we know the other, and the notion of a separate and independent ego is an illusion."[4] The sociological task was to study the interaction between self and society; that is, to analyze the ways in which the two relate to effect a totality.

Social consciousness and self-consciousness are located in human imagination. By imagination Cooley wished to emphasize that the interpretive locus of behavioral facts was in the minds of individuals. For Cooley, all the phenomena of human life and all the data of social science are located in the imaginative properties of the mind. As he emphasized, ". . . the imaginations which people have of one another are the *solid facts* of society, and that to observe and interpret these must be a chief aim of sociology." [5]

Since self-consciousness and social consciousness originate and exist only in the mind, their interaction can only occur therein. Here is the way Cooley expressed this important point:

> Society, then, in its immediate aspect, is a relation among personal ideas. In order to have a society it is necessary that persons should get together somewhere; and they get together only as personal ideas in the mind. Where else? What other possible *locus* can be assigned for the real contacts of persons, or in what other form can they come in contact except as impressions or ideas formed in this common *locus*? Society exists in my mind as the contact and reciprocal influence of certain ideas named "I," Thomas, Henry, Susan, Bridget, and so on. It exists in your mind as a similar group, and so in every mind.
>
> I do not see how one can hold that we know persons directly except as imaginative ideas in the mind. [6]

To Cooley, the self is an imaginative reconstruction (but not necessarily an irrational or make-believe creation) of the way in which a person perceives others to imaginatively interpret his appearance. Cooley referred to the self as a "looking-glass self" and said: "A self idea of this sort seems to have three principal elements: the imagination of our appearance to the other person; the imagination of his judgment of that appearance; and some sort of self-feeling, such as pride or mortification." [7]

To uncover the imaginations of people, Cooley prescribed the method of sympathetic introspection. The social psychologist was to place himself actually and/or imaginatively in the functioning milieu of his subjects and then imaginatively reconstruct the relationship between identified stimuli and observed behavioral activity. "In general," said Cooley, "the insights of sociology . . . are imaginative re-

constructions of life whose truth depends upon the competence of the mind that makes them to embrace the chief
factors of the process studied and reproduce or anticipate
their operation." [8] The data of social science are not only
in the imaginations of subjects, but also in the imaginative
interpretive thoughts of investigators. Although interrelated,
the two types of thought are not identical. To apply the
method of sympathetic introspection effectively, one was advised to be careful to differentiate one's own thoughts, their
sources and forms, from those of others. As might be expected, Cooley did not view the method to be effective for
everyone as not all could be expected to possess the proper
combination of native ability and factual knowledge.

In expressing a preference for the method of sympathetic
introspection, Cooley did not rule out the usefulness of
other methods. Consistent with his basic liberal philosophy,
he emphasized the need for an "open-ended" as opposed to a
restrictive methodological orientation. In his words: "Knowledge requires both observation and interpretations, neither
being more scientific than the other. And each branch of
science must be worked out in its own way, which is mainly
to be found in the actual search for truth rather than by *a
priori* methodology." [9]

He did not inveigh against the use of statistics. As Dewey
has interpreted Cooley's position: "There is no essential antagonism between statistics and sympathetic observation and
interpretation. Social science becomes exact, not through the
substitution of statistics for the latter method but through a
supplementation of it by the mathematical manipulation of
data." [10]

The idea of sympathy had more than methodological significance in Cooley's thought. His study of social organization is very much oriented around envisioning a structure
conducive to the generation of sympathetic understanding
among individuals. He hoped that development of the means
of communication and transportation would someday make
it possible for the members of an entire nation to behave
toward one another in the manner of members of a close-
knit family. The heart of Cooley's view on meaningful social

organization is located in his conception of the "primary group." He defined primary groups in the following way:

> By primary groups I mean those characterized by intimate face-to-face association and cooperation. They are primary in several senses, but chiefly in that they are fundamental in forming the social nature and ideals of the individual. The result of intimate association, psychologically, is a certain fusion of individualities in a common whole, so that one's very self, for many purposes at least, is the common life and purposes of the group. Perhaps the simplest way of describing this wholeness is by saying that it is a "we"; it involves the sort of sympathy and mutual identification for which "we" is the natural expression. One lives in the feeling of the whole and finds the chief aims of his will in that feeling.[11]

As Philip Rieff observed, "The primary group is Cooley's Godterm, at once the principle of analysis and that which is the object of analysis." As Rieff continued,

> Cooley tried, by the personal force of his analytic understanding, to help extend the "primary ideals" (i.e., the sentiments generated by primary group living) into areas of society where they cannot be carried directly by primary groups themselves. Cooley's essential conservatism—and, indeed, the essential conservatism of sociology—is most evident here. Implicit in all his intellectual work is the purpose of preserving the ideal values of small, pre-industrial communities in the period of massive, industrial societies.[12]

Cooley, then, sought to combine the micro and macro levels of analysis. He was as much interested in the actions of large social aggregates as he was in the unit acts of individuals. Cooley, says Rieff, knew what he was after and intended to accomplish his goal by regularly shifting theoretical perspectives. It is hard to overemphasize the value of this strategy. Today, as in Cooley's time, the study of the same phenomenon from different vantage points is the most important test of observational reliability available to the sociologist. Many agree with Rieff that only by increasing and alternating analytic perspectives is it possible for sociology to keep from sliding into narrow ideology.

This is not to suggest that Cooley did not have certain ideological inclinations and value biases. His political position has been described as liberal. As Angell has written,

> Provided that the system is an open one, he believed in altering it through gradual, not revolutionary, change. Although he found much that was crude and selfish in the capitalism of his day and much that was admirable in socialism (especially its humane spirit), he was in no sense a radical. He believed too strongly in a ramified tentative process to favor monolithic organization and too strongly in the need of guidance and control to embrace anarchism.[13]

Basically, Cooley was a thoroughgoing humanitarian. The sociologist, he thought, ought to be concerned with portraying the human condition as it is, with sympathetic concern. He wrote,

> A sociologist must have the patient love of truth and the need to reduce it to principles which all men of science require. Besides this, however, he needs the fullest sympathy and participation in the currents of life. He can no more stand aloof than can the novelist or the poet, . . . He cannot be a specialist in the same way that a chemist or a botanist can, because he cannot narrow his life without narrowing his grasp on his subject. To attempt to build up sociology as a technical tradition remote from the great currents of literature and philosophy, would, in my opinion, be a fatal error. It cannot possibly avoid being difficult, but it should be as little abstruse as possible. If it is not human it is nothing.[14]

Cooley's social-psychological orientation was widely acknowledged, particulary for its heuristic implications. His concern with the nature of social order and the manner in which patterns of behavior evolve out of social interaction was and continues to be of basic importance to social psychologists in particular and sociologists in general.

During the last decade of Cooley's life, there was a growing emphasis on the collection of data tied to observables and capable of verification by any trained investigator. The individual continued to be the object of investigation; and the analysis of the growth of self-consciousness and the development of personality were central topics of concern.

Symbolic Interaction and the Social Self: George Herbert Mead

Cooley's contemporary, George Herbert Mead (1863–1931), was very much attuned to the temper of the times and applied a behavioristic orientation to the study of interaction processes. Mead taught at the University of Chicago from 1893 until his death. He was a dynamic and engaging personality who evidently preferred to express and develop his ideas verbally in the classroom setting rather than by means of the written word and formal publication. Most of his ideas were published posthumously in four volumes put together by "devoted students from stenographic notes of his lectures, fragmentary manuscripts, and tentative drafts." [15]

In 1930 Mead published an article in which he critically appraised Cooley's contributions to social thought. In much the same way as Marx disagreed with Hegel's idealism, Mead took issue with Cooley's emphasis on the mind as *the* independent variable in the study of human behavior. In his view, the mind was best viewed as "an outgrowth of primitive human communication." Self-consciousness and personality growth were the product of the human ability to communicate by means of physical gestures and symbolic sounds (language). As Angell put it, "Whereas Cooley saw communication arising within mind, Mead saw mind arising in communication; he held that communication begins in gestures and preverbal sounds to which words are gradually added to create mind." [16]

From Mead's perspective, then, social psychology was concerned with the study of the relationship between group membership and patterns of individual behavior. Society was taken to be the prior variable. "For social psychology, the whole (society) is prior to the part (the individual), not the part to the whole; and the part is explained in terms of the whole, not the whole in terms of the part or parts." [17]

Consistent with his behavioristic approach, Mead's unit of analysis was the "social act." "Social psychology," Mead said, "is behavioristic in the sense of starting off with an observable activity—the dynamic, on-going social process, and the social acts which are its component elements—to be studied and analyzed scientifically." [18] But he was quick to assert that behavioristic social psychology should not ignore the "inner experience of the individual." In his view, ". . . it is particularly concerned with the rise of such experience within the process as a whole." [19]

A social act was defined as a transaction between two or more individuals who possess an established division of labor. Language, the distinctive human attribute, developed when individuals began to interact with one another in a cooperative and rational way. Language begins, said Mead, in expressions of emotions called gestures. Gestures refer to "any part of a social act which stands for, or is a sign of, those parts of the social act yet to occur." [20] In Mead's words, gestures are either "preparatory—beginnings of acts—social acts, i.e., actions and reactions which arise under the stimulation of other individuals, such as clenching the fists, grinding the teeth, assuming an attitude of defense—or else . . . outflows of nervous energy which sluice off the nervous excitement or reinforce and prepare indirectly for action." [21]

To Mead, gestures become significant when they permit symbolic interaction. Significant symbols are gestures whose meaning is known to all members of a social group. They are not only the building blocks of language, but also the essential prerequisites of intellectual activity.

Only in terms of gestures as significant symbols is the existence of mind or intelligence possible; for only in terms of gestures which are significant symbols can thinking—which is simply an internalized or implicit conversation of the individual with himself by means of such gestures—take place. The internalization in our experience of the external conversations of gestures which we carry on with other individuals in the social process is the essence of thinking; and the gestures thus internalized are significant symbols because they have the same meanings for all individual members of the given society or social group, i.e., they respectively arouse the same attitudes in the individuals making them that they arouse in the individuals responding to them: otherwise the individual could not internalize them or be conscious of them and their meanings.[22]

Ultimately, however, the main function of gestures in Mead's perspective is to facilitate rational behavior and stable social organization.

Rational, adjusted behavior is a concomitant of mature self-consciousness. Self-consciousness occurs when one is able intellectually to interpret the symbolic meaning of one's own gestures. In other words, and as Mead put it, the self has the unique quality of being an object to itself. The question was, "How can an individual get outside himself (experimentally) in such a way as to become an object to himself?" He sought the answer by means of an analysis of the "social conduct or activity in which the person is located."

In the manner of Cooley, Mead proceeded on the assumption that the individual cannot experience himself except through the eyes or gestures of others. The individual "enters his own experience as a self . . . , not directly or immediately, not by becoming a subject to himself, but only in so far as he first becomes an object to himself just as other individuals are objects to him or in his experience; and he becomes an object to himself only by taking the attitudes of other individuals toward himself within a social environment or context of experience and behavior in which both he and they are involved." [23]

It is important to note that Mead was referring to the initial stages in the development of self-consciousness. He did not imply that the self is a mere replica, or a mirrored reflection of a standard type. The capacity of the self to be an object to itself in combination with individual differences in social circumstance, perceptive and intellectual ability, physical prowess, and a host of other factors, permit considerable variation in forms of self-consciousness. Actually, the forms of self-consciousness were of secondary importance to

Mead. The primary subject of concern was the general process by which self-consciousness occurs.

The basic process was, of course, human interaction in a group context. "The self," insisted Mead, "is something which has a development; it is not initially there, at birth, but arises in the process of social experience and activity, that is, develops in the given individual as a result of his relations to that process as a whole and to other individuals within that process." [24] Mead concerned himself primarily with the genesis of the self in the socialization process of children.

Initial self-consciousness emerges in three evolutionary stages: the stage of imitative acts, the play stage, and the game stage. The first typically occurs during the second year of life and involves aping the mannerisms of one's significant others, i.e., parents, siblings, and other members of the family of orientation. The play stage begins in about the third year and is marked by the child's inclination to assume various roles. "A child plays at being a mother, at being a teacher, at being a policeman; that is, it is taking different roles, as we say." [25] It is during the play stage that the child begins to get "outside himself"; that is, he begins to manifest sensitivity to the attitudes of others toward himself as object. Role playing eventuates in the acquisition of a series of selves which become integrated during the game stage. The game stage, the period of the emergence of the unified self, occurs when the child is able to take the attitude of all members of the groups to which he belongs. To be an integrated member of a baseball team, for example, one must know the roles of all members of the team and their interdependence with one's own role. As Mead points out,

> The organized community or social group which gives to the individual his unity of self may be called "the generalized other." The attitude of the generalized other is the attitude of the whole community. Thus, for example, in the case of such a social group as a ball team, the team is the generalized other in so far as it enters—as an organized process or social

activity—into the experience of any one of the individual members of it.[26]

For Mead, the basic question was the manner in which man the rational and adjusted being was created. As Charles W. Morris phrased it, ". . . Mead endeavored to carry out a major problem posed by evolutionary conceptions: the problem of how to bridge the gap between impulse and rationality, of showing how certain biological organisms acquire the capacity of self-consciousness, of thinking, of abstract reasoning, of purpose behavior, of moral devotion; the problem in short of how man, the rational animal, arose." [27]

Mead's interest in the study of human behavior went beyond the point of acquisition of knowledge for its own sake. He was much involved in practical politics and was deeply interested in social reconstruction. His approach to social reform was expressed in an article entitled "The Working Hypothesis in Social Reform." Herein he revealed an aversion to utopian solutions and a preference for an experimental approach. He did not think that men could ever sufficiently predict the future course of evolution to be able to govern themselves accordingly. As he saw it,

It is always the unexpected that happens, for we have to recognize, not only the immediate change that is to take place, but also the reaction back upon this of the whole world within which the change takes place, and no human foresight is equal to this. In the social world we must recognize the working hypothesis as the form into which all theories must be cast as completely as in the natural sciences. . . . We can never set up a detailed statement of the conditions that are to be ultimately attained. What we have is a method and a control of application, not an ideal to work toward.[28]

Mead's approach was comparable to that of Cooley and Durkheim. All three men shared a pragmatic orientation and a decidedly tempered evolutionary perspective. None viewed progress toward a definite and ideal stage to be an inherent quality of social organization. Another who shared these ideas, but who emphasized the situational factors in human behavior, was William Isaac Thomas.

The Situational Approach: William Isaac Thomas

In 1886, W. I. Thomas (1863–1947) was awarded a doctorate in English and modern languages by the University of Tennessee. After spending four years at Oberlin College as a professor of English, he entered the University of Chicago to pursue a second doctorate in sociology which he received in 1896. He remained at the University of Chicago until 1918. In that year Thomas was dismissed from the university largely as a result of his having been arrested for an alleged violation of the Mann Act and false hotel registration. As Janowitz appraised the situation, W. I. Thomas was fifty-five years of age and had completed his major piece of research.[29]

The major research work was *The Polish Peasant in Europe and America* done in collaboration with Florian Znaniecki. This work was in four volumes and covered 2,244 pages. In the methodological note to volume 1 Thomas and Znaniecki presented their basic theoretical orientation.

As they saw it, two fundamental problems have confronted social thinkers from time immemorial: (1) the problem of the dependence of the individual upon social organization and culture, and (2) the problem of the dependence of social organization and culture upon the individual. Two kinds of data are involved in the analysis of these problems: "objective cultural elements" or values and "subjective characteristics of the members of the social group" or attitudes. Values and attitudes are the behavioral facts of sociology and social psychology.

"By a social value," they said, "we understand any datum having an empirical content accessible to the members of some social group and a meaning with regard to which it is or may be an object of activity." [30] As examples they referred to a foodstuff, an instrument, a coin, a piece of poetry, a university, a myth, and a scientific theory. The meanings of each become explicit when they are seen in the context of human activity.

> The meaning of the foodstuff is its reference to its eventual consumption; that of an instrument, its reference to the work for which it is designed; that of a coin, the possibilities of buying and selling or the pleasures of spending which it involves; that of the piece of poetry, the sentimental and intellectual reactions which it arouses; that of the university, the social activities which it performs; that of the mythical personality, the cult of which it is the object and the actions of which it is supposed to be the author; that of the scientific theory, the possibilities of control of experience by idea or action that it permits.[31]

An *attitude* is "a process of individual consciousness which determines real or possible activity of the individual in the social world." [32] For example, "hunger that compels the consumption of the foodstuff; the workman's decision to use the tool; . . . the interest in creating, understanding, or applying a scientific theory and the ways of thinking implied in it . . . these are attitudes." [33] To Thomas and Znaniecki, an attitude is the psychological counterpart of a social value. The link between the two is to be observed in activity.

To the field of social psychology, Thomas and Znaniecki assigned the task of studying attitudes—primarily as they are manifested in the concrete acts of members of specific social groups. Values were to be the subject matter of sociology and the other cultural sciences. Sociology was to study one type of values in particular: "social rules." *Social rules* referred to what Durkheim called social facts and what Sumner called folkways, mores, and institutions. Here is how Thomas and Znaniecki explained their interpretation of the relationship between social rules:

> The rules of behavior, and the actions viewed as conforming or not conforming with these rules, constitute with regard to their objective significance a certain number of more or less connected and harmonious systems which can be generally

called social institutions, and the totality of institutions found in a concrete social group constitutes the social organization of this group.[34]

Social psychology and sociology were subsumed under the general designation *social theory*, "as they are both concerned with the relation between the individual and the concrete social group. . . ." The function of social theory is the study of social change, or as they put it, "the process of becoming."

> The chief problems of modern science are problems of causal explanation. The determination and systematization of data is only the first step in scientific investigation. If a science wishes to lay the foundation of a technique, it must attempt to understand and to control the process of *becoming*. Social theory cannot avoid this task, and there is only one way of fulfilling it. Social becoming, like natural becoming, must be analyzed into a plurality of facts, each of which represents a succession of cause and effect. The idea of social theory is the analysis of the totality of social becoming into such causal processes and a systematization permitting us to understand the connections between these processes.[35]

For the study of the process of becoming, Thomas and Znaniecki prescribed a situational frame of reference. "Every concrete activity," they said, "is the solution of a situation." Primarily they wished to capture behavior where and when it occurred. In their view, after-the-fact analyses could only be interpreted as rationalized hearsay. The study of *situational behavior* was viewed as the behavioral scientist's chief opportunity to approximate the experimental method. They felt that human activity had to be observed as it unfolds in a natural setting, and that it was possible to identify the variables which combined to result in particular types of behavior. Accordingly, they conceived of behavioral situations as including three essential elements: (1) the objective value conditions which affect either directly or indirectly the conscious status of the individual actor; (2) the attitudes that an individual brings into a situation on the basis of past experience; and (3) the individual's "definition of the situation," that is, his more or less conscious interpretation of the proper combination of values and attitudes to respond to in the form of a specific act or set of actions.

The definition of the situation was viewed as a necessary preliminary (in most cases resolved in a matter of seconds) at times when the individual must select from among a variety of attitudes and values those he perceives to be appropriate to apply in the circumstances in which he finds himself. Sometimes, of course, a certain value can provoke an automatic response. Upon sight, for example, we often experience an immediate and undeniable urge to consume an article of food. However, said Thomas, in the usual situation "there is a process of reflection, after which either a ready social definition is applied or a new personal definition worked out."

Thomas thought individual attitudes to be influenced by certain inherent "wishes" (which are comparable in function to the social forces concept in the schemes of Ward and Sumner). The wishes were enumerated as follows: (1) the desire for new experience; (2) the desire for recognition, for example, sexual response and social status ("secured by devices ranging from the display of ornament to the demonstration of worth through scientific attainment"); (3) the desire for mastery, or the "will to power" ("exemplified by ownership, domestic tyranny, political despotism, based on the instinct of hate, but capable of being sublimated to laudable ambition"); and (4) the desire for security, which is an emanation of the instinct of fear.[36]

Countering Durkheim's basic methodological principle ("The determining cause of a social fact should be sought among the social facts preceding it and not among the states of the individual consciousness"), Thomas adhered to the following tenet:

> The cause of a social or individual phenomenon is never another social or individual phenomenon alone, but always a combination of a social and an individual phenomenon.
> Or in more exact terms:

The cause of a value or of an attitude is never an attitude or a value alone, but always a combination of an attitude or a value.[37]

One of the most penetrating analyses of the difference between Thomas' conceptual orientation and that of Durkheim, Sumner, and others of a more sociologistic disposition, was performed by Edmund Volkart. According to Volkart,

One of the most important features of human existence is the fact that each individual is born into a group which possesses a going way of life, or a culture. In Thomas' terms a culture is composed of . . . "definitions of situations" which have been arrived at through the consensus of adults over a period of time. As a product of social life, these definitions are embodied in codes, rules, precepts, policies, traditions and standardized social relationships. They are external to individuals, exercise some control over them, and have an existence of their own which makes them amenable to study in and of themselves. In this respect Thomas' approach is similar to that of Durkheim, Sumner, and others.

He differed from them, however, in at least one respect. Whereas Durkheim conceived of "social facts" as being caused by prior social facts, and Sumner conceived of the mores as representing "automatic" adjustments to life conditions, Thomas credited individuals with some power to form these common definitions. . . . By acknowledging the influence of individuals on culture he avoided the mechanistic implications of such doctrines as Sumner's "automatic adjustment," yet retained the possibility of scientific understanding.[38]

The situational idea is very much a part of contemporary social-psychological research. However, Thomas and Znaniecki's distinction between the two essential components of the situation, attitudes and values, has come under severe criticism. In a thorough critique of *The Polish Peasant in Europe and America*, Herbert Blumer, though in favor of distinguishing between attitudes and values, felt that the authors had used the terms in a vague and ambiguous manner. Frequently, he pointed out, the terms were used in reference to the same thing, and, therefore, all too often could be used interchangeably. Consequently, Blumer was led to question the validity of the overall methodological scheme.

> This scheme declares that a value playing upon a pre-existing attitude gives rise to a new attitude, or an attitude playing upon a pre-existing value gives rise to a new value. With terms that are uncertain and not clearly disjunctive, the presumed causal relation becomes suspect.
>
> The questionable character of the scheme is increased by the problem as to how a value operates on an attitude, or an attitude on a value. This problem is either ignored or not admitted by the methodological principle itself, for the principle implies that an attitude and a value give rise in a deterministic way to a new attitude or value. Yet in the discussion which the authors have devoted to what they term "the definition of the situation," they do deal with the question as to how values act on attitudes, and they admit that instead of a predetermined outcome, multiple possibilities are present.[39]

In commenting on Blumer's critique, Thomas observed, "I approve our separation of attitudes and values, or psychological sets and tendencies to act, on the one hand, and the external stimuli to action on the other, and of our general description of the interaction of these factors, but I think we went too far in our confident assumption that we shall be able to lay bare the complete and invariable nature of this interaction and thus determine the *laws* of 'social becoming.'"[40] He came to the view that human material was too unstable to make the search for laws in human behavior a practical endeavor. Instead, he said, we should "seek to establish high degrees of *probability* in the interaction of attitudes and values."

The writings of W. I. Thomas mark a major turning point in the orientation of American sociological theory. Up to his work, theory had been heavily directed toward the organization of all available knowledge of human behavior in terms of the evolutionary perspective. Social facts were conceptualized as the emergent phenomena of an inherently progressive evolutionary process. The clash of competitors throughout nature's realm was postulated to be the effective mechanism behind the process. The aim was to uncover the laws of nature so that nature's course could be either improved by deflection or more efficiently adapted to.

A number of factors combined to undermine confidence in this world view. The advent of World War I signaled the fact that nature was not as smoothly deterministically progressive as had been presumed. At the same time, a growing body of information on human societies around the world pointed to the diversity of social institutions in spite of the implied determinism and uniform applicability of the "natural social forces." Thomas, as Durkheim, was impressed by both these facts,[41] and it is not surprising that he should prescribe a more concentrated focus for the sociological perspective.

Thomas's reconstruction or reorientation of social theory is in the vein of a dialectical reaction. In place of theory as high level intellectual discourse based on a deterministic principle, Thomas substituted a conception of theory as an adjunct of micro analytic field research. Theory as imaginative extrapolation became suspect beyond interpretations of the interaction between specified and observable behavioral variables. It is with Thomas that methods of research and theory construction became highly interdependent subjects.[42] Of the two, methods of research began to attract the greatest amount of attention. Thomas's methodological distinction between the subjective (inherent motivational facts) and objective (social facts) sides to the study of human behavior became the subject of a spirited debate between Robert MacIver and George Lundberg.

The "Dynamic Assessment" and Objectivity: Robert M. MacIver and George A. Lundberg

Where Thomas spoke of the definition of the situation, Robert M. MacIver (1882–1970) referred to the dynamic assessment of the situation. The dynamic assessment was viewed as a key focus of attention in the study of social causation. Its essential features were outlined in the following manner:

1. A preliminary to conscious activity is a decision between alternatives—to do this or to do that, to do or not to do. In the process of decision-making the individual assesses a situation in the light of these alternatives.

2. The decision once taken, the other purposes or valuations of the individual are accommodated to it. Preparatory action follows. . . .

3. The dynamic assessment . . . rests on a predictive judgment of the form: if this is done, this consequence will (is likely to) follow *and* if this is not done or if this other thing is done, this other consequence will (is likely to) follow.

4. The selectivity of the dynamic assessment, as it reviews the situation prior to decision and as it formulates the alternatives to action, makes it subject to several kinds of contingency and practical hazard. First, the dominant objective registered in the decision to act may not persist throughout the process leading to its attainment. Second, the means-ends nexus envisaged in the decision to act may be misapprehended. Third, the physical order assumed to be under control as the means and conditions of action may "erupt" into the situation in unanticipated ways. All conscious behaving is an implicit reckoning of probabilities which may or may not be justified by the event.[43]

The individual's "definition of the situation," said MacIver, is to be viewed as a "dynamic assessment." It is something subject to constant reconstruction, primarily because of the unforeseen consequences of much of our actions. Upon first entering a cocktail party, for example, one may, simply because of the overwhelming presence of hunger, decide that the first order of business is to help oneself to the displayed hors d'oeuvres only to be checked en route by the hostess who declares that she had hoped they would not be touched until the arrival of a certain guest.

However, MacIver emphasized, the social sciences are not concerned primarily with how particular individuals behave, but how "we" behave. The study of social causation focuses on the "converging dynamic assessments that underlie group activities, institutional arrangements, folkways, in general the phenomena of social behavior." Three causal types of phenomena were seen as constituting the subject matter of sociology:

1. Distributive Phenomena—Directly expressive of the like or converging assessments of a number of people, as they issue in separate activities of a like nature, together constituting an aggregate or ratio of the same order, such as a crime rate or an opinion trend.
2. Collective Phenomena—Directly expressive of the like or converging assessments of a number of people, as they issue in concerted and unified action, such as a legal enactment or an organizational policy.
3. Conjunctural Phenomena—Arising from the variant assessments and activities of interdependent individuals and groups, as they issue in unpurposed resultants, such as the business cycle under a capitalistic system.[44]

MacIver, then, postulated the aim of sociological inquiry to be the identification of the causes and forms of human behavior. Toward this end, he, like Thomas, prescribed the application of a frame of reference which included both intraindividual stimuli (motivation) and extraindividual stimuli (social facts, values, physical and geographical facts, and so on). As with Thomas, the problem was to determine how these two orders of facts combine to produce patterns of behavior. To those like George A. Lundberg who would deny the necessity of including the motivational component in the sociological perspective, MacIver addressed the following statement:

We shall . . . not spend time on the purely metaphysical objection of those who reject the language of "motives and goals" and require a common frame of reference for physical and social causation—which in effect means that they would restate the problems of social causation in the language of physics. Thus one writer seems to object to our drawing a distinction between the type of causality involved when a paper flies before the wind and that revealed when a man flies from a pursuing crowd. When we mention the surely obvious fact that "the paper knows no fear and the wind no hate, but without fear and hate the man would not fly nor the crowd pursue," this writer takes it as an illustration of "the tendency to regard familiar words as essential components of situations." He informs us that "the principle of parsimony requires that we seek to bring into the same framework the explanation of all flying objects." He suggests that because we can describe the amoeba's approach to its food without reference to fear and hate we should learn to abandon such references when applied to human beings! And he expresses an almost mystical hope that by resort to "operationally defined terms" science may attain this goal. Presumably in this new synthesis science will still have goals, but not human beings. But until that brave new world is disclosed, we must continue to regard the physico-chemical nexus as one manifestation of the nature of things and the psychological nexus as another, as a different manifestation. No operational defining can charm away a difference that nature itself reveals.[45]

Lundberg (1895–1966) did not deny the possibilities of a dynamic assessment in human behavior; he merely emphasized that until its details could be defined by reference to observables, the idea was scientifically meaningless. He identified the following as the basic postulates upon which all science proceeds:

1. All data or experience with which man can become concerned consist of *the responses of the organisms-in-environment*. This includes the postulate of an external world and variations both in it and in the responders to it.

2. Symbols, usually verbal, are invented to represent these responses.

3. These symbols are the immediate data of all communicable knowledge and therefore of all science.
4. All propositions or postulates regarding the more ultimate "realities" must always consist of inference, generalizations, or abstractions from these symbols and the responses which they represent.
5. These extrapolations are in turn represented symbolically, and we respond to them as we respond to other phenomena which evoke behavior.[46]

According to these postulates, said Lundberg, ". . . all statements about the nature of the universe or any part of it are necessarily a verbalization of somebody's responses to *that which* evoked these responses." His point is that though the "things" we react to may exist, our interpretations of them are always incomplete and a function of available symbolic means. (Here Lundberg was saying something consistent with Sumner's point that "Everyone of us is a child of his age and cannot get out of it," and Max Weber's assertion that ". . . the choice of the object of investigation and the extent or depth to which this investigation attempts to penetrate into the infinite causal web, are determined by the evaluative ideas which dominate the investigator and his age [*The Methodology of the Social Sciences*, p. 84])." Thus, Lundberg concluded, "All assertions about the ultimate 'reality,' 'nature,' 'essence,' or 'being' of 'things,' or 'objects' [and he means that those, such as MacIver, who emphasize the study of human motivation, presuppose an ability to uncover the "real" or "final" cause of individual behavior] are therefore unverifiable hypotheses, and hence outside the sphere of science." [47]

Accordingly, here is the way Lundberg reacted to the writings of Robert MacIver:

The following illustration from contemporary sociological literature further illustrates the tendency to regard familiar words as essential components of situations: "There is an essential difference, from the standpoint of causation, between a paper flying before the wind and a man flying from a pursuing crowd. The paper knows no fear and the wind no hate, but without fear and hate the man would not fly nor the crowd pursue. If we try to reduce fear to its bodily concomitants we merely substitute the concomitants for the reality experienced as fear. *We denude the world of meanings for the sake of a theory itself a false meaning which deprives us of all of the rest."*

Note the essential nature of the words *hate* and *fear* in this analysis. Even their translation into terms of their behavior-referents is alleged to "denude the world of meanings." Now if anyone wishes to interpret the flying of a paper before the wind in terms of fear and hate, . . . I know of no way of refuting the analysis for it is determined by the terms, the framework, and the means adopted. *These categories* are not given in the phenomenon. Neither are the categories I should use in scientific description so given. In fact, I have no objection to the words "fear" and "hate" if they are defined in terms of physicochemical, biolinguistic, or sociological behavior subject to objective verification. I have no doubt, either, that descriptions in these terms would vary widely in different cases of flying objects. For this reason, I do not declare MacIver's analysis of the man and the crowd *false*. I merely point out that possibly I could analyze the situation in a frame of reference not involving the words "fear" or "hate" but in operationally defined terms of such character that all qualified observers would independently make the same analysis and predict the behavior under the given circumstances.[48]

In regard to the peculiar subject matter of sociology, Lundberg agreed with Sorokin's statement that "Sociology is interested only in those aspects of social phenomena and their relations which are repeated either in time or in space or both; which consequently exhibit some uniformity or constancy or typicality." [49] Like Lester Ward, Lundberg viewed sociology as the general social science. Hence, all behavioral phenomena were to be included within the scope of the sociological enterprise. "The characteristics and relationships common to all societal phenomena or social situations are . . . the proper concern of the field of general sociology." [50]

For the analysis of social phenomena, Lundberg prescribed

a perspective along the lines developed by the physical sciences. Thus, he said, "Having chosen to regard interhuman behavior in its most generalized form as a system of energy operating within a field of force, we next postulate that similarities and differences of characteristics, behavior, intensity of interaction, attractions, and repulsions—imbalances of whatever sort—within this total system determine the direction and the vigor of the flow of this energy." [51] Individuals, then, were to be observed as interacting with one another as a consequence of their being exposed to the social forces present in a situation. The social forces, as in the case of Lester Ward, included the entire range of behavioral stimuli. "The similarities and the differences or imbalances which determine the flow of societal energy may be of any kind—social-spatial (status), temporal (e.g., age), sexual, economic, esthetic, temperamental, developmental, ideational, or any other." [52]

William Catton, a student and colleague of Lundberg's, recently analyzed the MacIver-Lundberg interchange as a function of the difference between animistic and naturalistic sociology. He describes what he has in mind by animistic thinking in the following manner:

> For convenience, I will use the term "animism" as an antonym for "naturalism." By saying that man and society are (at least partly) outside "nature," animistic thinkers appear to mean that there are some aspects of human behavior that are exempt from the laws of nature. The exemptions they apparently have in mind are these: man can allegedly modify his actions (or at least change his mind) without cause, and he can act without being acted upon, or he can be acted upon without responding. To the participants in a culture that includes belief in "free will," such propositions seem almost self-evident. That people can act "at will" seems to be plain common sense and unquestionable fact. But these notions would clearly set men apart from other entities such as those whose behavior is described in physical mechanics, for example, where unmoved movers are assumed an impossibility, and where action persists unchanged unless modified by a force.[53]

The animistic sociologist, says Catton, believes that common-sense interpretations of the nature of human nature are valid and should be used to develop basic sociological propositions. For example, he says, "To many people it is a matter of common sense that human nature involves something more than the aspects science can study, and this extra-material part includes a 'will'—thought to be intrinsically immune to scientific analysis and prediction because it allegedly does not conform to the principle of inertia and now and then does act as an unmoved mover." [54]

From the naturalistic point of view, the basic assumption is that phenomena do not change unless they are acted upon by identifiable forces and that all actions are interactions. The following describes the naturalistic perspective:

1. A study is naturalistic to the extent that it asks questions whose answers depend on sensory observation (with the aid of instruments when necessary). Thus naturalism stresses "objectivity"—in the sense that the conclusions of a study are subject to corroboration in parallel research by other investigators.

2. A study is naturalistic only if it seeks to explain given phenomena by reference to data that are or could be available prior to (or at least concurrently with) observations of the phenomena to be explained. . . .

3. A study is naturalistic only if it considers change, rather than continuity, to be the problem requiring explanation. This third element of naturalism may be called the "axiom of inertia"; . . .

4. Finally, a study is naturalistic only if it posits no "unmoved movers"—i.e., never explains a change in terms of something that does not itself change. . . . [55]

In Catton's scheme, Lundberg is depicted as a thorough-going naturalistic sociologist whereas MacIver appears as a marginal man. "Although in *Social Causation* he [MacIver] had nearly crossed the divide between animism and naturalism, his understanding of the distinction between these two kinds of thought was still far from clear." [56] While stressing the need to study human behavior as causally determined, MacIver is seen to be ambivalent about his commitment to naturalistic principles because of his emphasis on there being a difference between physical and social causation.

Catton surely has a point, but he seems to have underestimated a problem that was very clear to MacIver and that continues to be troublesome, namely, the fact that when applied to human behavior, the stimulus-response frame becomes uniquely complex. To MacIver, both stimulus and response, that is, individual and society, may be simultaneously independent and dependent variables. What, he asked, would be an appropriate perspective from which to include the analysis of the individual's unique impact on social facts and vice versa? One may, to be sure, discern something unsatisfactory in MacIver's analysis of how deterministic an influence one side of the equation has on the other. But this may be more objectively interpreted as the consequence of his inability to resolve the problem rather than a mere instance of a misinterpretation of the nature of science because of animistic thinking.

In any event, once committed to an epistemological position, one still has the task of conceptualizing a specific frame of reference suitable for the analysis of a particular class of phenomena. It is not at all clear that a naturalistic perspective is less arbitrary when applied to the analysis of human behavior than an animistic approach. The naturalistic perspective was borrowed from the physical sciences largely because it was assumed that all science is of one piece. While this is a meaningful axiomatic position, it is not self-evident that the subject matter of the different sciences lend themselves to a single epistemological interpretation. No satisfactory explanation has ever been given to justify empirically the assumption that the phenomena of the physical and the social sciences behave the same way for the same reasons. There is just as much justification for the view that human behavior is in some way singular (in the language of Durkheim, something sui generis) and in need of unique treatment. This was the particular side of the issue which engrossed MacIver and which Catton largely ignored.

Summary

The social-psychological perspectives of Cooley, Mead, Thomas, and MacIver reveal certain underlying assumptions. To begin with, all four assumed that man is not at birth a social animal. That is, the human child must be nurtured in the "ways of mankind" to become civilized. Second, each assumed that human beings are born into a social context: society and its norms are taken as a reality. Third, they were all basically concerned with the process of social interaction —its various forms and its consequences for organized human conduct. Concomitantly they assumed that the individual is both an actor and a reactor. For them, man was more than a mere reflection of his physical and social environment. He had, each and every one but some more than others, an idiosyncratic contribution to make, the limits of which were to be determined. Fourth, all assumed a rational motive force behind both individual maturation and societal evolution because they perceived a quest for order in both spheres.[57] Of course they recognized the prominence of irrationality in human behavior, but nevertheless the assumption of rationality was basic to the line of analysis pursued by each. Finally, they all adhered to the methodological principle that "the investigator must see the world from the point of view of the subject of his investigation."[58]

Lundberg also held many of these assumptions, but unlike the others, he emphasized that only interpretations of observables could be accorded scientific status. One could refer to mind, attitudes, empathy, and so on as much as one wanted; but if such terms could not be translated into something observable, they could only be interpreted as scientifically meaningless.

Although much affected by the contributions of all five men, the contemporary interactionist framework differs somewhat from its initial formulations. As Stryker has noted, for example, the study of socialization is no longer restricted to the study of children. All types of "recruit training" are now studied: from the army induction process to "the marriage game." But more importantly, current proponents of the perspective strongly emphasize the claim that it is anti-reductionist (that is, against treating human behavior as the product of nonhuman forces, e.g., geographical factors) and in favor of the principle of emergence (which means basically that human behavior is unique). As Stryker has put it,

> . . . man must be studied on his own level. . . . There are valid principles of human behavior as the product of social interaction which cannot be derived from, or inferred from, the study of non-human forms. This assertion rests on the principle of emergence. Emergence suggests the existence of qualitative differences as well as quantitative continuities among the precipitates of the evolutionary process.[59]

The theoretical basis for the axiomatic acceptance of the notion of emergence is not entirely clear. Just how much of it is a manifestation of an arbitrary anthropocentric bias (mankind reveals an arrogant penchant for elevating itself to supreme status among the realms of nature) as opposed to logically or empirically defensible criteria is not known. It is certainly not based on Lundbergian criteria; that is, the process of emergence has not been accounted for by reference to the precise combination of observables.

Epistemologically, the emergence thesis is based on a view of nature as composed of hierarchically organized levels of complexity. The question is: are the levels to be viewed as autonomous layers or simply different products of a continuously evolving whole? Put another way, should man be viewed as a detached "thing" or an integrated component of nature?

Depending upon how the emergence thesis is interpreted, one may proceed in at least two general directions: (1) one can adopt the view that phenomena of a particular level can be explained only in terms of other phenomena from that level (Durkheim, for example, held this view); or (2) one can accept the view that emergence is an event in nature to be explained by reference to any and all other possibly related phenomena (Ward leaned in this direction).

In sociology, the first alternative, the antireductionist point of view, leads toward the adoption of a sociologistic perspective (like that of Durkheim and Marx). The second alternative may or may not lead toward the adoption of an antireductionist stance. Some interactionists, like J. Milton Yinger, wish to explain human behavior by reference to all the variables (physical, biological, psychological, sociological, and so on) that can be accounted for. From this point of view (one aspect of which is the field-theoretical perspective which will be discussed in chapter 6) the referent is human behavior in all of its manifestations and the goal is to explain its forms and formulations by reference to any and all known behavioral variables.

Other interactionists, such as Peter Blau, accept the antireductionist perspective and confine their analytic focus to either the micro (that is, the study of the behavior of an individual or a few individuals) or macro (for example, the relational patterns among the various institutional structures of society) level, or take a perspective in which the two levels are viewed as both unique and interrelated. Those who combine a micro-macro orientation tend to follow the lead developed by Talcott Parsons. In particular, Parsons has sought to examine the relationship between the sociologistic perspective and the action frame of reference. The Parsonian world view is the subject of the next chapter.

FIVE · From social action to social system: the Parsonian perspective and its critics

There is little doubt that the contributions of Talcott Parsons are pivotal in the development of sociological theory. In Parsons' works one can discern syntheses of a great many strands of thought. Of special interest in the present context is Parsons' attempt to develop a conceptual scheme appropriate to the analysis of the unit acts of individuals as well as the complex actions of nation-states. The entire range of human behavior comes within the range of his system's frame of reference.

Early in his career Parsons pointed to a theoretical convergence in the writings of a group of European scholars, in particular, Alfred Marshall, Vilfredo Pareto, Emile Durkheim, and Max Weber. According to Parsons, all, by means of a variety of routes, arrived at a "voluntaristic theory of action." Of the group, Max Weber developed the rudiments of an action frame of reference that has had the most apparent impact on Parsons' thinking.

The Weberian Action Scheme

Max Weber's lifetime spanned the years from 1864 to 1920. As a university student, his major field of study was law, but as Reinhard Bendix has noted, he also studied and attained professional competence in economics, history, and philosophy.[1] His two university appointments, one at Freiburg and the other at Heidelberg, were as professor of economics. It was while a student at Heidelberg that Parsons was first exposed to Weber's writings.

The Weberian action scheme was outlined in an uncompleted work, *Wirtschaft und Gesellschaft*. The English version of the book is entitled *The Theory of Social and Economic Organization* and was translated by A. M. Henderson and Talcott Parsons.

Weber defined sociology as "a science which attempts the interpretive understanding of social action in order thereby to arrive at a causal explanation of its course and effects." [2] The concept *action* described all human behavior to which an actor attaches "subjective meaning." "Action is social," said Weber, "in so far as, by virtue of the subjective meaning attached to it by the acting individual (or individuals), it takes account of the behavior of others and is thereby oriented in its course." [3]

Meaning referred to the rationalized reasons developed by an individual or individuals for particular actions. "In no case," Weber emphasized, "does it refer to an objectively 'correct' meaning or one which is 'true' in some metaphysical sense." Furthermore, it was difficult to distinguish between meaningful and nonmeaningful action. Nonmeaningful behavior was defined as "reactive behavior to which no subjective meaning is attached." [4] Weber was certain that a large part of human behavior fell somewhere between these two categories.

Weber prescribed two interrelated methods to employ in order to develop an "understanding" of the meaning of social action. First of all, one can practice, he suggested, and in the manner of Cooley, *sympathetic introspection*. "For the verifiable accuracy of interpretation of the meaning of a phenomenon, it is a great help to be able to put one's self imaginatively in the place of the actor and thus sympathetically to participate in his experience. . . ." [5] As George Simpson interpreted Weber,

The sociologist must interpretatively grasp the meaning of the actor or actors. Crucial to the understanding of social action is the grasp of the motive behind it. A motive is a complex of subjective meaning which seems to the actor himself or to the observer an adequate ground for the conduct in question.[6]

Second, and concomitant with the first, *typological analysis* is to be employed; that is, and as discussed in chapter 1, one can delineate a limited number of "ideal types" of behavior to be used as benchmarks from which to gauge the form and development of actual behavior. It must be noted that Weber conceived of his ideal-type constructs as aids to research rather than conclusive interpretations of observable uniformities. The problem with "actual types" was that their relevance must be restricted to limited historical circumstances; that is, they were of necessity descriptions of something as of a given moment in time. Weber's ideal type was an attempt to deal with the problem of the historical relativity of conceptual types by means of the construction of a limited number of terms which could be used as constant generalizable abstractions. Only by means of such constant tools did Weber see it possible for the sociologist to gauge behavioral change and make comparative analyses. Simpson has neatly summarized the nature and intent of ideal-typical analysis in the following statement:

> As far as individual social action is concerned the sociologist seeks to arrive at an understanding of individual motives; in groups he seeks to arrive at motives which are typical of the group. In both cases the sociologist seeks to arrive at ideal types which establish what the action of individuals or groups would be if it were strictly rational, unaffected by errors or emotional factors, and if, furthermore, it were completely and unequivocally directed to a single end. Actual behavior of individuals and groups is then studied as a deviation from such ideal-typical behavior.[7]

The idea here is to identify the factors which intervene to prevent the ideal type from being realized in actual behavior. As Julien Freund noted, by the use of the ideal type the sociologist "is able to measure the gap between the ideal-typical objectively possible action and the empirical action, and ascertain the part played by irrationality and chance or by the intrusion of accidental, emotional and other elements." [8] In this way, hypotheses may be derived and theory developed.

Weber identified four ideal types of social action: (1) action is *zweckrational* when an individual is able to rationally select his own behavioral goals and the means for their attainment; (2) action is *wertrational* when, though the goals of action may be highly restricted, one is, nevertheless, free to rationally select the most efficient means for their attainment; (3) action is *affectuell* when the means and ends of action are selected on the basis of emotional criteria; and (4) action is *traditional* when custom prescribes the selection of the means and ends of action.[9] As Martindale has pointed out,

> Any regularities in interhuman conduct represent no more than the stabilization of behavior in terms of rationality, ethical fixity, emotionality, or habit. To be sure, behavior will always display an admixture, for people are not merely rational or emotional; they are both, and the question is often one of determining which will be paramount.[10]

Consistent with his interpretation of the goals of sociological analysis, Weber hoped his action scheme would facilitate the identification of the causes of human behavior. He did not see the emerging functional approach as appropriate to the task. To quote Weber,

> . . . it is the method of the so-called "organic" school of sociology to attempt to understand social interaction by using as a point of departure the "whole" within which the individual acts. His action and behaviour are then interpreted somewhat in the way that a physiologist would treat the role of an organ of the body in the "economy" of the organism, that is from the point of view of the survival of the latter. . . . this functional frame of reference is convenient for purposes of practical illustration and for provisional orientation. In these respects it is not only useful but indispensable. But at the same time if its cognitive value is over-

estimated and its concepts illegitimately "reified," it can be highly dangerous . . . in certain circumstances this is the only available way of determining just what process of social action it is important to understand in order to explain a given phenomenon. But this is only the beginning of sociological analysis as here understood.[11]

Strikingly comparable to the viewpoint of his American contemporary W. I. Thomas, Weber wrote: "A correct causal interpretation of a concrete course of action is arrived at when the overt action and the motives have both been correctly apprehended and at the same time their relation has become meaningfully comprehensible." [12]

Overt action leading to interindividual contact was the next subject of typological analysis. The concept *social relationship* was coined to describe meaningful patterned human interaction. A social relationship occurs between two individuals when the actions of each take account of the actions of the other. Weber identified six types of social relations which he designated as "modes of orientation of social action," that is, patterns of human behavior attributable to the recognition of normative expectations: (1) *usage* described behavior performed simply to conform to a style or pattern, e.g., social etiquette; (2) *custom* described habitual practices with roots in antiquity; (3) *rational orientation* designated that variety of social action which is the consequence of actors orienting themselves to one another on the basis of "similar ulterior expectations," e.g., mutual self-interest; (4) *fashion* described social action which is the result of adherence to contemporary fad; (5) *convention* designated that type of social action performed in recognition of strong moral obligation in the manner of Sumner's "mores"; and (6) *law* described that type of social action performed in recognition of codified expectations and restrictions.

Weber was particularly interested in *conventional* social action; that is, behavior recognized as related to an acknowledged and legitimate moral order. He identified the bases of legitimate authority in the form of three further ideal types: (1) *rational legitimacy*, "resting on a belief in the 'legality' of patterns of normative rules and the right of those elevated to authority under such rules to issue commands (legal authority)"; (2) *traditional legitimacy*, "resting on an established belief in the sanctity of immemorial traditions and the legitimacy of the status of those exercising authority under them (traditional authority)"; and (3) *charismatic legitimacy*, "resting on devotion to the specific and exceptional sanctity, heroism or exemplary character of an individual person, and of the normative patterns or order revealed or ordained by him (charismatic authority)." [13]

Weber used the ideal type not only as a device for the identification and classification of particular components of human behavior, but also as a general theoretical frame for the analysis of society writ large. In the manner of a Hegelian idealist, he saw the way of life of a people as an attempt to realize certain idealistic aims. This orientation is evident in *The Protestant Ethic and The Spirit of Capitalism*, a work considered by many to be Weber's masterpiece.

Behind the material achievements of capitalistic societies, America in particular, Weber discerned a unique and compelling idealistic spirit. To him the spirit of capitalism was exemplified by the typical writings of Benjamin Franklin. In *Necessary Hints to Those That Would Be Rich* and *Advice to a Young Tradesman*, Franklin preached maxims such as "Remember, that time is money," "Remember, that credit is money," "Remember this saying, The good paymaster is lord of another man's purse," and "He that loses five shillings, not only loses that sum, but all the advantage that might be made by turning it in dealing, which by the time that a young man becomes old, will amount to a considerable sum of money." To Weber, "The peculiarity of this philosophy of avarice appears to be the ideal of the honest man of recognized credit, and above all the idea of a duty of the individual toward the increase of his capital, which is assumed as an end in itself." [14] What impressed him about Franklin's statements was their ethical tone. Money was to be made not as a means of attaining specified material ends, but as a way of conforming to a moral calling. Along lines prescribed by Durkheim, Weber sought to account for this anomalous social fact by reference to an antecedent social fact, a "peculiar" religious ethic whose origins could be traced to the Protestant Reformation.

To Martin Luther, the German leader of the Reformation, Weber attributed one very important part of the spirit of capitalism, namely, the moral justification for compulsory worldly activity. The selling of indulgences to rich nobles and other such practices of the church led Luther to reject obedience to its commands as either a sufficient or a necessary means of salvation. What he required of the believer was a lifetime of devoted work in a "calling." A calling was defined as a task sent by God; it was a task to be fulfilled by continuous labor as an end in itself rather than as a means of material gain and self-indulgence. Luther did not sanction upward social mobility, constant striving to rise above one's station in life. Luther believed, said Weber, that "the individual should remain in the station and calling that God had placed him, and should restrain his worldly activity within the limits imposed by his established station in life." [15] To pursue material gain beyond what was necessary to satisfy basic personal needs was symptomatic of a lack of grace. In essence, Weber had to look elsewhere for the ethical basis of the acquisitive motives of a Ben Franklin. It was in the teachings of John Calvin that he found what he was looking for.

At the heart of Calvinism was the doctrine of predestination. This meant that whether or not one was saved or damned was a foregone conclusion. Man could do nothing to alter the inexorable will of God. Most people were damned, but a select few were saved. Although it was impossible to prove one's inevitable fate, there was a way to alleviate the fear of being among the condemned. Success in worldly pursuits was defined as an indication that one may be among the favored few. The sign of worldly success was continuous material achievement. The more one acquired, the less the fear of being among the damned. As Weber put it, material achievements "are the technical means, not of purchasing salvation, but of getting rid of the fear of damnation." [16] Here, then, was the ideal type that Weber believed to be the motivational force behind the spirit of capitalism, a religious ethic that he regarded as having extraordinarily powerful psychological effects.

The Protestant Ethic and The Spirit of Capitalism was a reflection of Weber's lifelong interest in the relationship between religion and economics. It was also intended to be a counterpoise to the materialistic world view of Karl Marx. Weber made it clear, however, that his goal was not so much to challenge the validity of Marxian theory as to make a case for the value of studying social processes from both idealistic and materialistic viewpoints. In his words,

> it is, of course, not my aim to substitute for a one-sided materialistic an equally one-sided spiritualistic causal interpretation of culture and of history. Each is equally possible, but each, if it does not serve as the preparation, but as the conclusion of an investigation, accomplishes equally little in the interest of historical truth.[17]

To summarize, the function of the ideal type was to facilitate the goal of uncovering the causes of human behavior. Toward this end, Weber further prescribed a sociological perspective which combined the data of empirical observation with the interpretive insights gained from sympathetic introspection. It was not enough to chart the observable activities of individuals or groups in the manner of an astronomer plotting the movements of the variety of celestial bodies. To interpret human behavior causally, one also had to obtain an understanding of the motives of acting individuals. As Julien Freund put it, to Weber "a human activity is unintelligible to us unless we understand its meaningful orientation to objects, means and ends." [18]

Finally, it is worth noting that,

> In the opinion of some sociologists, Max Weber was the greatest social scientist of the first half of the twentieth century. Certainly Weber formed the starting point for the careers of many contemporary sociologists; among leading social scientists who took their point of departure in con-

siderable measure from Weber are Karl Mannheim, Hans Speier, Hans Gerth, Talcott Parsons. . . .[19]

To a considerable degree, Parsons' work can be interpreted as an attempt to extend the structure and content of the Weberian perspective.

The Parsonian Perspective

Talcott Parsons (1902–) received his undergraduate training at Amherst College. He graduated in 1924 with a degree in biology. Though not exposed formally to sociology at Amherst, it was there that he admits to being converted to the social sciences.

To pursue the study of institutional economics, Parsons enrolled at the London School of Economics (1924–25). It was while there that he received his first exposure to formal sociology and the personality and ideas of the anthropologist Bronislaw Malinowski. At the time, Malinowski was proposing the reorientation of anthropological theory along the lines of a functional frame of reference. Malinowski acknowledged the works of Durkheim to be a prime source of much of his thinking.

The following year (1925–26) was spent in Germany. Parsons obtained a national scholarship and was assigned to Heidelberg University. At Heidelberg, Parsons was immediately exposed and attracted to the works of Max Weber. He began a dissertation "on the subject of the treatment of the idea of capitalism as a conception of a socio-economic system in German social science literature" and as revealed in the works of Karl Marx, Werner Sombart, and most of all, Weber. Parsons received his doctorate from Heidelberg in 1927. The degree was not in a specific major, but Parsons' initial academic appointments were in departments of economics—briefly at Amherst and later at Harvard. He went to Harvard in 1927 and began to teach sociology there in 1931; in 1944 he was made professor of sociology and he is currently a professor in the department of social relations.

Parsons' initial theoretical efforts were heavily oriented toward the Weberian action frame of reference. The Parsonian version has been variously described but most succinctly so by Edward C. Devereux:

> Where others talk of organism and environment, Parsons talks of actor and situation. Where others talk of behavior or response, Parsons talks of action. All action, to be sure, is behavior; but not all behavior is action. If the flight of a moth toward a candle is conceived simply as a mechanistic response of its organism to the stimulus of light, there is behavior but not action. On the other hand, if we were to conceive of some subjective process of orientation as an essential link in the chain . . . as if the moth, for example, were to reason with itself: "What pretty light! I would like to be closer to it. I will fly there as directly and quickly as possible. . . ," then we should be dealing with action.[20]

Action as opposed to behavior is viewed essentially as the intervention of the element of decision making (Thomas's "definition of the situation" or MacIver's "dynamic assessment") between stimulus and response. The unit of analysis is an actor. An actor may be an individual, a group, or a society. A situation may be thought of as a stage, an arena, or a setting in which an actor is obliged to decide between alternative roles to play. The situation includes a variety of potential stimuli—in particular, objects (both human and nonhuman), norms (expected patterns of behavior), and values ("certain conceptions of the desirable"). It is the task of the investigator to determine how and why it is that actors respond to certain stimuli rather than others.

To Parsons, behavior typically occurs under conditions which pose varying amounts of circumstantial dilemma for the actor. He has conceptualized circumstantial predicaments as "pattern-variables," which are "a set of five dichotomous variables conceived as constituting universal and basic dilemmas confronting any actor in any social situation." [21]

In orienting ourselves to another, we must determine whether we are to be emotionally involved (affectivity) or emotionally detached (affective neutrality). Also, we are often faced with the problem of having to decide between orienting ourselves to another as a total personality (diffuseness) or in a partial or secondary way (specificity). Generally, one is concerned with a spouse in a diffuse way but a druggist in a specific or strictly functional sense. We should select a doctor on the basis of standards of competence (universalism) rather than because he happens to be handsome (particularism). Furthermore, and again generally speaking, we orient ourselves to our children because of who they are (quality) rather than because of what they do (performance). Finally, we may be required to make a choice between acting on our own behalf (self) or in the interests of a group (collectivity). Overall, all possible combinations of roles of these five dichotomies yield thirty-two possible behavioral orientations.

Parsons described the utility and purposes of the pattern-variables in the following way:

> . . . in certain crucial areas of social structure we do not find that empirically observable structures cover anything like the whole range of theoretically possible variability; . . . Actual structures are . . . concentrated in empirical "clusterings." . . . If the existence of such clusterings can be validated, even only in a rather rough way, this validation serves a two-fold purpose for the sociologist. On the one hand, it justifies his short-cutting investigation of the *whole* range of structural possibilities and concentrating on a fraction of them; thus it enormously simplifies arriving at least at a first approximation of a systematic classification of empirically significant ranges of differentiation and structural variation of societies. On the other hand, it can serve as a highly important lead into the formulation, and hence testing, of fundamental dynamic generalizations, of laws of social process, since the explanation of *why* the logically possible range of variability is empirically restricted can be found only in terms of such laws.[22]

What Parsons has attempted to do, then, with the action frame of reference, and as illustrated by the introduction of the pattern variables, is to develop a conceptual scheme—by means of constructed typologies—in order to narrow the range of relevant phenomena to be analyzed within its borders. As he described it,

> . . . a generalized conceptual scheme is a genuinely technical analytical tool. It ensures that nothing of vital importance is inadvertently overlooked, and ties in loose ends, giving determinancy to problems and solutions. It minimizes the danger, so serious to common-sense thinking, of filling gaps by resort to uncriticized residual categories.[23]

Other elements in the Parsonian conceptual scheme include such Weberian elaborations as "modes of action or motivational orientation" and "modes of value orientation." "Motivational orientation refers to those aspects of the actor's orientation to his situation which are related to actual or potential gratification or deprivation of the actor's need-dispositions."[24] There are three modes of motivational orientation: (1) the *cognitive mode* includes "the 'location' of an object in the actor's total object-world, the determination of its properties and actual and potential functions, its differentiations from other objects, and its relations to certain general classes"; (2) the *cathectic mode* "involves the various processes by which an actor invests an object with affective significance"; and (3) the *evaluative mode* which "involves the various processes by which an actor allocates his energy among the various actions with respect to various cathected objects in an attempt to optimize gratification."[25]

First of all, there is the problem of identifying the objects in a situation in which one must act. For example, in order to adapt to conditions on earth, men have had to learn to distinguish between nutritious and poisonous plant life. Second, though many plants in a habitat may be edible, people tend to develop a discriminating devotion to some rather than others. In fact, says Parsons, the foods and other objects preferred by people invariably come to be invested with emotional significance. Parsons would like to determine how it is that people develop emotional attachments to certain objects rather than others. Lastly, Parsons would like to be able to identify the criteria people apply to discriminate between the situational worth of valued objects. Though a person may be both hungry and angry, why, for example, might he choose to focus his attention on objects to vent his anger rather than on those which might gratify his hunger?

Modes of value orientation refer to cultural standards, or to those "aspects" of an actor's orientation which compel him to recognize the applicability of particular norms and the criteria for their selection whenever he is in a situation which permits and requires him to decide his own behavior. There are three modes of value orientation: (1) the *cognitive mode* "involves the various commitments to standards by which the validity of cognitive judgments is established"; (2) the *appreciative mode* "involves the various commitments to standards by which the appropriateness or consistency of the cathexis of an object or class of objects is assessed"; and (3) the *moral mode* "involves the various commitments to standards by which certain consequences of particular actions and types of action may be assessed with respect to their effects upon systems of action." [26]

Essentially, the modes of value orientation represent Parsons' attempt to articulate the influence of social expectations on a person's definition of a situation. Societal values —the expectations people share about the proper means to attain respected ends—affect cognition by restricting the range of objects perceived and the manner (that is, the attitude toward and the method of approach) of an actor's response. A person feels he must address himself to certain people and things in certain ways. Societal values also influence the individual by giving him a general sense of the worth of particular objects. Some things simply require more careful treatment than others. Finally, social values influence the actor's orientation by imposing on him a feeling of responsibility for his action in terms of its possible positive and negative repercussions for society.

By means of these and other typologies, Parsons strives to fill in the behavioral landscape by identifying basic points about which human activity pivots. In keeping with the

Weberian tradition, Parsons applies the typological method as a means to approach the empirical world. In his scheme, useful systematic types should permit the kind of focused observation that leads to the derivation of working and testable hypotheses. Fundamentally, then, Parsonian types are instruments for the observation of reality rather than exact interpretations of its various forms.

Initially, Parsons proceeded to develop his action perspective by examining the social-psychological conditions of individual behavior. Eventually, he began to direct his attention more to the problems surrounding the patterned interaction of several individuals. For the analysis of social interaction, Parsons prescribed a structural-functional, social systems frame of reference. In 1945, Parsons had structural-functional analysis in mind when he wrote,

> . . . the thesis may be advanced that sociology is just in the process of emerging into the status of a mature science. Heretofore it has not enjoyed the kind of integration and directed activity which only the availability and common acceptance and employment of a well-articulated generalized theoretical system can give to a science. The main framework of such a system is, however, now available, though this fact is not yet very generally appreciated and much in the way of development and refinement remains to be done on the purely theoretical level, as well as its systematic use and revision in actual research.[27]

The essential components of the Parsonian structural-functional theory of social systems were identified as follows: (1) a *frame of reference*—"For the social system in question it is quite clear that it is that of 'action' or perhaps between 'actor-situation' in a sense analogous to the organism-environment frame of reference of the biological sciences"—and (2) *units of analysis*—"The unit of all social systems is the human individual *as actor* [i.e., role player] as an entity which has the basic characteristics of striving toward the attainment of 'goals,' of 'reacting' emotionally or affectively toward objects and events, and of, to a greater or less degree, cognitively knowing or understanding his situation, his goals and himself. . . . A goal is by definition a 'desirable' state of affairs. . . ." [28]

Structure refers to stable patterns of role behavior. A stable pattern of role relationship is called an *institution*. The special province of sociology is the study of social institutions, their growth and behavioral effects. *Function* describes the effect of structures in terms of their positive and negative impact on the maintenance of "going concerns" called social systems. As Parsons put it,

> Functional significance in this context is inherently teleological. A process or set of conditions either "contributes" to the maintenance (or development) of the system or it is "dysfunctional" in that it detracts from the integration, effectiveness, etc., of the system. [29]

Parsons' reference to teleology in his writings has been often pointed to as proof positive of his metaphysical predilections. *Teleology* refers to the "philosophical study of manifestations of design or purpose in natural processes or occurrences, under the belief that natural processes are not determined by mechanism but rather by their utility in an overall natural design." [30] Quite obviously, there is a thin line between teleological assumption and metaphysical conviction. While not dismissing the possibility that Parsons harbors metaphysical assumptions, his reference to teleology is undoubtedly most appropriately to be viewed as evidence of his maintaining a phenomenological position consistent with the Durkheimian postulate which asserts that social facts are sui generis phenomena.

Parsons, following Durkheim, takes the view that human behavior can be and is considerably influenced by extrasomatic social facts. Thus, by reference to the term teleology, Parsons can be interpreted as meaning to emphasize the role and importance of social facts as independent variables and to deemphasize the anthropocentric idea that the only (or the most important) behavioral variables emanate from the unique intrasomatic character of the human organism. His use of the concept of social system is in large measure to be seen as his way of treating in a theoretically organized way the influence of social facts on human behavior.

A *social system* is defined as "two or more actors occupying differentiated statuses or positions and performing differentiated roles, some organized pattern governing the relationships of the members and describing their rights and obligations with respect to one another, and some set of common norms, or values, together with various types of shared cultural objects and symbols." [31] In addition to the attribute of social differentiation, Parsons postulates two other distinguishing characteristics of social systems: (1) a tendency toward boundary maintenance, i.e., for system components to retain a high degree of integration in spite of environmental pressures; and (2) an equilibrium tendency, or the possession of mechanisms which serve to maintain component functioning and interrelationships.

Parsons views social systems as having four basic problems to solve in order to continue their existence: adaptation, goal attainment, integration, and pattern-maintenance and tension-management. First of all, any complex social organization must adapt to a physical habitat and develop the economic means necessary to sustain the lives of its members. Second, for the attainment of a variety of goals, some form of political organization (concentration of power) is required. Third, during periods when politically organized goal attainment is not of overriding importance, social systems tend to have a problem of maintaining their organizational effectiveness. As protection against dissolution, a body of rules and regulations is invariably enacted (which prescribe appropriate and unappropriate conduct for both extraordinary and routine conditions) and a legal apparatus constructed to enforce them. Finally, social systems have the perpetual problem of recruitment. New members must be continually socialized and motivated to participate in their operation. It is the function of the family and the educational institution to provide the emotional support and practical training necessary to meet this problem.

The system problems are conceptualized as social facts

which coerce and constrain the behavior of actors in the Durkheimian sense. Robert Dubin has illustrated how they mesh with four pairs of pattern-variables [32] conceptually to effect an actor's evaluation of and orientation toward objects as follows:

SYSTEM PROBLEMS		ACTOR'S EVALUATION OF OBJECTS	ACTOR'S ORIENTATION TOWARD OBJECTS
Adaptive	$\longrightarrow$	Universalism	Specificity
Goal Attainment	$\longrightarrow$	Performance	Affectivity
Integrative	$\longrightarrow$	Particularism	Diffuseness
Pattern-maintenance—Tension-management	$\longrightarrow$	Quality	Neutrality

SOURCE: Robert Dubin, "Parsons' Actor: Continuities in Social Theory," *American Sociological Review* (August 1960): 463.

To execute the adaptive function successfully, actors should orient themselves to certain objects and evaluate their unique qualities on the basis of objective criteria, e.g., general survival value. To effect goal attainment, actors must have a spirited attitude and the capacity to select and apply the most appropriate means to accomplish particular ends. To resolve the integrative problem, actors should direct themselves toward others as whole beings with unique needs. Pattern-maintenance is best achieved and tension-management most effectively handled when objects, both human and non-human, are judged for what they are and by remaining emotionally detached.

In summary, and to quote Parsons,

The logical type of generalized theoretical system under discussion may thus be called a "structural-functional system." . . . It consists of the generalized categories necessary for an adequate description of states of an empirical system. On the other hand, it includes a system of structural categories which must be logically adequate to give a determinate description of an empirically possible, complete empirical system of the relevant class. One of the prime functions of *system* on this level is to ensure completeness, to make it methodically impossible to overlook anything important, and thus explicitly to describe *all* essential structural elements and relations of the system.[33]

Critical Reactions

1. Level of Analysis   One of the first critical reactions to the Parsonian perspective alleged it to be a premature effort to construct a unified social theory. Robert K. Merton, a former student of Parsons, has been the most influential critic of this point of view. To Merton, "Some sociologists still write as though they expect, here and now, formulation of *the* general sociological theory. . . . This I take to be a premature and apocalyptic belief. . . . Not enough preparatory work has been done." [34]

To acquire the kind of knowledge that he thinks is prerequisite to valid generalization, Merton prescribes the application of "middle-range" theory. Theories of the middle range lie between everyday working hypotheses and all encompassing social theories. His examples include "a theory of reference groups, of social mobility, of role-conflict, and of the formation of social norms." [35] Whatever the substantive focus (for example, the study of role-conflict in the home or at the office) or level of analysis (for example, the study of role-conflict in a family as opposed to families in general), middle-range theories, insists Merton, should be close enough to the real world to be put into propositional form and subjected to empirical test.

For unspecified reasons, Merton claims that middle-range theory (and by this he apparently means sociological theory in general) should be addressed to the problem of social order. In his words, "middle-range theory is not concerned with the historical generalization that a degree of social order or conflict prevails in society but with the analytical problem of identifying the social mechanisms which produce a greater degree of order or less conflict than would obtain if these mechanisms were not called into play." [36]

For the study of social order, Merton proffers "A Paradigm for Functional Analysis." His notion of a paradigm coincides with what was defined in chapter 1 as a frame of reference and a conceptual scheme. Merton's frame is what he refers to as "a given system." As he does not define what he means by this, one must infer that he wishes the sociologist to study enduring groups with a certain degree of structural complexity. The units of analysis are standardized social and cultural items such as norms, roles, and institutions. In the study of these items Merton suggests the use of certain conceptual distinctions. Above all, one is to observe their *functions*. Functions are those observed consequences of units of analysis that make for the adaptation or adjustment of a given system. It is also important to note *dysfunctional* items. Dysfunctional social and cultural facts have observed consequences that lessen the adaptation or adjustment of a given system. It is also possible for standardized items to be *nonfunctional*, that is, not to have consequences that either contribute toward or militate against the continuation of a given system. Lastly, in order to avoid confusing motives and consequences of behavior, what people intend as opposed to what they effect, Merton distinguishes between *manifest* and *latent* functions. Manifest functions have consequences that make for the continuation of a given system and that are intended and recognized by its members; latent functions also have positive consequences, but they are neither intended nor recognized by the members of a given system.

Some scholars have taken issue with Merton's use of the criteria of intention and recognition to distinguish manifest from latent functions. It is argued that intention and recognition are different variables. For example, it is possible to intend to do something without conscious awareness of the desire. Habitual behavior, such as smoking, is often to be described in this way. Furthermore, one can recognize having brought about a result without consciously intending to do so. This is, after all, the meaning of accidental behavior. With these distinctions in mind, Isajiw saw the need to introduce an intervening category between manifest and latent functions, namely unmanifested functions. Accordingly, he advised the following modifications of the Mertonian distinction:

> First, Merton's distinction between manifest and latent functions more properly should be a distinction between intended and unintended consequences or effects. Secondly, the intended effects can be subdivided into those consciously intended and those subconsciously or unconsciously intended. For the sake of retaining Merton's terminology, the former can be called, at least for the present, the "manifested functions" and the latter "unmanifested functions." The term "latent functions" can remain to identify the unintended effects. Thirdly, all of these, the manifested, the unmanifested and the latent functions can be divided into effects which are either recognized by the participants in the system or unrecognized by them.[37]

Elaborations such as Isajiw's are consistent with Merton's view of his paradigm as a provisional structural guide to functional research. In discussing the functions of paradigms, Merton emphasized that

> ... the paradigm is the foundation upon which the house of interpretations is built. If a new story cannot be built directly upon this foundation, then it must be treated as a new wing of the total structure, and the foundation of concepts and assumptions must be extended to support this wing. ...[38]

To Merton, then, the purpose of middle-range functional analysis is to provide the structural orientation necessary to lay the foundation of the sociological enterprise. The foundation is to be composed of numerous building blocks which, presumably, will eventually add up to permit the construction of a single sociological edifice. Merton is not altogether clear as to what the final product should look like. The immediate aim is the identification of all standardized cultural items and their functional interrelationships. Once a table of sociological elements can be determined, it will then be possible to perform the precise observations necessary for the application of deductive theory and the discovery of laws.

However, for Parsons the question is: in the absence of general theory, how is sociological knowledge to be accumulated to the point where lawful statements about human behavior can be derived? To him,

> The basic reason why general theory is so important is that the cumulative development of knowledge in a scientific field is a function of the degree of *generality of implications* by which it is possible to relate findings, interpretations, and hypotheses on different levels and in different specific empirical fields to each other. If there is to be a high degree of such generality there *must* on some level be a common conceptual scheme which makes the work of different investigators in a specific sub-field and those in different sub-fields commensurable.[39]

The debate between these two men concerns first principles. Parsons calls for a single social science frame of reference and conceptual scheme. For him, there is little doubt that the explanation of human behavior *writ large* is the constant referent. Merton, on the other hand, presses for the construction of multiple and independent sociological theories. Both work within a general systems perspective, but only Parsons has attempted to spell out the theoretical components of the term.

Whereas Parsons has a conception of scientific progress as movement toward a particular goal by certain means, Merton opts for the view that scientific development should proceed cautiously from primitive beginnings. Particularly in terms of the goals of science, Merton believes that neither structure nor content should be granted priority. The two essential elements of theory must be viewed as organically interrelated. In Merton one discerns the fear that the elaboration of structural schemes beyond or without specific content may eventuate in the arbitrary constraint of subject matter to suit the demands of a fanciful if not stereotypical scheme. But, one is likely to ask, how is it possible to generate new theory without thinking beyond what is presently known or observable? Merton's answer is that sufficient theoretical challenge will be generated if one remains constantly in touch with actual behavioral referents.

In spite of their theoretical differences, both, but particularly Parsons, have been attacked for their alleged ideological bias toward the study of social order rather than social change. It is pointed out that the functional frame of reference is inherently static and virtually compels a conservative orientation.

2. Ideological Bias To the extent that sociologists continually apply a single theoretical perspective in their studies —for example, by taking social structure as a constant and examining its effects on the behavior and attitudes of people —to that extent they lend themselves to charges of ideological bias. Sociologists have not been unaware of their inclination to focus attention on certain kinds of problems rather than others. Rather, they have attempted to identify the sources of their own biases.

The basic substantive problem that Parsons has concerned himself with is the nature of social order. As he says, ". . . the empirical-theoretical problem which was at the focus of my own theoretical 'takeoff' was the problem of the bases of social order." [40] Lewis Coser believes that Parsons' interest in social order is colored by the biased way in which he applies his conceptual scheme. In Coser's view,

> Terminology often provides a clue to orientation. Parsons prefers to speak of "tensions" and "strains" where earlier theorists would have used the term "conflict," and this choice does not appear to be fortuitous. Both "tension" and "strain" connote injury due to overexertion, overtasking or excessive pressure, thus connoting some form of "sickness" in the system. [41]

Why does Parsons use such terminology? Because, says Coser, he "is primarily interested in the conservation of existing structures." Andrew Hacker also sees an ideological bias in Parsons' work but thinks that it should be labeled as *liberal* rather than *conservative*. In his words,

It should be pointed out . . . that the epithet "conservative" is a deceptive one, and one undeserved by Parsons. While he shares some of the philosophical assumptions of a man like Edmund Burke . . . he is on the whole a "liberal." This ideological commitment appears at two levels. On the more transitory plane Parsons' liberalism expresses itself in a partisan sense: in his approach to the proper functions of government he is sympathetic to a greater—but not overextended—assumption of public responsibilities for the general welfare. . . . In a more profound sense his liberalism is more historically based: it is the ideology of John Locke and John Stuart Mill, the ideology of political liberty and a free society.[42]

Parsons' use of the concept *equilibrium* is undoubtedly the most frequent target of those who accuse him of being ideologically biased. Edward Devereux has defended Parsons' use of the term. From his vantage point,

To this reviewer, it appears that Parsons' concern with equilibrium does not reflect the view that everything is automatically integrated and adjusted to everything else in this best of all possible worlds. It reflects instead the view that society represents a veritable powder keg of conflicting forces, pushing and hauling in all ways at once. That any sort of equilibrium is achieved at all, as it evidently is in most societies most of the time, thus represents for Parsons something both of miracle and challenge. Far from taking equilibrium for granted, he sees it as a central problem demanding detailed analysis and explanation.[43]

Here is Parsons' view on the matter:

Equilibrium . . . is nothing but the concept of regularity under specific conditions as applied to the internal state of an empirical system relative to its environment. This regularity of course should always be treated as relative rather than absolute; indeed, it is generally subject to considerable ranges of tolerance, and of course its maintenance is by no means inevitable but, if the conditions on which it depends are changed beyond certain limits, it will disappear, again most probably giving way to other regularities than to sheer randomness. Thus in my opinion this concept is an inherently essential part of the logic of science. . . . The denial of its legitimacy . . . is at the least, in my perhaps not very humble opinion, symptomatic of the denial that social science itself is legitimate, or realistically possible. On this point I have thus remained completely unimpressed by the barrage of persistent criticism.[44]

To counter what he considered to be the misguided influence of certain prevalent sociological perspectives such as Parsonian structural-functionalism, C. Wright Mills urged the study of problems that "are of direct relevance to urgent public issues and insistent human troubles."[45] By means of the application of the "sociological imagination," which he claimed "enables us to grasp history and biography and the relations between the two within society," one will be able to discern and analyze relevant problems appropriately. Those who possess this imagination (and not all sociologists were attributed with its possession) have been concerned, said Mills, with the relationship between "the personal troubles of milieux" and "the public issues of social structure." How, then, are we to distinguish a personal problem from a public issue? According to Mills,

When, in a city of 100,000, only one man is unemployed, that is his personal trouble, and for its relief we properly look to the character of the man, his skills, and his immediate opportunities. But when in a nation of 50 million employees, 15 million men are unemployed, that is an issue, and we may not hope to find its solution within the range of opportunities open to only one individual. The very structure of opportunities has collapsed. Both the correct statement of the problem and the range of possible solutions require us to consider the economic and political institutions of the society, and not merely the personal situations and character of a scatter of individuals.[46]

Taking a cue from Mills, Ralf Dahrendorf also opted for a problem-oriented approach and a frame of reference in which the Parsonian equilibrium-integration theory of society would be supplemented with, if not made subordinate to, a neo-

Marxian coercion-conflict theory of society. The following were identified as the basic tenets of the two perspectives:

I. Equilibrium-Integration Theory
   1. Every society is a relatively persistent, stable structure of elements.
   2. Every society is a well-integrated structure of elements.
   3. Every element in a society has a function. i.e., renders a contribution to its maintenance as a system.
   4. Every functioning social structure is based on a consensus of values among its members.

II. Coercion-Conflict Theory
   1. Every society is at every point subject to processes of change; social change is ubiquitous.
   2. Every society displays at every point dissensus and conflict; social conflict is ubiquitous.
   3. Every element in a society renders a contribution to its disintegration and change.
   4. Every society is based on the coercion of some of its members by others.[47]

Dahrendorf postulates that in every social organization there is a differential distribution of power. Some people, by virtue of the position they occupy, always have the right to coerce others. The first task in conflict analysis, he pointed out, is to identify the "variously equipped authority roles" in social organizations. In place of the concept of social system as the general unit of reference, he would substitute the Weberian concept of "imperatively coordinated association." Authority in all imperatively coordinated associations, he asserted, is dichotomized into relations of superordination and subordination. Superiors and subordinates have opposing latent interests (the one to maintain and the other to acquire authoritative control of their association) and are, to Dahrendorf, *quasi* or potential conflict groups.[48] Actual conflict groups, or *interest* groups, are those in which latent interests have become manifest. The goal is to identify the conditions that are sufficient or necessary for the emergence of overt conflicts of interest within and among imperatively coordinated associations. In any event, to Dahrendorf,

> There are sociological problems for the explanation of which the integration theory of society provides adequate assumptions; there are other problems which can be explained only in terms of the coercion theory of society; there are, finally, problems for which both theories appear adequate. For sociological analysis, society is Janus-headed, and its two faces are equivalent aspects of the same reality.[49]

From this and other statements, one gathers that Dahrendorf is not so much interested in devising a scheme to rid sociology of ideological intrusions as he is in making sure that its thrust is not simply ideologically one-sided. If this is a correct reading of his work, one might well wonder whether he believes that ideology should enter into the selection of problems to study and the interpretation of data, or that ideology is an ineradicable component of sociological work and that the best that can be done is to identify its many forms and juxtapose their diverse claims.

Apparently, the best that can be said is that to handle the problem of ideological bias, Dahrendorf recommends the diversification of the sociological frame of reference along the lines suggested by the first two stages of the dialetical method. Thus, wherever there is a thesis there should also be an antithesis. If there is a male sociology there should also be a female sociology, and so on. The third phase of the dialectic presented Dahrendorf with some difficulties. He did not think it possible to reconcile the diverse claims of "integration theory" and "coercion theory." "It seems at least conceivable," he argued, "that unification of theory is not feasible at a point which has puzzled thinkers ever since the beginning of Western philosophy."[50] It did not seem possible to Dahrendorf that the sociologist could look in opposite directions simultaneously. In this he is obviously correct. It is possible to look at different subject matter from the same structural vantage point, however. It was with this idea in mind that Pierre van den Berghe took issue with Dahrendorf's conclusion and presented some thoughts toward a theoretical synthesis of Marxian conflict theory and Parsonian integration theory.

To van den Berghe it was not enough to say that the two theories were not capable of synthesis and had to be used in a complementary way for different purposes. He believed one had to examine the possibilities of their reconciliation. He did not pretend to have accomplished this goal, but did feel that he had identified important points of convergence in their orientations which might eventually point the way to a solution.

First of all, said van den Berghe, both theoretical perspectives are holistic; that is, they are based on the idea that societies can be viewed as systems composed of interrelated parts. Second, even though integration theory may be interpreted as regarding consensus to be a primary source of system stability, and coercion theory may be viewed as regarding conflict as the source of system instability and change, both facts can have the exact opposite effect. For example, consensus on a norm of extreme competition may lead to the growth of an amount of suspicion sufficient for the disintegration of stable social relationships. Furthermore, Lewis Coser has demonstrated ways in which social conflict may be conducive to social solidarity. He has shown, for example, that a number of independent conflict groups in a society can promote its cohesiveness by preventing conflict from stabilizing about a point of primary cleavage.[51]

Third, both positions adhere to an evolutionary notion of social change. In coercion theory, change is viewed as a dialectical process in "an ascensional spiral towards progress." The integration theory concept of social differentiation is predicated on the assumption of a gradual advance in structural complexity and functional specificity. Finally, and herein, said van den Berghe, lies the opportunity for reconciliation, both theoretical perspectives are heavily influenced by the idea of equilibrium. In the case of integration theory the point is obvious. But the threefold dialectical sequence is also based on an ideal of equilibrium. As he stated his case,

The dialectic conceives of society as going through alternating phases [of] equilibrium and disequilibrium: the thesis is the initial equilibrated stage of the cycle; the emergence of the antithesis leads to the intermediate disequilibrated phase; finally, as the contradiction resolves itself in the synthesis, one enters the terminal, balanced stage of the cycle, which then starts anew. While this model is different from the classical notion of dynamic equilibrium, the two views are not contradictory nor incompatible with a postulate of long-range tendency towards integration.[52]

According to van den Berghe, then, the integration approach and the conflict approach differ not so much in their theoretical structure as in their subject-matter orientation. In effect, theoretical structures—particularly frames of reference—can be so general and abstract as to accommodate quite diverse content and even opposing ideological perspectives. Therefore, to deal with problems such as ideological bias, it is not enough to vary the subjects studied. Theoretical structures of different types and varying degrees of flexibility in terms of the range of phenomena to which they are applicable must also be applied. But even these measures are not sufficient to control for ideological bias. Hopefully, however, they might serve to mitigate its influence.

To balance the influence of the structure as opposed to the content of theory in the study of human behavior, Parsons has worked toward the differentiation of levels of analysis (in particular, the biological, the psychological, the sociological, and the culturological) and the construction of frames of reference appropriate to the subject matter of each. In the Parsonian scheme, each level of analysis is simultaneously an independent and dependent variable, i.e., is at the same time causal agent and effected unit. Thus, at certain times an individual's biological constitution will exert a dominating influence on his psychological disposition and vice versa. At still other times, "outputs" from different levels will come into conflict and neutralize each other. Hopefully, Parsons says, the general structure of the theoretical orientation will permit the acquisition of knowledge of the various types of interaction between and within all levels and essential components of a social system.

3. The Unit of Analysis and the Validity of the Causal Perspective In 1964, George Homans wrote,

> In the early 'thirties a distinct school of sociological thought was beginning to form. Its chief, though certainly not its only, intellectual parents are Durkheim and Radcliffe-Brown. I call it a school, though not all its adherents accepted just the same tenets. . . . The school is usually called that of structural-functionalism, or functionalism for short. For a whole generation it has been the dominant, indeed the only distinct, school of sociological thought. I think it has run its course, done its work, and now positively gets in the way of our understanding social phenomena.[53]

The school, said Homans, took as its point of departure the study of norms, or how men ought to behave. Of special interest were clusters of norms called rules and clusters of roles called institutions. It was claimed that the basic unit of analysis was the role, not the acting individual per se. As Homans saw it, the problem was that functionalists never asked why there should be roles in the first place.

To Homans, it was not so much the method as the theoretical usefulness of functionalism that had run its course. For him, the office of theory is to explain, and functionalism does not permit the discovery of explanations of behavioral events. "To look for the consequences of institutions is not the same thing as explaining why the interrelationships are what they are." [54]

As Homans saw it, whenever sociologists actually get down to the business of trying to explain human behavior, whether they are professed functionalists or not, they end up seeking to account for the actions of human beings, not roles. As he observed,

> If a serious effort is made to construct theories that will even begin to explain social phenomena, it turns out that their

general propositions are not about the equilibrium of societies but about the behavior of men. This is true even of some
good functionalists, though they will not admit it. They keep
psychological explanations under the table and bring them
out furtively like a bottle of whiskey, for use when they really
need help. What I ask is that we bring what we say about
theory into line with what we actually do, and so put an end
to our intellectual hypocrisy.[55]

Not all, of course, agree with Homans' viewpoint. Some
neither agree nor disagree with it because they are not sure exactly what he meant. It is one thing to say that social scientists
must observe actual human behavior to derive adequate explanations for its dynamics. It is something else to say that
human behavior can be scientifically observed without the application of some kind of conceptual scheme on the order of
the role perspective. While Homans acknowledges the latter,
it is not clear whether he means to emphasize that (1) behavioral roles should not be conceived of and studied as dis-
embodied phenomena, or (2) that social facts cannot be
treated as sui generis phenomena with independent causal
relevance. In other words, one cannot be sure whether he is
saying that human behavior must be viewed as the effect of
the interaction of the variety of behavioral variables and that
these must be weighed simultaneously in the actions of concrete individuals; or that social facts should be viewed as
dependent variables until their origins have been more clearly
delineated. If Homans is not explicit as to the theoretical implications of these questions, he is not alone. Their ramifica-
tions have not been satisfactorily identified and resolved and,
thus, they represent points of confusion and debate.

A subject of great concern to sociologists has been the relationship between social facts and behavioral causation. Of
particular interest is the question of whether or not the structural-functional frame of reference can be viewed as pre-
scribing a scientifically defensible causal level of analysis.

Parsons has described functional causation as teleological
in character. As Isajiw has stated, "Parsons states at one point
that functionalism has an inherently teleological significance
inasmuch as it views processes of the social system as either

contributing to its maintenance or development or detracting from its integration and effectiveness." [56] Parsons postulates the existence of a social system as a self-regulating unit in the nature of a living organism. The activity of components is viewed as being "caused," i.e., determined, by the "need" demands of the system. As Isajiw notes,

> Parsons' meaning of teleology here is not that of the motives or purposes of the individual actor, but rather that of the end of action itself. . . . In other words, the question of finality in functionalism [that is, the manner in which the behavior of the parts is determined by the whole] is not of the ends or motives of the individuals, but one of the ends of the system itself, regardless of the motives of the individuals participating in it. . . . Critics of teleology in functionalism agree that this is methodologically inadmissible. To hold that there are ends in the social system which are independent of those of the individuals participating in it is according to them, an illegitimate transferral of concepts.[57]

The first major objection to "telecausality" is, then, "that imputation of ends to phenomena other than individual human beings is, in effect, anthropomorphism and cannot be tested empirically." [58] The second is that to assume that human activity is a function of predetermined ends one must employ value judgments.

Isajiw does not consider either of these criticisms wholly legitimate or sufficient reason to eliminate the use of telecausal analysis in sociology. The first objection, says Isajiw, would confuse action directed toward ends with the purpose, intention, i.e., motives, of the acting agent. "It is one thing to say that things act for a purpose—it is another thing to say that they act toward an end." [59] Applied to human behavior, the former concerns the motives of individuals, whereas the latter relates mostly to the goals of action, regardless of motives. One can, for example, pursue a singular goal for any number of purposes. To Isajiw, telecausality in Parsonian functionalism emphasizes the behavioralistic assumption [in many ways compatible with the position argued by George Lundberg in chapter 4] that human activity is pushed and pulled by observable pressures of attraction and repulsion. Telecausality in functionalism, then, does not prejudge the motives of individuals. It emphasizes instead the causal impact of system demands.

Actually, says Isajiw, the anthropomorphic criticism of telecausal analysis is of questionable validity for an even more basic reason. As he put it, ". . . what concepts in the methodological tool-kit of science are not anthropomorphic?" [60] Since all the tools of science are man-made, who is to say which are not influenced by anthropomorphic bias?

Isajiw admits that the assumption of a self-regulating system does involve questions of value judgment. To speak about a part whose action ends either contribute to the maintenance or disruption of a system is to evaluate its worth. In his view,

> . . . to steer clear of all or any value-judgments we could reject the model of a self-regulating system. From the standpoint of logic there is nothing which tells us that we should assume a model of a self-regulating system, but there is also nothing which tells us that it should be rejected. It is hence a question of methodological values; ultimately, a question of fruitfulness of the approach. [61]

To Isajiw, the fruitfulness of the Parsonian perspective is to be gauged in terms of its use as a generalized model. The value of a model, he says, is heuristic. That is, "It directs and organizes research, it shows how a theory is to be built and even if the propositions of the model are ultimately substituted by others which are not isomorphic with them, nevertheless the model, through its logic, provides scaffolding for the connection between these new propositions, as well as suggests what type of propositions to look for." [62] He identifies the basic "elements or propositions" of the Parsonian model as follows: "(1) integration of diverse elements into a unity, (2) interdependence of these elements, so they can be treated as variables, (3) self-regulation, as represented by the notion of equilibrium, (4) pressure of needs of the whole system, (5) processes of need satisfaction." [63]

Each of these propositions may be applied toward the aim of generating deductive theory and empirical analysis.

Though the distinction was not important to Isajiw, it makes a great deal of difference to interpret Parsons' social system construct as a model or an ideal type. Both are heuristic devices but not in the same way. To interpret Parsons' social system as a model is to view it as an end in itself; that is, as an attempt to precisely duplicate "reality." In this case it is subject, at least eventually, to exact test and either confirmation or rejection. If, however, it is interpreted to be an ideal type, it is to be viewed as a means to gauge reality; that is, as an instrument to facilitate the observation of the empirical world. As a tool its scientific validity is to be judged solely in terms of its usefulness. From all indications, Parsons has endeavored to construct an ideal type rather than an isomorphic model. Presumably, the one may be used as a means to work toward the attainment of the other. Admittedly, his immediate goal is to devise an organized scheme or method of looking at reality. Hopefully, this will eventuate in precise interpretations of its patterning. The ideal-type quality of the Parsonian perspective has not been fully appreciated by many. Even a Weberian scholar such as Ralf Dahrendorf has erred in this respect.

In a lengthy critique of the Parsonian perspective, Dahrendorf wrote,

> . . . the social system as conceived by some recent sociological theorists appears to be characterized by the same features as those contained in utopian societies. This being so, the conclusion is forced upon us that this type of theory also deals with societies from which historical change is absent and that it is, in this sense utopian. To be sure, it is utopian not because some of the assumptions of this theory are "unrealistic"— this would be true for the assumptions of almost any scientific theory—but because it is exclusively concerned with spelling out the conditions of the functioning of a utopian social system. Structural-functional theory does not introduce unrealistic assumptions for the purpose of explaining real problems; it introduces many kinds of assumptions, con-

cepts, and models for the sole purpose of describing a social system that has never existed and is not likely ever to come into being.[64]

Had Dahrendorf not assumed Parsons' scheme to be an empirical model, but chose instead to interpret it as an analytical ideal type, his analysis would have amounted to little more then a descriptive truism. An ideal type is basically a utopian construct; and as previously noted, one of its primary functions is to gauge the extent of historical change. Parsons has stated that his is an analytical rather than an empirical scheme. "It should be made very clear . . . that the theory of action, so far as it is in any sense a logically closed system, which is an open question, can be so *only* on an analytical level, most definitely not as a system of empirical generalizations." [65] Dahrendorf is only one of many sociologists who have failed to consider the diverse possibilities of both the structure and content of the Parsonian perspective.

In terms of content, Parsons takes the view that the identification of the structural components of social systems and their interrelationships is prerequisite to the analysis of both social order and social change. Furthermore, isolation of the laws of general social system processes is a necessary preliminary to the construction of a theory of social change. As Parsons has stated,

> . . . *a general theory of the processes of social systems is not possible in the present state of knowledge.* The reason is very simply that such a theory would imply complete knowledge of the laws of process of the system and this knowledge we do not possess.[66]

It was on the basis of this rationale that Parsons reached the following conclusion: "If theory is *good theory*, whichever type of problem it tackles most directly, there is no reason whatever to believe that it will not be *equally* applicable to the problems of change and to those of process within a stabilized system." [67]

Summary

It is readily apparent that structural-functionalism, and particularly the Parsonian version, has been and continues to be a dominant theoretical guide in sociological analysis. One indication of the sociological importance of functionalism is the tremendous amount of criticism and elaboration to which it has been subjected. Though functionalism cannot be described as a full-fledged scientific paradigm, there is little doubt that it has served the important function of bringing sociologists together long enough for them to gain a sense of commonality and a feeling for the uniqueness of their discipline.

While Parsons has been deeply concerned with outlining the elements of a macroanalytic perspective, others have begun to move toward micro analyses as revealed, for example, in the vigorous interest in two-party interaction patterns in the form of "exchange theory." Furthermore, there is renewed interest in the study of individual behavior. Though not widely discussed or applied, the "field-theoretical" frame of reference is worthy of note in this respect. These subjects will be discussed in the next chapter.

SIX · Œxchange theory and field theory: from social interaction to variables in interaction

Social Behavior as Exchange: George C. Homans

George Homans' contributions to sociological theory have not been restricted to critiques of the structure and content of the functional frame of reference. Although not the first to recognize the existence of a quid pro quo motive in social life, Homans is the recognized initiator of the "exchange theory of social behavior." As will be seen, *exchange theory* is a combination of the action, functional, and situational frames of reference. It combines interest in the behavioral sources of social consensus and dissensus primarily by concentrating the analytical focus on two-party interaction patterns.

Homans begins the conceptual explanation of exchange theory by defining its subject matter as social behavior, "which means that when a person acts in a certain way he is at least rewarded or punished by the behavior of another *person*, though he may also be rewarded or punished by the non-human environment." Thus, the perspective is fundamentally concerned with human interaction of a face-to-face, give-and-take nature. Furthermore, "the behavior must be actual behavior and not a norm of behavior." [1] In other words, Homans is more interested in identifying the process by which norms are created than in studying their impact on human behavior.

In order to begin the development of a conceptual scheme, Homans, even as the behavioral psychologists, focuses his interest on "what determines changes in the rate of emission of learned behavior." [2] Pointing to laboratory experiments on pigeons, Homans proceeds to explore factors involved in the maintenance and termination of pigeon pecking behavior. For example, the more hungry the pigeon, the more often it is likely to peck for food. If the pecking behavior is rewarded by the acquisition of considerable food, the pecking rate will drop off as *satiation* increases. On the other hand, if pecking to relieve hunger is not reinforced by the ingestion of food, the pecking rate will eventually become *extinguished*. Finally, the emission of behavior, no matter how rewarding, entails *cost*. Cost may be calculated in a number of ways. For example, as energy expended in a foot race, or in terms of financial resources depleted in order to make a profit. "Extinction, satiation, and cost, by decreasing the rate of emission of a particular kind of behavior, render more probable the emission of some other kind of behavior, including doing nothing." [3]

Although human learning potential is much greater than that of pigeons, Homans believes that the behavior of the two may be regarded as comparable after a behavior pattern has been established. It is assumed that people bring into interaction situations a set of consciously and unconsciously developed response patterns. The goal is to identify not only the alternative response patterns available to individuals receiving observable behavioral stimuli, but also to determine how alternative response patterns change (by alteration, elimination, and substitution) as a result of particular experiences.

The key components of Homans' conceptual scheme are descriptive terms and variables. *Descriptive terms* name kinds of behavior, such as the pecking activity of a pigeon; *variables* describe properties of behavior that vary in quantity, such as rate of pecking.

Homans relies heavily on three basic descriptive terms: activities, sentiments, and interaction. *Activity* denotes to Homans what "action" denotes to Parsons. That is, Homans, like Parsons, is singularly interested in that type of human behavior which results from an individual's having to select from a plurality of behavioral choices the most appropriate to apply in response to the presence or action of others.

By *sentiment*, Homans means a type of activity. "The activities that the members of a particular verbal or symbolic community say are signs of the attitudes and feelings a man takes toward another man or other men—these we call sentiments." [4] Many activities represent institutionalized ways of expressing sentiment and are readily identifiable. For example, in Western culture, kissing denotes sentiments of love and affection. The raining of blows with clenched fists by one person on another signifies hostility. Many other human activities, however, are not so easily interpretable for the sentiments they are designed to represent. A "joker," for example, usually means to display himself in a casual and carefree light. But the target of his jokes, for instance, women drivers, may well be the focus of more hostility than jocularity.

Sentiments, then, though capable of assuming various forms, are always expressions of overt behavior. Sentiments of social approval and disapproval are of particular concern to Homans. "We hold that all activities and sentiments emitted by one man in response to the behavior of another are more or less reinforcing or punishing to the behavior of the other or, as we shall say, more or less valuable to him." [5] *Interaction*, the last of the descriptive terms, refers to the mutual influence of two or more individuals.

Homans' variables have to do with the quantity and value of expressed activities and sentiments. *Quantity* can be measured in a variety of ways including frequency counts of the gestures and verbal symbols employed by interacting individuals. One can also record the amount of time devoted to certain activities by interacting parties. For example, "Within an eight-hour day at the office, how many minutes did Other spend giving help to Person, and how many minutes of approval did Person give Other in return." [6]

Value is defined as the positive and negative worth attached by one individual to the actions of another. Certain factors must be kept in mind in the measurement of human values. First of all, in many instances one will not be able to determine the extent to which an object or a stimulus is valued by a person. Though we would like to know exactly how much one person values another, perhaps all we can determine in a given instance, for example, in the case of a married couple, is that the husband values the companionship of his wife more than that of any other woman. Often the best we can do in such cases is to record the types of stimuli to which an individual responds and attempt to differentiate values of constant concern from those of temporary interest. Second, when it is possible to determine the degree to which a stimulus is valued by an individual, we can begin to probe questions such as why it is that he values something more at one time than another.

By analyzing elementary conditions such as these, Homans was able to develop five major theoretical propositions. First of all, and in line with the principle of inertia, he makes the assumption that a man will tend to react to a present stimulus the way he has in the past. "If in the past the occurrence of a particular stimulus-situation has been the occasion on which a man's activity has been rewarded, then the more similar the present stimulus situation is to the past one, the more likely he is to emit the activity, or some similar activity, now." [7]

Second, "The more often within a given period of time a man's activity rewards the activity of another, the more often the other will emit the activity." [8] Quantity or frequency of activity is, as has been noted, only one of Homans' key variables. The second concerns the value of activity and this variable is the subject of his third proposition, which is, "The more valuable to a man a unit of the activity another gives him, the more often he will emit activity rewarded by the activity of the other." [9]

Fourth, under certain conditions the fact of satiation may become of overriding importance and, hence, one may state that: "The more often a man has in the recent past received a rewarding activity from another, the less valuable any further unit of that activity becomes to him." [10]

Proposition five is based on the presumption that stable patterns of exchange entail a notion of distributive justice. As Homans puts it, "A man in an exchange relation with another will expect that the rewards of each man be proportional to his costs—the greater the rewards, the greater the costs—and that the net rewards, or profit, of each man be proportional to his investments—the greater the investments, the greater the profit." Proposition five reads: "The more to a man's disadvantage the rule of distributive justice fails of realization, the more likely he is to display the emotional behavior we call anger." [11] It is here that Homans could have delved into the dynamics of exploitation, power, conflict, and change. But instead the discussion turns toward a consideration of the basic question: what are the interaction processes behind the evolution of balanced or equilibrated exchange patterns? As he summarized his theoretical perspective,

> Social behavior is an exchange of goods, material goods but also non-material ones, such as the symbols of approval or prestige. Persons that give much to others try to get much from them, and persons that get much from others are under pressure to give much to them. This process of influence tends to work out at equilibrium to a balance in the exchanges.[12]

Reciprocity and Social Exchange: Alvin W. Gouldner

The subjects of exchange, exploitation, and equilibrium in social life have been discussed by Alvin Gouldner in his article, "The Norm of Reciprocity: A Preliminary Statement." As Gouldner sees it, functionalists have failed to distinguish between the concept of reciprocity and the concept of complementarity. To Gouldner, *complementarity* "connotes that one's rights are another's obligations, and vice versa." *Reciprocity*, on the other hand, "connotes that *each* party has rights *and* duties." In elaboration he says,

> . . . were there only rights on the one side and duties on the other, there need be no exchange whatsoever. Stated differently, it would seem that there can be stable patterns of

reciprocity *qua* exchange only insofar as *each* party has both rights and duties.[13]

His point is that social exchange is in good measure to be observed as the consequence of the existence of "a generalized moral norm of reciprocity which defines certain actions and obligations as repayments for benefits received." [14] To Gouldner, the norm of reciprocity is a cultural universal; that is, in one form or another, it is likely to be found in any and every cultural system.

The norm makes two demands of people: (1) to be helpful to those who have been helpful, and (2) not to inflict harm on those who have been helpful. The task of the sociologist is to uncover the various forms of the norm of reciprocity and the conditions of its application and interpretation.

In pursuing the conceptual clarification of reciprocity in social life, Gouldner notes that many, including Homans, have implied that reciprocity must entail an exchange of equivalents. Equivalence, he suggests, can assume at least two forms: heteromorphic or homeomorphic reciprocity. In the former case, though the subjects or exchange may be different in kind, their values should be equal to the transacting parties. In the latter case, the objects exchanged "should be concretely alike, or identical in form, either with respect to the things exchanged or to the circumstances under which they are exchanged." [15] The question is, says Gouldner, "can we find reciprocity norms which, in fact, require that returns be equivalent in value and are these empirically distinguishable from norms requiring that returns be concretely alike?" [16] The answers, he says, lie in future empirical investigation.

The focus of Gouldner's discussion is admittedly on the bearing of the norm of reciprocity on the stability of social systems. He believes that social stability is in good measure the consequence of the mutual indebtedness of those who live by a norm of reciprocity. As he explains,

It is obviously inexpedient for creditors to break off relationships with those who have outstanding obligations to them. It may also be inexpedient for *debtors* to do so because their creditors may not again allow them to run up a bill of social indebtedness. In addition, it is *morally improper*, under the norm of reciprocity, to break off relations or to launch hostilities against those to whom you are still indebted.[17]

If the line of reasoning is correct, says Gouldner, we might expect to find not only "mechanisms" which drive men to pay their debts, but also "mechanisms" that "induce people to *remain* socially indebted to each other and which *inhibit* their complete repayment."[18] Thus, *rough equivalence* rather than exact equivalence of exchange may play an important part in maintaining system stability.

Gouldner argues that unequal exchange may be an important normatively sanctioned process and not, therefore, necessarily exploitative. Functionalists, he says, have tended to view unequal exchange as indicative of exploitation of the weak by the powerful and evidence of system instability. Though not denying the validity of the interpretation, Gouldner emphasizes that the norm of reciprocity constrains even the powerful. "The norm . . . safeguards powerful people against the temptations of their own status; it motivates and regulates reciprocity as an exchange pattern, serving to inhibit the emergence of exploitative relations which would undermine the social system and the very power arrangements which had made exploitation possible."[19]

Exchange and Power: Peter M. Blau

The relationship between exchange and power is a primary concern of Peter Blau's. Blau agrees with Homans that knowledge of social structure must be built up from analyses of "elementary" social behavior. "The problem," he states, "is to derive the social processes that govern the complex structures of communities and societies from the simpler processes that pervade the daily intercourse among individuals and their interpersonal relations."[20] However, he emphasizes, this is not to suggest that the whole is to be interpreted as the mere sum of its parts. Social structure is to be understood as an emergent phenomenon. Thus, although individuals who exchange commodities may be motivated to maintain their relationship because of the psychological reinforcement provided by the promise of continual attainment of satisfying rewards, "the psychological process of reinforcement does not suffice to explain the exchange relation that develops." A social relationship is an interdependent affair and the "emergent properties of social exchange consequent to this interdependence cannot be accounted for by the psychological processes that motivate the behavior of the partners." [21]

Where Homans suggests that the analysis of elementary social behavior is the means to *account* for the fact of emergent social structure, Blau contends that the best that can be obtained thereby is a *better understanding* of the process. Blau does not specify what he means by a "better understanding." Furthermore, it is not clear whether Blau means to convey the impression that he accepts the animistic view that the fact of emergence is not subject to empirical determination, or that emergence is subject to empirical determination but not by means of the close scrutiny of elementary social behavior. In the case of the latter, we are not given a clue as to what else might be involved.

Having merely touched upon important epistemological considerations, Blau goes on to declare that "Not all, human behavior is guided by considerations of exchange. . . ." Two criteria establish *exchange* in social life. First of all, the ends of action must be those that require the cooperation of two or more persons. Second, the interacting parties must have the common problem of selecting means for goal attainment. The act of exchange is to be viewed as a bargaining process between those who must given something to get something and who are motivated to attain their goals at minimal cost. "Excluded from consideration, therefore, is behavior resulting from the irrational push of emotional forces without being goal oriented, for instance, a girl's irrational conduct on dates that is motivated by her unconscious conflicts with her father." [22] Put another way, ". . . the concept of exchange re-

fers to voluntary social actions that are contingent on rewarding reactions from others and that cease when these expected
reactions are not forthcoming." [23]

Social exchange is not to be construed as a synonym for
human interaction. Rather, it is meant to describe that type
of interaction in which all parties who desire something in
the possession of one or another come together to work out
their own terms of reciprocity. Fundamentally, both the
means and ends of exchange must be worked out on a trial
and error basis. The subject of concern is the substance of
and criteria for the initiating and reacting strategies employed by transacting parties. Situations involving the application of adaptive wit, and rational and deliberate calcula-
tion—such as the bargaining process in an open economic
system—are of particular interest.

The affinity between Blau's conception of social exchange
and the economic transaction is not fortuitous. As he puts it,
"The very term 'social exchange' is designed to indicate that
social interaction outside the economic sphere has important similarities with economic transactions." [24] Nevertheless, there is a basic difference between the two. For him, a
fundamental part of the economic transaction is the spelling
out in advance of the conditions of exchange. Contrary to
economic transactions, he emphasizes, the terms of reciprocity in social exchange cannot be stipulated ahead of time.
As he explains,

> Social exchange . . . entails supplying benefits that create
> diffuse future obligations. The nature of the return is invari-
> ably not stipulated in advance, cannot be bargained about,
> and must be left to the discretion of the one who makes it.
> Thus, if a person gives a dinner party, he expects his guests to
> reciprocate in the future. But he can hardly bargain with
> them about the kind of party to which they should invite
> him, though he expects them not simply to ask him for a
> quick lunch if he has given a formal dinner for them. [25]

One variety of exchange is of special interest to Blau—that
involving imbalance, or the exchange of nonequivalents. In a

competitive society there is considerable pressure to maintain an imbalance in terms of one's exchanges with others. That is, it is to our advantage to have more people and/or certain kinds of people indebted to us than vice versa. In this way we are able to acquire sufficient power to maintain a measure of autonomy in our lives. As Blau reasons, "By providing unilateral benefits to others, a person accumulates a capital of willing compliance on which he can draw whenever it is to his interest to impose his will upon others, within the limits of the significance the continuing supply of his benefits has for them." [26]

The exchange of nonequivalents, then, may furnish the foundation for an unequal distribution of power. Furthermore, and as has been often noted, the nonequitable distribution of power is an important source of system stability and equilibrium. The question is, is it not also the source of the strain and tension that is conducive to system disequilibrium and social change? As Blau sees it,

> Power differences as such, analytically conceived and abstracted from other considerations, create such a pressure toward change, because it can be assumed that men experience having to submit to power as a hardship from which they would prefer to escape. The advantages men derive from their ruler or government, however, may outweigh the hardships entailed in submitting to his or its power, with the result that the analytical imbalance or disturbance introduced by power differences is neutralized. The significance of power imbalances for social change depends, therefore, on the reactions of the governed to the exercise of power.[27]

If the ruled interpret the power of their rulers as normatively legitimate, unequal exchange between them may be institutionalized as equitable policy and the measure of social equilibrium. "If the members of an organization, or generally those subject to a governing leadership, commonly agree that the demands made on them are only fair and just in view of the ample rewards the leadership delivers, joint feelings of obligation and loyalty to superiors will arise and bestow legitimating approval on their authority." [28]

In itself this line of reasoning is difficult to fault. But sociologically speaking, it leaves something to be desired. That is, if social facts are to be viewed as emergent sui generis phenomena, we should expect Blau to concern himself with identifying instances of social exchange which produce the kind of power relationships (for example, those which are unacceptably coercive and exploitative) that lead to predictable types of social change. One social fact should be accounted for in terms of another or other social facts. Instead, Blau postulates that the effect of social stimuli depends on the way people react to them. One is reminded of Homans' charge about some functionalists who "keep psychological explanations under the table and bring them out furtively like a bottle of whiskey, for use when they really need help." [29]

Blau believes that the exploitative and coercive power that provokes rebellion and revolution is more likely to result from intergroup rather than intragroup relations. Within organizations, the institutionalization of power serves to minimize the necessity for the application of force to gain compliance. However, intergroup contact (particularly in international relations) is seldom subject to a comparable degree of constraint. Interaction between groups may very well represent a clash of opposing conceptions of legitimate power and rules of reciprocity. Thus, the actions of one group are likely, for as many valid as invalid reasons, to be interpreted as attempts to coerce the response of the other.

Reformulating the work of Richard Emerson, Blau presents four conditions associated with the production of power imbalance. Individuals who want the services of another have four response options: (1) they can supply him with a service as inducement for him to reciprocate on their terms (for example, one morning we may volunteer our services to a neighbor by helping him paint his house in hopes of inducing him to play golf with us in the afternoon); (2) they can seek to satisfy their needs elsewhere; (3) they can attempt to force him to supply the desired service; and (4) they can choose to forgo the acquisition of the service. One may, of course, simply accede to the demands of another.

It follows that the conditions of autonomy in social life are, then: (1) the possession of all the desired and necessary resources to sustain life and gratify needs, (2) continual and direct access to the necessary and desired means of life, (3) the ability to coerce others into satisfying our needs, and (4) lack of a need for the provision of services that might necessitate submission to the will of another.

On the other hand, the requirements of power include: (1) the ability to restrict the behavioral options of others to those of our choosing; (2) the ability to prevent others from gaining access to other suppliers of services, i.e., the monopolization of needed rewards; (3) the ability to prevent others from forcing our compliance to their demands; and (4) the ability to make others need the benefits we have to offer.

Conflict between the powerful and their subjects centers on four types of issues. The first concerns the resources of subordinates vis-à-vis superordinates. If subordinates had sufficient resources to exchange for the benefits they require, their power relationship to others would not be problematic. "Granted," says Blau, "that every single subordinate's resources are inadequate for this purpose, the issue becomes that of pooling the resources of all subordinates who confront a superior or group of superiors to exact demands from him or them." [30] The second involves the alternative methods available to subordinates to satisfy their needs. As Blau notes, "Competition among superiors for the services of subordinates increases the subordinate's independence, whereas monopolistic practices increase the superiors' power." [31] Third, there is the political issue as to the proper and effective application of force to gain compliance or resist domination. The prototype, says Blau, is the dispute over the manner in which the legitimate coercive power of the state may be applied to regulate the development of factors conducive to exchange imbalance, such as the growth of unequal economic advantage. Finally, says Blau, there is the ideological conflict between social values that intensify the need for the services the powerful have to offer and counterideologies that mitigate the need. In the process of decreasing the need for some services, however, radical ideologies increase the need for other—namely, those that contribute to the reform movement—with the result that ideologies make adherents less dependent on the power of some but more dependent on the power of others.[32]

All of these issues have important implications for the analysis of structural problems. To begin with, to gain some insight into why certain people enter into exchange relationships, it is necessary to study the connection between the way in which resources are distributed and the observable types of exchange prevalent in a given society. Second, one must also be alert to the changes taking place in existing patterns of exchange and to the new types that may be coming into being. Third, the fact that all societies manifest some form of coercive power suggests the need to study the relationship between exchange processes and the development of differentiated power. Finally, the fact that people can learn to do without something "calls attention to the modification of social values that occur under various conditions, the formation of new ideologies, and conflicts between ideologies." [33]

Of central importance to Blau is the relationship between the process of social exchange and social integration. Blau has described the complexity of the relationship between social exchange and social integration as follows:

A group is cohesive if bonds of social attraction unite its members. For social integration to prevail in a group and a cohesive unit to develop, its members must be concerned with attracting one another. To prove himself an attractive associate, each member will seek to impress the others with his good qualities. But the resulting competition for popularity and defensive reactions against letting one's self be impressed by others threaten to lead to an impasse in which social integration would be impossible. If groups do not disintegrate, and many obviously do not, it is because other social processes forestall it.[34]

As Blau sees it, to receive an invitation to become a member of a group, one must make oneself appear attractive to its membership. Seemingly, there are an endless number of ways to effect an attractive appearance. Whatever the particular strategy one may decide to employ, it is to be recognized that the demonstration of attractive qualities is a mixed blessing. "Paradoxically," Blau notes, "the very attributes that make a person an attractive associate for others also raise fears of dependence that make them reluctant to acknowledge their attraction." [35] An individual may demonstrate such superior qualities that he virtually compels the deference of others. For Blau, "Deference to another impedes relaxed sociability with him."

The relaxed interaction necessary for the development of strong peer relationships may also be impeded by the competition which group members often enter into in order to make evident their valuable and attractive qualities. Within groups, then, individuals may compete to differentiate themselves from the very people whose esteem and responsiveness they covet.

The potential divisiveness of this antithetical behavior is mitigated by several considerations. First of all, it must be recognized that competition has positive functions for group cohesion. Competition is a convenient method of discovering the different talents "members have for making needed contributions" to the attainment of group ends. Furthermore, competition is a useful means of discovering the most qualified group leader. Also, competition is a method for weeding out those whose membership is not functionally important.

Individuals who compete successfully can minimize the intimidation of their comrades by flaunting certain of their weaknesses. "By calling attention to his weaknesses, a person gives public notice that he withdraws from the competition for superior standing in the group and that he considers acceptance as a peer sufficient reward for his attractive qualities and for whatever contribution they enable him to make." [36] By means of self-depreciation the superior competitor acknowledges the social superiority of his peers. That is, by admitting that he has certain inferior characteristics, a leader can lessen his threatening influence on others by assuring them that they too possess superior qualities to which he must defer. Blau has summarized his theory of social integration in the following manner:

> Following Homans' suggestive conceptualization, these patterns of social interaction may be looked upon as exchange processes. A person with superior qualities which enable him to provide services that are in demand receives the respect and deference of others in a group, which bestows superordinate status upon him, in exchange for rendering these services. A person who is not able to offer services that are in demand must settle for a lower position in the group. He can exchange his ready acceptance of others like him and his conformity to group norms for their acceptance of him. To put it into a somewhat different perspective, he wins social acceptance in exchange for ceasing to compete for superior standing in the group and for the contribution to social integration he thereby makes.[37]

Summary and Critique

Of the three formulations discussed, the writings of Homans and Blau have attracted the greatest amount of attention because each has written a major work on social exchange. Even though Blau's work builds on that of Homans, the two theorists diverge at certain critical points.

To begin with, Homans is explicit about the kind of theory he aims to construct. He wishes to "explain" human behavior by relating key variables in propositional statements which form a deductive structure. In his scheme, the exchange frame of reference is a means to obtain information about the kinds of behavioral variables he deems important to his task. Blau, on the other hand, is mostly implicit about the theoretical structure toward which he is working. He considers his work "a prolegomenon of a theory of social structure" and, thus, the power of his work is meant to be its suggestiveness rather than its completeness. Even so, we are not told what the structure of the finished product should look like. Perhaps Blau will eventually build on *Exchange and Power in Social Life* the way Homans has on his *The Human Group*.

Homans and Blau make quite different epistemological assumptions. Homans believes that social institutions must be explained in terms of the actual behavior of individuals. He is not content to abide by the Durkheimian tenet that social facts must be explained, indeed, can only be explained, in terms of other social facts. Society may in fact be a sui generis phenomenon, but Homans would like to account for the process by which social facts emerge or arise out of elementary social exchange.

Homans' position has been somewhat controversial in sociology. Some have dismissed him as a foolish psychological reductionist. To those in this camp, the denial of the Durkheimian tenet is tantamount to the denial of the obvious. Here are the words of one of his critics:

> . . . the psychological perspective, adequate as it may be at its own level of abstraction, does not encompass sociological phenomena. . . . The psychologist understands the field of human behavior as it is affected by A's rewarding B or as B reinforces A. . . . To the sociologist, the relationship of A to B has its consequences on the field. It is probably true that A's relations to B may be learned according to reinforcement theory, but what is learned is another, a sociological phenomenon. Homans fails to see this and very early in his book [*Social Behavior: Its Elementary Forms*] rejects Durkheim's traditional position that social facts may be understood only in terms of other social facts. This rejection of social facts as having explanatory value in themselves is consistent with the assumptions Homans has made but is hardly to be viewed as a positive reinforcer by sociologists.[38]

While it is easy to dispute what an author "really said," it is not difficult to see that the appeal to tradition does not adequately confront the issue that Homans raises. Homans does not deny the existence or the independent effect of social facts. He believes that sociology ought to be concerned with the explanation of social facts by means of a behavioristic-empirical orientation. This point of view, though central in the formulations of those who initiated sociology in America, has long been given secondary attention in favor of the effort to demonstrate the independent effect of social facts in human behavior.

Blau wishes to have it both ways. He accepts Homans' idea that analysis of elementary social exchange is prerequisite to the analysis of complex social structures. At the same time, he holds that social facts are emergent phenomena and are not to be explained by knowledge of the precise linkage of their constituent elements. This is his way of making the point:

> Although the division of labor in a community refers ultimately to observable patterns of conduct of individuals, it is an emergent property of communities that has no counterpart in a corresponding property of individuals. Age distribution, similarly, is an attribute that exists only on the group level; individuals have no age distribution, only an age. The limitation of psychological reductionism is that it tends to ignore these emergent characteristics of social life and explain it exclusively in terms of the motives that govern individual behavior. The limitation of abstract conceptions of social structure that stress their distinctive "Gestalt," and do not analytically dissect the complex patterns into its simpler components, on the other hand, is not only that testable hypotheses can rarely be derived from such theories but also that the most complex aspects of social life cannot be fully explained without reference to its simpler aspects in which they are rooted.[39]

The epistemological issue here is more complex than might be apparent. In accepting the fact of emergence, Blau appears to have absolved himself from participating in its explanation. Nevertheless, we must consider whether *emergence* is to be a descriptive term for a perceived event we should like to explain, or simply a convenient label.

While no one has actually taken a vote on the subject, one gathers that the Durkheimian tenet is well ingrained in the sociological belief system. At one time, sociologists were in need of a conception of the "social factor" in which they could have faith in order to convince others and themselves of the importance of their discipline. By means of a persuasive example, Durkheim was able to demonstrate both the theoretical uniqueness and the empirical fruitfulness of a conception of the social factor as a sui generis, emergent phenomenon. In retrospect, it can be seen to have been more important to have demonstrated the existence and behavioral effect of sociological phenomena than their multidimensional genesis. It must be remembered that it took biologists some time to get around to the idea that the uniqueness of organic life might be capable of empirical determination by means of the unique combination of so-called inorganic substances.

Just as biological facts, so do social facts have a beginning, a developmental pattern, variable persistence, and a period of decline and death. They are both causal agents and effected results. To document the place of social facts in human behavior it is necessary to study the nature of their independence and dependence.

In summary, and as conceived by Homans and Blau, but particularly the latter, exchange theory is a restricted frame of reference from which to view the activity of interacting individuals. The aim is to identify the variable components within a limited social context. Exchange theory is fundamentally concerned with the analysis of those situations which involve bargaining between two or more individuals who need something from each other which they are motivated to acquire in the maximum amount and at the minimal expense.

Homans would like to identify precise linkages between identifiable behavioral variables within a limited social context with the goal of making lawful statements about human behavior. Blau is not explicit on this point. It would appear that his aim of obtaining a "better understanding" of elementary social processes is not the equivalent of Homans' effort to isolate laws of human behavior. Whatever the case, if one's goal is the discovery of laws of human behavior, it would appear logical to delineate for analysis a limited behavior area which one has reason to believe contains all the necessary factors that must be taken into account. Apparently, Homans feels that he has done precisely this. There are, however, grounds for doubting that the goal has been accomplished.

In spite of a declared antipathy for Durkheimian structural-functionalism and a professed predilection for psychological explanation, Homans has adhered basically to the Durkheimian tenet. That is, one social fact, exchange behavior, is viewed as the consequence of another, namely, two or more individuals with the "need" to get something in a socially induced way. Nonsociological variables, but important behavioral factors, such as biological endowment, are disregarded. Apparently, Homans believes that behavioral events can be conceived of as being caused by social-psychological variables regardless of the intrusion of other possible behavioral stimuli. If so, no justification for this position is stated. Consequently, it is difficult not to conclude that Homans has to a large extent employed a different terminology to describe the traditional sociological orientation. Though the exchange perspective has been suggestively developed by Homans and Blau, their exclusion of certain variables and problems from consideration means that the fruits of their analyses must fall short of the mark of uncovering lawlike generalizations.

To isolate laws of human behavior, one must devise a perspective from which to observe cause and effect relationships among all known behaviorally related variables. Some argue that the field-theoretical perspective, or something very much like it, is necessary for such an undertaking.

Field Theory: Kurt Lewin and J. Milton Yinger

As initially conceived by Kurt Lewin (1890–1947), field theory was a restricted psychological frame of reference. The subject of concern was the acting individual and the aim was to identify the variables in a field of action, or a situation, which could be documented to have affected his perceptual awareness by initiating predictable responses. In time, Lewin came to expand the perspective along the lines currently espoused by the sociologist J. Milton Yinger. To Yinger, field theory refers to that perspective concerned with the analysis of human behavior as it occurs and precisely where it occurs. Its scope is broader than the traditional situational perspective in that all the variables which may affect observable activity—from climatic conditions to biological endowment—are included within its purview.

Lewin's basic starting point was to psychology as Durkheim's basic tenet was to sociology. As Morton Deutsch has stated, Lewin "takes the stand that psychological phenomena must be explained in psychological terms just as physical phenomena must be explained in physical terms." [40] Psychological facts were to be thought of as sui generis phenomena and not, therefore, reducible to biophysiological elements.

Lewin's goal was the discovery of laws of individual behavior; field theory was to be the method by which the goal was to be attained. "Field theory is probably best characterized as a method: namely, a method for analyzing causal relations and of building scientific constructs." [41] For Lewin, field theory was not a theory in the sense of an explanation, but a theory in the vein of a frame of reference within which essential variables could be located, observed, and their interrelationships charted. The task of the psychologist was to grasp the underlying causes of human behavior by means of the art of conceptualization.

Fritz Heider has illustrated what Lewin had in mind by an analysis of the fable of the fox and the crow. According to the fable,

A hungry Crow stole a piece of cheese and flew with it onto the branch of a tree. Just as she was about to take the first bite, a sly Fox spied her and called from below.

"Good day, Mistress Crow, how well you are looking! How glossy your feathers, how shining your eyes! I am certain that your voice is lovely, too. Oh, if I could hear but one song from you I would surely greet you as the Queen of Birds."

The Crow, who was very vain, believed every word spoken by the Fox. Fluttering her wings, she lifted her head and opened her mouth to caw. With that, the cheese dropped to the ground and was immediately snapped up by the Fox.

As he walked away, well fed and well pleased with his cleverness, the Fox called back to the Crow, "In exchange for that delicious cheese, I will give you a bit of advice: *Remember not to trust those who praise you falsely.*" [42]

To Heider, the important underlying concepts of the fable are to perceive, belong to, want, cause, and can. The fox *perceives;* that is, something desirable in the outside world, the cheese, has been brought to his attention. However, the cheese is not immediately available to his possession as it *belongs to* the crow. Nevertheless, the fox *wants* it. The effective *cause* of the solution is a verbal trick. Thus, the fox *can* get the cheese and without being direct and brutal.

Though the same event may have more than one conceptual interpretation (for example, the fable of the fox and the crow may simply be interpreted as an example of one type of thievery), Lewin, in the manner of Parsons, hoped to identify concepts of general applicability. That is, he wished to develop a conceptual scheme useful for the analysis of all types of human behavior.

Behavioral concepts, said Lewin, should describe the general in the particulars, but not at the expense of being inapplicable to the particular. As he reasoned,

Like any science, psychology is in a dilemma when it tries to develop "general" concepts and laws. If one "abstracts from individual differences," there is no logical way back from these generalities to the individual case. Such a generalization leads from individual children to children of a certain age or certain economic level and from there to children of all ages and all economic levels; it leads from a psychopathic individual to similar pathological types and from there to the general category "abnormal person." However, there is no logical way back from the concept "child" or "abnormal person" to the individual case. What is the value of general concepts if they do not permit predictions for the individual case? [43]

To deal with the dilemma, Lewin urged the application of what he called *the constructive method*. By this he meant that concepts should be devised with a limited amount of abstraction. The level of abstraction should never be so great as to preclude the interpretation of a construct by means of reference to observables. For example, the life space of an individual should be capable of interpretation by means of reference to specific observables such as particular people and inanimate objects. The observables of key concern to Lewin were "the dynamic aspects of events." "What is needed," he said, "are scientific constructs and methods which deal with the underlying forces of behavior but do so in a methodologically sound manner." [44] The term *dynamic* referred to "an interpretation of changes as the result of psychological forces." The essential psychological forces were motivation, psychological conflict and change. Put another way, Lewin was invoking the naturalistic principle of inertia in which change in, rather than maintenance of, a steady state is taken as problematic.

To develop constructs from dynamic referents, one must, Lewin insisted, employ a psychological approach. "One of the basic characteristics of field theory in psychology . . . is the demand that the field which influences an individual should be described not in 'objective physicalistic' terms, but in the way in which it exists for that person at that time." [45] The individual's "field" was conceptualized as his "life space." Hall and Lindzey have diagramed the Lewinian concept of life space as follows:

Nonpsychological (**E** (**P**) **E**) Nonpsychological

(P + E = Life Space)

In their words,

> The region between the two perimeters [and surrounding the person, shown as P] is the psychological environment, E. The total area within the ellipse, including the circle, is the life space. . . . The space outside the ellipse, represented the nonpsychological aspects of the universe. For the sake of convenience, we shall call this region the physical world, although it is not restricted to physical facts alone. There are, for example, social facts as well in the nonpsychological world.[46]

As J. Milton Yinger has observed, "In Lewin's work, field means 'psychological field'—that part of the total series of forces that is perceived by an individual."[47] As Lewin says,

> To describe a situation "objectively" in psychology actually means to describe the situation as a totality of those facts and of only those facts which make up the field of that individual. To substitute for that world of the individual the world of the teacher, of the physicist, or of anybody else is to be, not objective, but wrong.[48]

Yinger disagrees. It may seem reasonable to the psychologically trained individual, he says, that a person cannot be influenced by something of which he is not aware. But this point of view "overlooks the fact that a person's perceptions are a function not only of his sensitivities but also of the available stimuli; many of them derived from culture and social structure." Hence, concludes Yinger, "Priority in determining behavior can be assigned neither to the sensitivities of the person nor to the facilitating forces in the environment, because both are always involved in the equation."[49]

In effect, Yinger calls attention to the fact that any behavioral variable may be taken as the independent point of reference with combinations of the others held constant, treated as dependent effects, or even temporarily disregarded for analytical convenience or some other calculated purpose.

For example, in attempting to explain why a particular individual has become a champion track star, an analyst may choose to treat the subject's biological endowment as of primary importance with psychological disposition (for example, self-confidence) and social background (for example, the particular groups to which the subject belonged as a youngster) given secondary importance. Another analyst may, of course, interpret the relevance of the variables as falling in reverse order. In the final analysis, Yinger insists that all behavioral variables will have to be taken into account simultaneously.

In making this important point, Yinger seems to have overlooked the problem of objectivity in the study of human behavior that Lewin was at pains to deal with. From Lewin's point of view, the only available way to maintain an objective posture in behavioral analysis was to study the individual from the perspective of his definition of the situation. It was by holding to this interpretation that Lewin felt that the observer could guard against (certainly not entirely prevent) imputing to a subject something that could not be refuted or verified by the actions of the latter. True, something important might be left out of the analysis, but better this than unrestricted conceptual interpretation.

Toward the latter part of his career, Lewin came to acknowledge the importance of including sociological variables in his field perspective and ended up at a position quite comparable to Yinger's. Finally, then, for the analysis of individual behavior, Lewin urged that the situation as a whole be taken into account. "Instead of picking out one or another isolated element within a situation, the importance of which cannot be judged without consideration of the situation as a whole, field theory finds it advantageous, as a rule, to start with a characterization of the situation as a whole." [50] Lewin, taking a cue from the then developing science of cultural anthropology, would have the analyst be aware of the general context within which action takes place before it is dissected for its particulars.

Concomitantly, Lewin emphasized that individual activity

must be accounted for in terms of the properties of the field when it occurs. This point, it should be noted, is consistent with the naturalistic principle that given phenomena must be explained by "reference to data that are or could be available prior to (or at least concurrently with) observations of the phenomena to be explained." As Lewin explained his position,

> It has been accepted by most psychologists that the teleological derivation of behavior from the future is not permissible. Field theory insists that the derivation of behavior from the past is no less metaphysical, because past events do not exist now and therefore cannot have effect now.[51]

As Deutsch put it, "Lewin rejected the notion of 'action at a distance' and stressed that past events can have a position only in the historical causal chains whose interweaving creates the present situation."[52]

In addition to these elements, Lewin made it clear that social factors also had to be included in his field perspective. In 1939, eight years before his death, he wrote, ". . . psychology has learned, particularly in the last decade, to realize the overwhelming importance of social factors for practically every kind and type of behavior."[53] Furthermore, he said,

> I am persuaded that it is possible to undertake experiments in sociology which have as much right to be called scientific experiments as those in physics and chemistry. I am persuaded that there exists a social space which has all the essential properties of a real empirical space. . . . The perception of social space and the experimental and conceptual investigation of the dynamics and laws of the processes in social space are of fundamental theoretical and practical importance.[54]

To illustrate his point, Lewin described the way one of his close colleagues, Ronald Lippit, was able to operationalize the concept of social space. On the assumption that successful leadership is related to the kind of *atmosphere* a leader can create among his charges, Lippit compared the effect on subjects exposed to an autocratic versus a democratic social climate. Two experimental groups were selected for a mask-making club and composed of boys and girls between ten and eleven years of age. The two groups were matched in terms of leadership qualities and other interpersonal characteristics. The democratic group was allowed to choose its own activities freely. Whatever the democratic group chose to do, however, the authoritarian group was ordered to do.

The leader in each group was an adult student. His job was to create the appropriate atmosphere in his group by emphasizing certain policy-making procedures and interpersonal behavioral practices. For example, the leader in the democratic group defined policy making as a group responsibility. In the autocratic group, the leader defined policy formation as the product of the will of the most forceful member of the group. Furthermore, in the democratic group each person was free not only to select his own work task but also his own work associates. In the authoritarian groups, individuals were told what to do and with whom to do it.

The findings of the experiment were not inconsistent with what might be expected. According to Lewin, member-to-member relationships in the two groups were quite different. Acts of hostile domination were thirty times as prevalent in the authoritarian group as in the democratic group. Hostile criticisms and demands for attention were also in greater evidence in the authoritarian environment. Relationships in the democratic group were much more cooperative and matter of fact than in the autocratic group. Lastly, in the democratic atmosphere, submissive behavior between members was much more evident than in the authoritarian atmosphere.

Though individual differences are always important, they could not, said Lewin, explain away the results of the study. To support his claim, Lewin described the effect on a child transferred from the authoritarian to the democratic group and another transferred from the democratic group to the authoritarian group. In his words,

Before the transfer the difference between the two children was the same as between the two groups they belonged to, namely, the autocratic child was more dominating and less friendly and objective than the democratic one. However, after the transfer the behavior changed so that the previously autocratic child now became the less dominating and more friendly and objective child. In other words, the behavior of the children mirrored very quickly the atmosphere of the group in which they moved.[55]

Overall, Lewin observed,

The social climate in which a child lives is for the child as important as the air it breathes. The group to which a child belongs is the ground on which it stands. His relation to this group and his status in it are the most important factors for his feelings of security or insecurity. No wonder that the group the person is a part of, and the culture in which he lives, determine to a very high degree his behavior and character. These social factors determine what space of free movement he has, and how far he can look ahead with some clarity into the future. In other words, they determine to a large degree his personal style of living and the direction and productivity of his planning.[56]

Summary and Conclusion

In summary, Lewin's work emphasized the importance of analyzing the nature of individual perception and cognition, and much psychological research into these subjects has been spurred by his ideas.[57] Mainstream sociology has been little affected by Lewinian field theory. Where Lewin was concerned with accounting for the variability and particularity of individual behavior, sociologists have devoted themselves to the identification of the general in social behavior. Yinger is the only contemporary sociologist to espouse the field-theoretical perspective in a major treatise.

To Yinger, the field perspective refers to the identification and analysis of any or all the variables in "some segment of the world as it exists" that can or have had an effect on the behavior of an individual or the interaction of individuals. As he sees it,

> . . . the final concern of most of us is not with the isolation of independent relationships but with the understanding and predicting of behavior. Not many are content with the type of proposition that states: This is the relationship of intelligence to delinquency, the influence of all other variables having been controlled. We want rather to be able to say: A given proportion of the youth under study became delinquent because of the *interaction* of these several variables.[58]

To Yinger, the referent is observable behavior (for the most part, that which occurs in a "natural" as opposed to a laboratory setting) and the approach is to be multidisciplinary in the integrated rather than eclectic sense. "Most interdisciplinary work today," says Yinger, "represents the adding together of separate points of view rather than the synthesizing of a new and more complex unity."[59] To Yinger, little more than haphazard amalgamation is likely to be gained by simply bringing together representatives from the several disciplines to get their separate viewpoints on a common problem. An approach is needed in which the several behavioral variables are conceptualized as part of a uniform perspective. All the variables, from biological facts to climatic stimuli, must be studied in combination in order to accomplish the twin objectives of explaining and predicting human behavior.

Yinger does not mean that all variables and their interrelations can or must be observed at a single glance. Nor does he suggest that all variables must be viewed at all times as of equal importance. Rather, he would urge that behavioral scientists: (1) learn to move easily from one perspective to another, (2) be attuned to the variety of possible combinations of variables and factors which contribute to the different explanatory effectiveness of particular variables, and (3) learn to work together on a continual and regular basis.

In conclusion, then, and even though efforts such as Yinger's are far from complete, there is little doubt that the contemporary social scientific mood is much inclined toward a multidisciplinary and synthesizing perspective. It should be recalled that this point of view is quite compatible with that proposed by the early proponents of the sociological perspective, such as Lester Ward. Initially, sociology was to synthesize the diverse findings of the several sciences: "physical" and "social." The subject of concern was human behavior conceived of as the product of the interaction of an individual's psychobiological disposition and his physical and cultural milieu. The goal was to uncover behavioral laws to enable the prediction, and for some, the control of individual activity and social organization. There is considerable evidence to indicate that interest in these subjects is also on the increase.

In time, and largely through the efforts of such notables as Durkheim, Marx, and Sumner, sociology acquired a particular subject matter and a restricted analytic scope. It became the task of the sociologist to identify and demonstrate the extent of the impact of social facts on human activity. However, the range of sociological analysis was variously interpreted. For many, the normative behavior of individuals and/or deviations therefrom was the sociological point of departure. For others, the object of sociology was to discover the variety of linkages between social and psychological facts.

As investigation proceeded it became apparent to some that if sociology was to be in the exclusive business of isolating and relating social facts to each other and/or to selected other behavioral facts, the search for laws of human behavior had to be abandoned. This, or resort to sociological determinism. Furthermore, though social facts may be sui generis phenomena, if they were not to be treated as static categories, attention had to be given not only to their effect on human behavior, but also to the manner in which they were created, ignored, discarded, and replaced by both interacting individuals and the lone individual. To study these kinds of problems, one must, says the field theorist, study the relationships among the variety of behavioral facts.

The future trends in the development of sociological theory can only be speculated about. There is strong indication, however, that the values, goals, and epistemological bases of the discipline will undergo considerable reexamination. The burgeoning growth of world physical and social problems compels greater concern with applied and integrated scientific technique. The last chapter is concerned with an examination of some of the implications of these facts.

SEVEN · Philosophical problems and issues in contemporary sociology

The topics of sociological analysis and the epistemological foundation of the discipline have always been heavily influenced by major social upheavals. The combined fruition of problems such as political unrest, racial conflict, urban crisis, and environmental pollution in America is forcing American sociologists to examine the validity of the subjects they study and why they study them. The purpose of this chapter is to identify the nature of this examination as it relates to the goals of the discipline, the value and ethical implications surrounding the study of people, and the dilemmas involved in the control of human behavior. Overriding the entire discussion is the relation of each of these three topics to the maintenance of scientific objectivity.

Goals

Traditionally, the overall objective of sociology was "to provide generalizations that explain how the relations among groups and individuals become socially organized." [1] In other words, social organization was taken to be the dependent variable, or the subject to be explained. Today, the emphasis is on the impact of structural variables (in particular, norms and roles) on the activities and attitudes of individuals.

Although contemporary sociology is heavily oriented toward the identification of the presumed effects of social structure, there is actually little empirical knowledge available as to which variables determine or suggest the presence of one kind of structure rather than another, and why different structures develop in certain directions rather than others. Because of the absence of knowledge of these subjects and the fact that little theoretical work has been done which might point the way to a remedy of the situation, it is difficult to determine what contribution current structural analysis makes to the understanding of human behavior. In order to place structural analysis in a meaningful context, its scope must be broadened and answers to questions such as the following must be pursued: When and how do structural variables such as norms and roles influence biological, psychological, and culturological variables? And inversely, how and when are structural variables influenced by other behavioral variables? Are there structural laws of human behavior? If so, how are they related to other types of behavioral laws? What, to summarize the point, are the boundaries of structural analysis?

Any systematic exploration of these questions must involve rigorous study of not only the consequences, but also the determinants of social structure. As Peter Blau describes one phase in this study,

> To investigate the characteristics of social structure as the dependent variables to be accounted for by various antecedents, including other aspects of the social structure, necessitates (1) that different organized collectivities be examined rather than individual differences within one, however the boundaries of organized collectivities are defined; (2) that organized collectivities be treated as units of comparative analysis; (3) that the empirical data, though usually referring to observed conduct of individuals, be converted into measures of social structure, such as division of labor, status hierarchy, or homogeneity of beliefs; and, ideally, (4) that a large sample of collectivities be studied, because the organization of collectivities differs in so many respects that only multivariate analysis of many cases can hope to distinguish causal connections from correlated biases.[2]

The several varieties and types of social structure (from forms of courting behavior to kinds of political systems) must be identified and comparatively analyzed. Fruitful comparisons for the purpose of uncovering causal connections among structural variables will require accurate conceptions and detailed classification of structural units of analysis. One must have some assurance that he is comparing comparable items and that the phenomena to be compared have a certain constancy in form and content. The evidence shows that sociologists have not isolated empirical criteria sufficient to determine the degree of persistence of structural variables. (It is not known, for example, how long male-female role expectations will remain in their currently documented forms.) Essentially, the reasons for the location, timing, and severity of structural change are only vaguely understood. Why certain grievances erupt into revolutionary behavior and follow a particular course is only dimly perceived by social scientists. Succinctly put, the fundamental units of structure and the catalytic agents that spark particular combinations and dissolve others are yet to be determined. Some attribute the lack of knowledge of these subjects to the relative newness of the science of society; others take the view that these problems are intrinsic to the discipline and, therefore, never to be resolved. Short of being fatalistic, however, one must examine the strengths and weaknesses of current perspectives not only within existing limits, but also with the flexibility required to consider different possibilities and experimental techniques that could widen the working boundaries of the discipline.

To begin with, it is quite clear that in a complex and heterogeneous society, the constancy of structural units is a relative matter. For some, social norms are easily conformed to; for others, conformity to some norms may require rejection of others. The rejection of norms may lead to important structural innovations. The rejection of subordinate status by black people in America has set the tone for a widespread attack on the general authority and social structure of the country. In order to grasp the relative status of structural units, one must know something about the real-life situations of people. In David Lockwood's terms, a balanced view of social dynamics requires knowledge not only of the "normative structuring of motives," but also of "the structuring of interests in the substratum." [3] If we wish to understand why patterns of behavior persist or change, we must analyze the relationship between generally expected patterns of behavior and the conditions under which people must implement them in order to get along with others and make a living.

In place of maintaining constant touch with all the people in their everyday social milieu, how is the sociologist to get an estimate of the variable condition of his structural units? Should he seek to acquire continuous firsthand information from his own strategically placed representatives or should he use key informants in all or selected types of structural settings? What kinds of data should be gathered and interpreted only by means of firsthand experience on the part of the investigator? Assuming the possibility of widespread participant observation, what kind of organization would be most effective in minimizing the time between field reporting and data processing? When and how would data be disseminated and to whom would it be made available?

Granting the tremendous odds against overcoming the ethical objections and methodological problems involved in a far-ranging and coordinated participant-observation program, what other strategies are possible to obtain at least a slant on the range of relevance of various structural concepts? Lacking the ability to acquire considerable and reliable information on structural conditions from the position of the insider, must the sociologist be forever content with after-the-fact analyses of behavioral events?

Whatever one's interpretation of these questions, it is certain that as a would-be behavioral scientist the sociologist assumes some obligation to determine not only *how* but also *why* individuals behave the way they do in the variety of their group experiences. This requires some ability to become a participant in the social world of those selected for study. As Herbert Blumer emphasizes, if sociologists are to be concerned with the behavior of individuals, they must learn "to catch the process of interpretation through which they construct their actions." Furthermore, he points out,

> This process is not to be caught merely by turning to conditions which are antecedent to the process. Such antecedent conditions are helpful in understanding the process insofar as they enter into it, but . . . they do not constitute the process. Nor can one catch the process by inferring its nature from the overt action which is its product. To catch the process, the student must take the role of the acting unit whose behavior he is studying. Since the interpretation is being made by the acting unit in terms of objects designated and appraised, meanings acquired, and decisions made, the process has to be seen from the standpoint of the acting unit. . . . To try to catch the interpretative processes by remaining aloof as a so-called "objective" observer and refusing to take the role of the acting unit is to risk the worst kind of subjectivism—the objective observer is likely to fill in the process of interpretation with his own surmises in place of catching the process as it occurs in the experience of the acting unit which uses it.[4]

One does not, to be sure, have to be a member of a group to accurately observe the behavior of its members. But it is difficult to see how the sociologist is going to be able to gain some understanding of the reasons for individual (or group) behavior without acquiring a firsthand view of their world from the "inside out."

On the other hand, by assuming the stance of the detached observer and remaining aloof from his subjects, the sociologist has contributed heavily to making his research activities seem suspicious. Partly for this reason there is a noticeable trend in the popular press toward interpreting the survey-interviewing technique as an invasion of privacy.[5] Sociologists are increasingly accused of gathering information to make it easier for people to be manipulated in ways they cannot control. It is not unusual for the survey researcher to gain the confidence of a respondent only to disregard entirely communicating to him or a responsible person what were the results of his survey and how they are or might be used, and by whom, and when. If sociologists and other survey researchers had been more responsibly concerned with communicating their information to their respondents rather than to their paying clients and themselves, much of the present suspicion regarding their activities might not have arisen. (While it is true that survey researchers often cannot communicate their results to local people without betraying the confidentiality of their respondents, it is also the case that they frequently wish to conceal the fact that their purposes are not altogether altruistic or in the best interests of their subjects.) As it is, in the not too distant future, legislation will likely be passed to curtail severely not only the content of door-to-door interviewing, but also the place, content, and timing of the publication of results.

Because of their concern with scientific method, behaviorists have been staunch advocates of an "objective" or distant approach to the study of human behavior. It has been the view of some that subjective or intraindividual phenomena cannot be scientifically probed by presently available techniques and instruments. As George Lundberg once put it,

> The assumed inaccessibility of the data of consciousness to objective study arises from the underdeveloped state of the technic for such study. . . . It is a problem of developing an objective terminology and instruments with which to observe and describe experience which is now very inadequately communicable or subject to verification.[6]

Myrdal has referred to such a line of reasoning as constituting "terminological escapism." That is, Lundberg suggests that objective terminology must be discovered and applied before subjective evaluation can be treated as scientifically meaningful data. Myrdal denies the possibility of an objective terminology and argues that any meaningful conception of objectivity must entail valuation. In his view, the idea is not to deny subjective evaluation and bias—either on the part of the subject or observer—but to identify them and treat them as knowledge. In his words,

> . . . there is nothing wrong, per se, with value-loaded concepts if they are clearly defined in terms of explicitly stated value

premises. If they are not so defined but the implied valuation is concealed, they are certainly providing entrance to biases. If this occurs, it is then not the result of their load of valuations but of their concealment of them; the valuations can then be kept vague. Inventing new terms is no way out. They can only serve to give us a false sense of security and to deceive the general public. If the new terms represent the same approach to reality to be studied as the old, familiar, value-loaded terms, there has been no change, and they will soon become equally value-loaded.[7]

Of course, behaviorists such as Lundberg have always recognized the omnipresence of valuation in social life and the need to identify it as data. They have also never denied that human beings can and do empathize with each other. Nevertheless, their point has been that analyses based on techniques such as sympathetic introspection cannot be admitted to scientific status until it can be empirically demonstrated that they have not been contaminated by the imaginative projections of the observer. Though Myrdal and others have made a good case for the viewpoint that it is not a question of contaminating or not contaminating data but how and why the inevitable contamination occurs, the behaviorist position has long provided a good rationalization for the virtual elimination of participant observation as a valid scientific method. There are many who argue forcefully that the goal of scientific sociology is to minimize, if not eliminate, the necessity for contact between the investigator and his subjects.

Behaviorists obviously have a valid point. The "inside view" is difficult to obtain and not easily interpretable. But the price of its neglect solely because of the limitations of existing scientific method may be one the social scientists can ill afford to pay. Failure to get to know people on their terms leads to the idea that social scientists do not like them or do not really want to understand them. Often they are made to feel that they are simply media for research and that their way of life is so different or distasteful as to require viewing from a comfortable distance rather than experienced close-up.[8] Needless to say, the creation of such feelings in people is not the best way to keep them in an objective frame of mind concerning the activities of social scientists.

There is, then, more than one reason why the inside view must be sought by social scientists. Furthermore, there is no reason to believe that the problems involved in its execution should be viewed as insurmountable. One of the major obstacles the sociologist must overcome in his quest to comprehend the attitudes and perspectives of people in their diverse structural milieus is his own professional way of life. When not in the classroom or writing in some hidden retreat, the sociologist is inclined to expend much time and energy in ascertaining the state of the discipline in terms such as the extent and content of recently published work in his areas of interest, the in-process research and writing activities of colleagues, the opportunities for funded research, and the like. Most sociologists probably spend more time studying and rubbing elbows with one another than with their subjects. In this regard, Myrdal has observed,

> The great tradition in social science and, particularly, in economics has been for the social scientists to take a direct as well as an indirect responsibility for popular education. There is a recent trend, with which I must register my dissatisfaction, to abandon this great tradition. Through generations even the greatest scholars—and they especially—managed to spare the time from their scientific work to speak to the people in simple terms that laymen could understand. Yet too many social scientists today are increasingly addressing only each other. . . .[9]

As academic professionals go, then, sociologists are not atypical in this respect. Yet, their fundamental task is to study human behavior not just the behavior of some humans. Hence, one must ask, if sociologists interact more with themselves than others, what effect does this have on who they study and how they interpret the behavior of those selected for study? Do sociologists reveal a proclivity for studying people like themselves? When they study people unlike themselves, what kind of precautions should they take to minimize the intrusion of bias into their interpretations? To what extent are the interpreations of sociologists arbitrary judgments rather than objective theories? What kind of factors do sociologists knowingly and unwittingly take for granted in their analyses?

Values and Ethics

Direct answers to these questions will most certainly hinge on the valued criteria of scientific objectivity and ethical responsibility. There are many elements to consider in constructing an appropriate definition of scientific objectivity. Whatever else may be included, it is generally accepted, as Catton pointed out, that *scientific objectivity* involves asking questions "whose answers depend on sensory observation (with the aid of instruments when necessary)" and seeking explanations of "given phenomena by reference to data that are or could be available prior to (or at least concurrently with) observations of the phenomena to be explained." [10]

To some, these and other features simply add up to the principle of value neutrality. It is, of course, doubtful that any scientist is actually capable of performing his work in a neutral or value-free manner. But while the goal may not be attainable in the most complete sense, it is still worth striving for. The question is: what are the theoretical and practical consequences for those who seek to effect the goal?

In pursuing a value-free and neutral approach, one may devise a program systematically to eliminate from consideration any values but those connected with contemporary practices. In other words, one may resolve the problem of values in research to one's own satisfaction by merely doing what everyone else is doing—no more and no less. For example, if one's colleagues are concerned only with gathering information supportive of existing institutions, one may unquestioningly accept this practice as setting the tone for his own research. Often those who react in this manner are unaware that they may not be engaging in value-free science. One may handle the problem by dismissing it as inherently unresolvable. In either case, the effect may be to create a wide gulf between scientists and the public. If each does not take the other into account in terms of mutual obligations and responsibilities, any number of misunderstandings and conflicts may occur with unpleasant results for all concerned.

The experience of J. Robert Oppenheimer and his team of physicists who were responsible for the first atomic explosion is an extreme example of what can happen to those who become so engrossed in their own research as to fail to give serious consideration to its possible consequences. Even after they had created an operational atomic bomb, the decision makers involved in the project were mostly caught up in the immediate problem of deciding how to introduce their creation to the world so that it might have the greatest intimidating effect on the Japanese war effort. Here is the way Philip Stern has recounted the initial reactions of those responsible for the first atomic explosion:

> In later years, the power that had been unleashed over the Southwestern desert would tear at Oppenheimer's conscience; a decade later, that power would be, in a large sense, a destroyer of Oppenheimer's world. But for the moment, it mainly brought relief and great satisfaction. . . . Oppenheimer was later to recall that at the time "it was hard for us in Los Alamos not to share that satisfaction, and hard for me not to accept the conclusion that I had managed the enterprise well and played a key part in its success."
>
> In the ensuing days, however, "the whole community [of Los Alamos] experienced a kind of cathartic shock," according to one authoritative account. "Unfaced issues suddenly loomed large. The scientists now talked of little else but the effect of the bomb upon the postwar world." But for Robert Oppenheimer and the other principals at Los Alamos, there could have been little time for such thoughts: there was still the task of readying the bomb for the drop on Japan. . . .[11]

The evidence indicates that it was not until the results of the Hiroshima bombing had been assessed—78,000 killed, 13,000 missing, and 37,000 injured—that the creators of the bomb felt the full weight of the moral and ethical implications of their accomplishment.

The case of the nuclear physicist ought to have been an

object lesson for the social scientist. It was not what it might have been. On June 8, 1965, Secretary of Defense Robert McNamara canceled Project Camelot—a proposed behavioral science study of the revolutionary vulnerability of certain Latin American countries. The study was to be sponsored by the army and the Department of Defense and called for an operating budget of over $6 million. The circumstances surrounding the cancellation of Project Camelot involve the major ethical problems which confront the behavioral scientist.

This is the way Project Camelot was outlined in a document released in 1964 through the Office of the Director of the Special Operations Research Office (SORO) of the American University in Washington, D.C.:

> Project CAMELOT is a study whose objective is to determine the feasibility of developing a general social systems model which would make it possible to predict and influence politically significant aspects of social change in the developing nations of the world. Somewhat more specifically, its objectives are:
>
> *First*, to device procedures for assessing the potential for internal war within national societies;
>
> *Second*, to identify with increased degrees of confidence those actions which a government might take to relieve conditions which are assessed as giving rise to a potential for internal war; and
>
> *Finally*, to assess the feasibility of prescribing the characteristics of a system for obtaining and using the essential information needed for doing the above two things. . . .
>
> A large amount of primary data collection in the field is planned as well as the extensive utilization of already available data on social, economic and political functions. . . . It seems probable that the geographic orientation of the research will be toward Latin American countries. Present plans call for a field office in that region.[12]

Gideon Sjoberg has summarized the events leading to the termination of the project as follows:

> The project was cancelled on June 8, 1965, by Secretary of Defense Robert McNamara as a result of adverse reactions to

the Project in Chile. Although the details of this incident are the subject of some debate, certain events seem clear. Johan Galtung, a Norwegian sociologist then in Chile, apparently called the nature of this Project to the attention of Chilean intellectuals and ultimately also certain members of the Chilean Senate and various left-wing elements in that country. Galtung's actions followed certain informal efforts by Project Camelot (through the anthropologist Hugo Nuttini) to establish working relationships with Chilean social scientists.

The Chilean left sharply scored the Project and hurled charges against American researchers and the United States. This controversy led the American Ambassador to Chile, who apparently had not been informed by the Army of its activities, to call for cancellation of the Project. Actually, the situation reflected long-standing tensions between the Departments of State and Defense concerning research in other societies. In the end, the controversy led to a Presidential communication giving the Department of State authority to review all federally financed research projects involving research activities in other nations and potentially affecting foreign policy.[13]

Social science reactions to the demise of Project Camelot ranged from fear of the end of access to all government funding of behavioral science research to the righteous indignation of those who could not understand why some of their most talented colleagues could ever be so naive as to get involved in something so obviously questionable ethically. There are few who actually confronted the complexity of the issues involved in the incident; and they met with more questions than answers.

The focal point of much of the criticism of Project Camelot was the claim that it involved the collection of information to be used to manipulate people by dubious means and for even more questionable ends. It seemed clear that the Department of Defense was not so much interested in finding ways to promote democratically the life chances of all Latin Americans as in obtaining reliable data and developing techniques to prevent the taking over of Latin American governments by those of anti-American sentiment. However, acknowledgment of this fact leads one to consider just when the findings of behavioral scientists are not subject to the possibility of serious interpretive abuse. As Robert Boguslaw stated,

"Who can or might distort the purposes of this research for his own political ends?" "Which interest groups can be made to see this research as in their own interest?" "To what extent can one risk acceptance of their support without destroying the basis of the research itself?" "How are the researchers to balance their own sense of traditional scientific morality against the tactics of those who will see this morality as a weakness and exploit it to the limits dictated by their own political purposes?" "Is it at all possible to conduct even the most 'basic' and 'non-applied' research using real world events as data without *some* risk of the results being taken over and used by 'bad guys'?" Such questions seldom, if ever, get asked. It is tempting to speculate about the extent to which the Camelot difficulties were ultimately attributable to the lack of a sophisticated social science tradition in these areas.[14]

In other words, who is to be served by behavioral science research? Is the client to be the granting agency, the profession, science, or the public? If all these plus other referents are involved, what criteria can be employed in a given circumstance to specify the order in which they should be acknowledged?

Questions such as these have been often neglected because of certain points of value consensus among the members of a social science discipline. Many sociologists, for example, tend to emphasize the suffering and the plight of the underdog to the virtual neglect of the problems of the overdog. In reference to this school of thought espoused by Howard S. Becker, Alvin Gouldner has written: "In one part, this school of thought represents a metaphysics of the underdog and the underworld: a metaphysics in which conventional society is viewed from the standpoint of a group outside of its own respectable social structures." Furthermore, says Gouldner,

. . . Becker's school of deviance is redolent of Romanticism. It expresses the satisfaction of the Great White Hunter who has bravely risked the perils of the urban jungle to bring back an exotic specimen. It expressed the Romanticism of the zoo curator who preeningly displays his rare specimens. And like the zookeeper, he wishes to protect his collection; he does not want spectators to throw rocks at the animals behind the bars. But neither is he eager to tear down the bars and let the animals go. The attitude of these zookeepers of deviance is to create a comfortable and humane Indian Reservation, a protected social space, within which these colorful specimens may be exhibited, unmolested and unchanged. . . .[15]

It is difficult to tell exactly how widespread is the romantic underdog syndrome in sociology, but it is not difficult to see how those who are a part of it might assume an anti-establishment stance. As Gouldner puts it, the Becker school of thought "conceives of the underdog as someone maltreated by a bureaucratic establishment whose remedial efforts are ineffectual, whose custodial efforts are brutal, and whose rule enforcement techniques are self-interested."[16]

The sociological underdog is overwhelmingly conceived of as the victim of circumstance and the manipulated pawn of those who care not and/or know not what they do. The managers of the establishment tend to be written off as either middle-class hypocrites or indifferent and outmoded elitists. Simply put, the role of overdog is seldom given either a sympathetic or objective hearing at the hands of a sizable segment of the sociological community.

There are, however, a large number of sociologists, the more "professionally" oriented and status conscious, who are rather pro-establishment and much in favor of acquiring financial support for their research from governmental agencies (or who stand ready to tailor their research to the needs of a granting agency) and a role in high level governmental decision making. In attempting to explain why so many social scientists readily involved themselves in Project Camelot, Gideon Sjoberg offered the following two tentative hypotheses:

First, American social scientists (including sociologists) have been socialized, both as citizens and scholars, to an almost unquestioning acceptance of the authority and power wielded by their own nation-state system and consequently the administrative controls of the national government. (Nationalism is perhaps the most pervasive, yet the least explored, of the influences that shape the research carried out by American social scientists in other nations.) Second, the increasing stress in social science upon achieving professional (as opposed to scientific) status serves to rationalize the acceptance of administrative controls emanating from the national level. The professional organizations of social scientists in fact encourage their members to maintain a position of "respectability" in the eyes of the broader society. And one means of achieving this image is to forge links with the major institutional systems in the society, notably those that exert administrative controls over citizen and scientist alike.[17]

Also in reference to Project Camelot, Herbert Blumer noted,

I observe among many of my colleagues in social science a sense of eminence in being connected with high-level federal agencies in either a consultant capacity or a contract research relationship. Many social scientists construe such a connection as a form of professional recognition or as a sign that one is exerting influence in governmental circles.[18]

Finally, in Horowitz's judgment,

Ultimately, the social scientists, to the extent that they become involved with policy-making agencies, become committed to an elitist ideology. They come to accept as basic the idea that men who really change things are on the top. Thus, the closer to the top one can get direct access, the more likely will intended changes be brought about.[19]

Horowitz's fear is that in their quest for power and status, social scientists may come to accept subordinate status to that of government officials and in the process forfeit their scientific autonomy. The anthropologist Ralph Beals shares Horowitz's concern and emphasizes that governmental officials and social scientists must learn to work together while recognizing each other's autonomous needs. Here is the way Beals threads his way through this complicated problem:

> Social scientists who completely deny responsibility for the needs of government and government that demands subordination of scientific goals and values breed trouble both for social science and government. My point of view is that social scientists have a responsibility to government even if they do not agree with government practices. They must face the implications of involvement with government, evaluate their responsibilities to government, consider the effects of government utilization of social science results, be more aware of the consequences of government policy, and act effectively if research possibilities are to be maintained. At the same time, social scientists must not abdicate their professional responsibility or their dedication to human welfare.[20]

Some feel that this point of view is rather naive when it suggests that one can have the best of two opposing worlds without suffering any negative repercussions. That is, one can cater to the needs of government, conform to the ethics of science and to broader values about human welfare without sacrificing anything of the latter to the former. It is argued that a line of reasoning such as Beals' belies the complexity and sublety of the problem. Blumer, for example, calls attention to the difficulties involved in avoiding the "eroding effect that agency-determined projects may have on the integrity of the scientific undertaking itself." In his view, agency-guided research discourages the social scientist from acquiring the "intimate familiarity" necessary to grasp the "sensitivities and orientations of the people under study, their world as they see it, and the content of their experience from their point of view." Blumer cites several conditions which he feels combine to support his contention, for example: the tendency to mold a research design to suit the kind of information desired by the agency; the temptation to rely upon standard research methods; the acceptance of time limitations on the completion of a study; and, concomitantly, the disinclination of project directors to allow much, if any, deviation from a preestablished plan of execution.[21]

"The primary source of the corrupting influence," says Blumer, "is the lure that agency-determined research casts in the form of sizable allotments of funds for research and in the form of the prestige that is seemingly yielded by connection with high-level governmental work." As he assesses the situation,

> Many of today's social scientists are highly susceptible to this lure. There is great pressure among social scientists not merely to do research but to have funds for research; the social scientist today who does not have research funds is likely to be regarded as a lowly figure. Under the pressure to have funds, many are ready to bend their research interests and efforts in the directions laid down by available funds.[22]

Blumer contrasts the restricted nature of agency-guided research to what he considers to be the virtually free situation of the independent researcher. Such a person, he claims, is not under any pressure to compromise his own interests or values or the canons of science. But he overstates his case by failing to take cognizance of the kinds of pressures which all scientists are constantly exposed to.

One of these pressures is the rigidity surrounding the professional journals and societies. As Robert Boguslaw points out, "scientific societies and scientific journals are notorious for their insistence upon dogmas of all kinds: the dogma of acceptable methodology, the dogma of report format, the implicit dogma of acceptable areas for investigation. . . ."[23]

Some might refer to these "dogmas" as necessary and inevitable "conventions." For example, Thomas Kuhn might interpret them to be the routine pressures of "normal," or paradigm-guided science. However, they may also come to be viewed by the individual scientist as threats to his ethical integrity and intellectual autonomy. Unfortunately, there are no established criteria for determining when to conform to or rebel against an existing practice. The two sides of the issue constitute the horns of an omnipresent and seemingly irresolvable dilemma.

The major guidelines for dealing with this issue stem from the lessons of the past such as Camelot and from conceptions of ideal scientific norms. Neither is entirely satisfactory. The unique combination of variables that eventuated in an historical event cannot be counted on to repeat themselves in present or future situations. Historical experiences are useful mostly as reminders of what can happen to the ethically naive and the ethical activist.

The trouble with ideal scientific norms is that they are situationally unspecific and, when upheld, often provoke additional difficulties for the scientist. As Ralph Beals pointed out,

> The necessity of officially affirming the basic principles of freedom, truth, and honesty is an indication of the challenges confronting social scientists. Men have debated the meaning of freedom and truth perhaps since the beginning of human time. Both are relative, not absolute, concepts. In general, the degree of honesty desired and required or expected in a given context varies with the circumstances, as does the value of freedom. Complete honesty may be disastrous, as Galileo discovered; complete freedom may inspire irresponsibility.[24]

The applicability of ideal scientific norms is often based on the assumption of known conditions and specifiable alternative courses of action. For example, in dealing with the social scientist's problem of maintaining scientific objectivity while remaining ethically concerned with the human condition, George Lundberg wrote:

> Have scientists . . . no special function or obligation in determining the ends for which scientific knowledge is to be used? As scientists, *it is their business to determine reliably the immediate and remote costs and consequences of alternative possible courses of action, and to make these known to the public.* Scientists may then *in their capacity as citizens* join

with others in advocating one alternative rather than another, as they prefer.[25]

In response to Lundberg's position, Boguslaw wrote,

The notion of science as a means for providing an exhaustive analysis of all possible alternatives from which the nonscientist can select is simply not viable for the world I know. . . . Lundberg's concept of science is one that postulates only established situations. He implicitly omits consideration of the possibility of an emergent situation science.[26]

That is, as Boguslaw sees it, Lundberg does not treat the crucial problem, which is what to do in situations where the parameters do not lend themselves to comprehension by known methods. In effect, says Boguslaw, how can one really be ethically involved without taking unsafe chances and risking possibly unfavorable consequences? The point was made several years ago by Robert Lynd. As he put it,

. . . social science is confined neither to practical politics nor to things whose practicality is demonstrable this afternoon or tomorrow morning. Nor is its role merely to stand by, describe, and generalize, like a seismologist watching a volcano. There is no other agency in our culture whose role is to ask long-range and, if need be, abruptly irreverent questions of our democratic institutions; and to follow these questions with research and the systematic charting of the way ahead. The responsibility is to keep everlastingly challenging the present with the question: But what is it that we human beings want, and what things would have to be done, in what ways and in what sequence in order to change the present so as to achieve it.[27]

Alongside the great diversity of opinion on the topic of the proper relationships of values, ethics, and scientific objectivity, there is near-universal consensus that there is no such thing as value-free science. Most likely, Herbert Kelman expressed the position of many when he wrote,

A total separation of the role of scientist from the role of valuing man, of the definition of the research problem from the investigator's value preferences, of the investigator from his human subjects and subject matter, and of research findings from ideas about these findings and about the world into which they fit cannot be achieved and, what is more, the effort to achieve such separation leads to an impossible social science. What is necessary, however, for the enhancement of scientific objectivity, is that the investigator deliberately take his values, attitudes and expectations into account and systematically analyze their effects on the definition of the research problem, the observations obtained, and the interpretations placed on these observations.[28]

In the pursuit of scientific impartiality, then, one should not lose sight of the fact that partiality will influence and decide the manner in which social science research is evaluated and used. This problem is of unusual importance today. If all people held the same values and possessed equal amounts of power in more than the legal sense, the uses and abuses of social science information would not constitute the problem that it does. As conditions now exist, it is highly probable that human beings will become increasingly manipulated on the basis of social science findings. To Kelman, this means that,

> The social scientist is, therefore, confronted ever more sharply with the question of what kind of social force his research represents. What is the nature of the social processes that it is helping to foster, the quality of the social values it is helping to promote? [29]

In addition, he notes,

> On the one hand, there is the danger that the findings of social research may be used for the suppression of human freedom and the dehumanization of social life. On the other hand, there is the potential that social science knowledge may contribute to the advancement of human welfare, the rationality of social decisions, and the achievement of constructive social change.[30]

Because of his subject matter, the social scientist should be much closer to the problem of value judgments and conflicts than the "physical" scientist. Social groups and private individuals have values and so do social scientists as members of particular disciplines and as citizens of a particular nation. What are the reciprocal obligations of social science and society? How are they to interact without one attempting to dominate or impose its values on the other? When conflicts occur between the values of social science and the values of society, what factors must the social scientist consider in deciding whose values should take precedence in a given situation? There are no easy and timeless answers to these questions. In fact, one must seriously entertain the possibility that for the good of all concerned, they should never be permanently resolved.

Control

Lack of ability permanently to resolve the problem of the ethical and moral responsibilities of social scientists to society and vice versa does not mean that studies to anticipate the possible forms of its future development should not be undertaken or that strategies for its confrontation should not be continually examined and tested. There is a tendency to retreat from analyses of issues that admit of no immediately apparent resolution. Yet, if world social and physical problems continue to multiply and evolve at current rates, such a stance could very well be suicidal for the human race, let alone social science. Alarmist statements, pleas, and analyses are, of course, readily challengeable by those not presently living in a state of crisis. (Ironically, those with the resources to deal with problems before they get out of hand are invariably the ones who possess the ability to shield themselves from their immediate effects.) But the luxury of ignoring a possible threat of extinction until it becomes an overwhelming reality is hardly the most rational human response. It is, after all, one of the traditional functions of science to anticipate the future and to develop means to control factors actually and potentially inimical to the interests of mankind. To what extent, then, should social scientists concern themselves with the control of human behavior? When do human beings knowingly and unwittingly become their own worst enemies? Should social scientists attempt to manipulate an entire social organization in order to prevent it from endangering if not extinguishing human life on earth? If yes, what are the criteria for the timing of intervention? Succinctly put, under what circumstances and with what justification should social scientists participate in an attempt to harness the activities of individuals and collectivities?

Not too long ago, questions such as these would have seemed to most "right thinking" social scientists entirely irresponsible; today, their statement appears to be mostly anticlimactic. The times are too threatening for their phrasing not to be recognized as an attempt to be entirely responsible. Even so, the role of social science in human organization is not at all clear to most social scientists. Essentially, they are not sure what should be the rank order of their diverse responsibilities. Social scientists do not know when the application of their knowledge might or should take precedence over that of the other sciences. They are also unsure as to when political conviction or humanistic and moral principles should be accorded higher recognition than scientific norms and vice versa. All these values have their place. The question is: what are the criteria by which their rank order can be specified? So far, it appears that the best answer one can give is to allude to the demands of an obviously overwhelming situation. It must be asked, however, under what conditions should and/or must social scientists not wait for situations to dictate the nature of their responses? Is it possible and likely that the knowledge of certain other sciences —for example, biology or physics—will so far outstrip the accomplishments of the social sciences as one day to eliminate their functional utility? What are the possibilities that in the not too distant future political power will become so concentrated worldwide that social scientists will be compelled either to do the bidding of the powers that be or disband? Should social scientists collectively attempt to prevent such a situation from arising? Should social scientists attempt to make the world safe for their continual existence? If so, should they work to establish some form of sociocracy; that is, a society organized and controlled by social scientists? If not, who and what should they support?

Many social scientists consider such questions pretentious as they are convinced that the level of knowledge of their several disciplines has not and will not become so advanced as to constitute much of a threat or asset to human organization. Unfortunately, many physical and biological scientists have maintained the same position until it has been too late to do much more than express regrets. It has become obvious that for the good of all concerned some kind of balance must be maintained between the level of scientific achievements and the state of social organization. In the immediate future, if not already, the achievements of science may place unbearable adaptive demands on society. Some scientists are so concerned about this possibility that they are seriously willing to consider placing a moratorium on certain types of research altogether. As one scientist has stated: "Is science reaching a frontier beyond which its progress might be more harmful than advantageous?" [31] But who is to decide when scientific freedom is to be curtailed in favor of social equilibrium? According to Gordon Rattray Taylor,

> Scientists themselves are hardly likely to be unbiased about such a notion. . . . Such decisions will have, naturally, to be taken by governments—but governments feel kindly towards industry and its research efforts, and are unlikely to go very far in this direction. Some powerful and farsighted body is needed to advise them—a body so prestigious that they will think twice before refusing its advice. With the growth of the social sciences, it is just possible that a strong Social Sciences Council may emerge in some countries, such as the U.S.A., but it is hardly likely to gain sufficient status in time.[32]

It appears, then, that the question is not simply to control or not to control social and scientific activity, but when, how, and by whom this control is to be effected. The social scientist must analyze not only the possibilities of the direct and conscious control of human behavior, but also the likely forms of indirect and inadvertent control exerted by the accomplishments and research activities of his immediate colleagues as well as those in the other sciences. Furthermore, the social scientist must face the fact that science and its achievements have become independent variables in the study of human behavior.

Summary and Implications

The interrelationship among the goals of science, its ethical problems, and its responsibilities regarding control are obviously close and complex. Having once decided on the attainment of particular goals (that is, the phenomena to be studied and the level of explanation sought), a discipline is confronted by a host of value and ethical problems. For example, at some point it must be decided (criteria will have to be worked out) when the ends of science are to be accorded greater recognition than societal needs, and vice versa. Also, scientific method, particularly in the social sciences, will have to be reconciled with general standards of social propriety. Which methods, if employed, would result in a violation of an individual's rights of privacy? Furthermore, sooner or later a scientific community will be faced with deciding what is to be defined as malpractice and what is to be gauged as proper conduct on the part of its members. Under what circumstances should a discipline be held responsible for the conduct of its members by society, and when and how should a discipline attempt to protect its members against societal abuse? In short, what are to be the criteria by which the ethical behavior of a scientist is to be judged?

In addition to these problems, a group of scientists must also at some point develop some conception as to when they should attempt to exert control over the implications, interpretations, and use of their research methods and findings. It is obvious that not just anyone should practice science and can accurately appraise the scientific significance of research. Some training is required to do both, and it is by means of a certification process that scientists have exerted some control over the application of their methods and the interpretations of their research. However, if the techniques and the results of science are to be public information, to what extent should and must scientists attempt to educate the public, or carry out some other means of control, to prevent the misapplication of their methods and findings?

Social scientists are and will be confronted increasingly with some other thorny questions. To begin with, there is no doubt that the social sciences need society. The opposite, however, is not as readily apparent. Societies have existed, can exist, and do exist without the services of the formal social sciences. The question is, therefore, of what use is social science to society? Obviously, social science information may be useful to some for the manipulation of others; hence, under what circumstances might the instruments and findings of social scientists be used to control human behavior with and/or without the prior consent of those involved? Granting that human behavior is and will continue to be both directly and indirectly controlled—most certainly by economic and political functionaries and the several social institutions they may represent—should not social scientists hold themselves responsible for ensuring that their tools and contributions will be implemented toward the end of improving the general condition of all rather than the particular situation of a select few? If the answer is in the affirmative, what values—that is, which social and scientific means and ends—should social scientists support? For example, should they seek to liberalize opportunity structures and/or stabilize social relationships? Additionally, should social scientists actively seek political influence to accomplish whatever valued ends—should social scientists support? For example, should interventionist role in society, what strategies should and can they employ to prevent their subversion and cooptation by societal pressures? Inversely, what strategies should be adopted by society in order to protect its integrity from subversion at the hands of social scientists and scientists in general?

These are the questions and problems of the immediate future. Many were also the preoccupation of those who initiated sociology both in Europe and America.

Notes

Chapter One: The Components of Sociological Theory and Their Interrelationship

1. George C. Homans, "Bringing Men Back In," *American Sociological Review* 29 (1964): 811.
2. Barney G. Glaser and Anselm L. Strauss, *The Discovery of Grounded Theory* (Chicago: Aldine Publishing Co., 1967), p. 2.
3. Ibid., p. 3.
4. C. Wright Mills, *The Sociological Imagination* (New York: Oxford University Press, 1959), p. 26.
5. Claude C. Bowman, "Ordinary Parlance for the Phenomena Falling Within its Purview," a letter to the editor, *American Sociologist* 3 (1968): 157.
6. Mills, *Sociological Imagination*, p. 33.
7. G. Duncan Mitchell, ed., *A Dictionary of Sociology* (Chicago: Aldine Publishing Co., 1968), p. 211.
8. Clement S. Mihanovich et al., *Glossary of Sociological Terms* (Milwaukee: Bruce Publishing Co., 1957), p. 24.
9. See Webster's *New International Dictionary*, 2nd ed. (Springfield, Mass.: G. & C. Merriam Co., 1961), p. 2620.
10. Ely Chinoy, *Sociological Perspective* (New York: Random House, 1954), p. 3.
11. Chester I. Bernard, "The Acceptance of Authority," in *Sociological Theory: A Book of Readings*, ed. Lewis A. Coser and Bernard Rosenberg (New York: Macmillan Co., 1957), pp. 143–52.
12. John Greenway, *The Inevitable Americans* (New York: Alfred A. Knopf, 1964), p. 14.

13. Ibid., p. 14.
14. Max Black, ed., *The Social Theories of Talcott Parsons* (Englewood Cliffs, N.J.: Prentice-Hall, 1961), pp. 272–73, 279.
15. Ibid., p. 279.
16. See Ralf Dahrendorf, "Out of Utopia: Toward a Reorientation of Sociological Analysis," *American Journal of Sociology* 64 (1958): 115–27.
17. William Whewell, *The Philosophy of the Inductive Sciences*, vol. 1 (London: John W. Parker, 1843), p. 207.
18. John Stuart Mill, *Philosophy of Scientific Method* (New York: Hafner Publishing Co., 1950), pp. 177–78.
19. John C. McKinney, *Constructive Typology and Social Theory* (New York: Appleton-Century-Crofts, 1966), p. 9.
20. Ibid., pp. 9–10.
21. Hans Reichenbach, *The Rise of Scientific Philosophy* (Berkeley and Los Angeles: University of California Press, 1962), pp. 263–64.
22. William R. Catton, Jr., *From Animistic to Naturalistic Sociology* (New York: McGraw-Hill Book Co., 1966), p. 46.
23. McKinney, *Constructive Typology*, p. 3.
24. Ibid., p. 12.
25. Julius Gould and William L. Kolb, eds., *A Dictionary of the Social Sciences* (New York: Free Press of Glencoe, 1964), p. 312.
26. H. H. Gerth and C. Wright Mills, eds., *From Max Weber: Essays in Sociology* (New York: Oxford University Press, Galaxy Book, 1958), pp. 196–98.
27. Max Weber, *The Theory of Social and Economic Organization*, trans. A. M. Henderson and Talcott Parsons (New York: Free Press, 1947), p. 111.
28. Gould and Kolb, *Dictionary*, p. 694.
29. Talcott Parsons, "The Present Position and Prospects of Systematic Theory in Sociology," in his *Essays in Sociological Theory* (New York: Free Press of Glencoe, 1964), chap. 11, p. 214.
30. Gould and Kolb, *Dictionary*, p. 275.
31. Talcott Parsons and Edward A. Shils, eds., *Toward a General Theory of Action* (New York: Harper and Bros., 1951), p. 53.
32. Melvin H. Marx, *Theories in Contemporary Psychology* (New York: Macmillan Co., 1963), p. 13.
33. Dagobert D. Runes, ed., *Dictionary of Philosophy* (New York: Philosophical Library, 1960), p. 134.

34. William J. Goode and Paul K. Hatt, *Methods in Social Research* (New York: McGraw-Hill Book Co., 1952), p. 56.
35. Hans L. Zetterberg, "On Axiomatic Theories in Sociology," in *The Language of Social Research*, ed. Paul F. Lazarsfeld and Morris Rosenberg (New York: Free Press of Glencoe, 1955), p. 533.
36. Norman Campbell, *What is Science?* (New York: Dover Publications, 1952), p. 40.
37. R. B. Braithwaite, *Scientific Explanation* (New York: Harper & Row, 1960), p. 10.
38. Webster's *New International Dictionary*, p. 1401.
39. Albert Einstein, *Essays on Science* (New York: Philosophical Library, 1934), p. 14.
40. Hans L. Zetterberg, *On Theory and Verification in Sociology* 3rd ed. (Totowa, N.J.: Bedminster Press, 1965), pp. 69–74.
41. Webster's *New International Dictionary*, p. 194.
42. Zetterberg, *On Theory and Verification in Sociology*, p. 22.
43. George C. Homans, "Contemporary Theory in Sociology," in *Handbook of Modern Sociology*, ed Robert E. L. Faris (Chicago: Rand McNally & Co., 1964), chap. 25, p. 951.
44. Zetterberg, *On Theory and Verification in Sociology*, pp. 6–7.
45. See Herbert L. Costner and Robert K. Leik, "Deductions from 'Axiomatic Theory,'" *American Sociological Review* 29 (1964): 819–35.
46. May Brodbeck, "Methodological Individualisms: Definition and Reduction," in *Readings in the Philosophy of the Social Sciences*, ed. Brodbeck (New York: MacMillan Co., 1968), chap 16, p. 294.
47. Kent P. Schwirian and John W. Prehn, "An Axiomatic Theory of Urbanization," *American Sociological Review* 27 (1962): 814.
48. Robert B. Nordberg, "Modus Model—Some Problems about the New Jargon," *American Behavioral Scientist* 9 (1965): 14.
49. See Webster's *New International Dictionary*, p. 1567.
50. Ibid., p. 1576.
51. See James D. Watson, *The Double Helix* (New York: Signet Books, 1969).
52. Nordberg, "Modus Model," p. 14.
53. May Brodbeck, "Models, Meaning, and Theories," in *Symposium on Sociological Theory*, ed. Llewelyn Gross (New York and Evanston: Row, Peterson and Co., 1959), p. 379.

54. Melvin H. Marx, *Contemporary Psychology*, p. 14.
55. It is not always clear which of these interpretations a given author has in mind.
56. Brodbeck, "Models, Meaning, and Theories," p. 381.
57. John Ziman, *Public Knowledge: The Social Dimension of Science* (Cambridge, England: Cambridge University Press, 1968), p. 9.
58. Thomas S. Kuhn, *The Structure of Scientific Revolutions* (Chicago: University of Chicago Press, 1952), p. 23.
59. Ibid., p. 102.
60. Ibid., pp. 169–70.
61. Ibid., p. 91.
62. Ibid., p. 61.
63. Ibid., p. 10.
64. Ziman, *Public Knowledge*, pp. 27–28.
65. Emile Durkheim, *The Division of Labor in Society* (New York: Free Press, 1964), p. 64.
66. William R. Catton, Jr., "The Development of Sociological Thought," in *Handbook of Modern Sociology*, p. 922.
67. Crane Brinton, *The Shaping of Modern Thought* (Englewood Cliffs, N.J.: Prentice-Hall, 1950), p. 178.
68. C. Wright Mills, *Sociological Imagination*, p. 8.
69. For a review of works concerned with this issue and many others in contemporary sociology, see Tom Bottomore, "Has Sociology a Future?" *New York Review of Books*, 11 March 1971, pp. 37–40.
70. Robert A. Nisbet, *Emile Durkheim* (Englewood Cliffs, N.J.: Prentice-Hall, 1965), p. 9.

Chapter Two: The Sociologistic Perspective and the Works of Marx and Durkheim

1. Otto Rühle, *Karl Marx: His Life and Work* (New York: Viking Press, 1928), p. 14.
2. For a review of Marx's intellectual development, see Isaiah Berlin, *Karl Marx* (New York: Oxford University Press, 1963), particularly chaps. 4 and 5.
3. Karl Marx, *Capital* (Moscow, Russia: Foreign Languages Publishing House, 1959), 1:254–55.
4. Ibid., pp. 258–59.
5. Robert Freedman, *Marxist Social Thought* (New York: Harcourt, Brace & World, 1968), pp. 69–70.

6. Joseph Stalin, *Dialectical and Historical Materialism* (New York: International Publishers, 1940), p. 9.

7. David Caute, ed., *Essential Writings of Karl Marx* (New York: Macmillan Co., 1967), p. 32.

8. Jerome Balmuth, in the Introduction to *Marxist Social Thought*, ed. Robert Freedman (New York: Harcourt, Brace and World, 1968), p. xxxi.

9. Stalin, *Materialism*, pp. 7–11.

10. Ibid., p. 17.

11. Ibid., p. 15.

12. Maurice Cornforth, *Historical Materialism* (New York: International Publishers, 1954), p. 49.

13. Caute, *Karl Marx*, p. 122.

14. Cornforth, *Historical Materialism*, pp. 58–59.

15. Ibid., p. 60.

16. Karl Marx and Frederick Engels, *The Communist Manifesto* (New York: New York Labor News Co., 1934), p. 8.

17. Freedman, *Marxist Social Thought*, p. 321.

18. Caute, *Karl Marx*, p. 235.

19. Edmund Wilson, *To The Finland Station* (New York: Doubleday Anchor Books, 1953), p. 182.

20. Cornforth, *Historical Materialism*, p. 114.

21. Some recent exceptions are Peter Berger, ed., *Marxism and Sociology: Views from Eastern Europe* (New York: Appleton-Century-Crofts, 1969), and Raymond Aron, *Main Currents in Sociological Thought*, vol. 1 (New York: Doubleday Anchor Books, 1968), pp. 145–236.

22. T. B. Bottomore, "Marxist Sociology," in *The International Encyclopedia of the Social Sciences*, vol. 10, ed. David L. Sills (New York: Macmillan Co. and Free Press, 1968), p. 46.

23. See, for example, Robert A. Nisbet, "Conservatism and Sociology," *American Journal of Sociology* 58 (1952): 167–75.

24. Emile Durkheim, *The Rules of Sociological Method*, ed. George E. G. Catlin (New York: Free Press, 1964), p. 13.

25. Ibid., p. 1.

26. Ibid., p. 2.

27. Emile Durkheim, *The Division of Labor in Society* (New York: Free Press of Glencoe, 1964), p. 79.

28. Ibid., p. 106.

29. Ibid., p. 131.

30. Ibid., p. 257.

31. Ibid., p. 266.

32. Ibid., p. 286.
33. Ibid., p. 111.
34. Durkheim, *Rules of Sociological Method*, p. 27.
35. Ibid., p. 110.
36. Emile Durkheim, *Suicide* (New York: Free Press, 1951), p. 46.
37. Durkheim, *Rules of Sociological Method*, pp. 79–80.
38. Durkheim, *Suicide*, p. 209.
39. Robert Bierstedt, *Emile Durkheim* (New York: Dell Publishing Co., 1966), p. 160.
40. Durkheim, *Suicide*, p. 258.
41. Bierstedt, *Durkheim*, pp. 161–162.
42. Durkheim, *Suicide*, p. 243.
43. Ibid., p. 246.
44. A useful discussion of the subject of causation is contained in William R. Catton, Jr., *From Animistic to Naturalistic Sociology*, (New York: McGraw-Hill, 1966), pp. 60–65.
45. The efficient cause of a social fact was to be sought strictly within the human milieu or society. To Durkheim, it was not necessary for the sociologist to account for the causal origin of society (in Aristotelian terms the "final" or "first" cause of human organization) before seeking causal relationships among social facts. As he summed up his view on the matter: ". . . the significance attributed by us to the social and, more particularly, the human milieu does not imply that we must see in it a sort of ultimate and absolute fact beyond which there is no reason for inquiry. It is evident, on the contrary, that its condition at each moment of history is itself a result of social causes, some of which are inherent in the society itself, while others depend on interaction between this society and its neighbors. Moreover, science is not concerned with first-causes, in the absolute sense of the word. For science, a fact is primary simply when it is general enough to explain a great number of other facts. Now, the social milieu is certainly a factor of this kind, since the changes which are produced in it, whatever may be their causes, have their repercussions in all directions in the social organism and cannot fail to affect to some extent each of its functions" (*Rules of Sociological Method*, pp. 115–16).
46. Durkheim, *Rules of Sociological Method*, p. 103.
47. May Brodbeck, "Methodological Individualisms: Definition and Reduction," in *Readings in the Philosophy of the Social*

Sciences, ed. May Brodbeck (New York: Macmillan Co., 1968), p. 283.

48. George C. Homans, "Bringing Men Back In," *American Sociological Review* 29 (1964): 815.

49. Ibid., p. 817.

50. Irving M. Zeitlin, *Ideology and the Development of Sociological Theory* (Englewood Cliffs, N.J.: Prentice-Hall, 1968), p. 235.

51. Ibid., p. 241.

52. Robert A. Nisbet, *Emile Durkheim* (Englewood Cliffs, N.J.: Prentice-Hall, 1965), p. 55.

53. Ibid., p. 62.

54. Ibid., p. 63.

55. Zeitlin, *Ideology*, p. 234.

56. Joseph Neyer, "Individualism and Socialism in Durkheim," in *Emile Durkheim*, ed. Kurt H. Wolff (Columbus, Ohio: Ohio State University Press, 1960), p. 51.

57. Ibid., p. 52.

58. Ibid., p. 51.

59. Durkheim, *Division of Labor in Society*, p. 375. To combat the alienating effects of the advanced division of labor characteristic of industrial society, Durkheim proposed the development of occupational groups composed of individuals who pursue the same type of work. He described their function as follows: "What we especially see in the occupational group is a moral power capable of containing individual egos, of maintaining a spirited sentiment of common solidarity in the consciousness of all the workers, of preventing the law of the strongest from being brutally applied to industrial and commercial relations." Emile Durkheim, *Socialism*, ed. Alvin W. Gouldner (New York: Collier Books, 1962), p. 10.

60. Durkheim, *Socialism*, p. 61.

61. Neyer, "Individualism," p. 55.

62. Durkheim, *Socialism*, p. 23.

63. Durkheim, *Division of Labor in Society*, pp. 203–4.

64. Ibid., p. 211.

65. Durkheim, *Socialism*, p. 27.

66. Ibid., p. 25.

67. Pitirim A. Sorokin, *Contemporary Sociological Theories* (New York: Harper & Row, 1928), p. 476.

68. Roscoe C. Hinkle, Jr., "Durkheim in American Sociology," in Wolff, *Durkheim*, p. 267.

69. Nisbet, *Emile Durkheim*, pp. 3–4.
70. Hinkel, "Durkheim," p. 289.
71. Nisbet, *Emile Durkheim*, p. 1.
72. Durkheim, *Suicide*, p. 38.
73. Marx, *Capital*, 1:331.

Chapter Three: The Ward-Sumner Controversy

1. For a penetrating discussion of the contrasting views of Ward and Sumner placed in historical context, see Richard Hofstadter, *Social Darwinism in America*, rev. ed. (Boston: Beacon Press, 1955).
2. In his biography of Lester Ward, Samuel Chugerman made the following statement of dedication: "Dedicated to the memory of Lester F. Ward—The founder of sociology in America." See his *Lester F. Ward: The American Aristotle* (Durham, N.C.: Duke University Press, 1939).
3. Harold W. Pfautz, "Lester F. Ward," in *The International Encyclopedia of the Social Services*, vol. 16, ed. David L. Sills (New York: Macmillan Co. and Free Press, 1968), p. 473.
4. Ibid., p. 474.
5. Lester F. Ward, *Dynamic Sociology*, vol. 1 (New York: Appleton and Co., 1911), p. 5.
6. Ibid., pp. 10–11.
7. Lester F. Ward, "The Human Mind Does Make the World Over," in *Darwinism: Reaction or Reform?* ed. Bert James Loewenberg (New York: Rinehart and Co., 1957), p. 21.
8. Israel Gerver, *Lester Frank Ward* (New York: Thomas Y. Crowell Co., 1963), p. 11.
9. Ibid., p. 12.
10. Lester F. Ward, *Outlines of Sociology* (New York: Macmillan Co., 1898), p. 175.
11. Ibid., p. 176.
12. Ibid., p. 175.
13. Chugerman, *Lester Ward*, pp. 163–64.
14. For example, see Fay Berger Karpf, *American Social Psychology: Its Origins, Development and European Background* (New York: McGraw-Hill Book Co., 1932).
15. Ward, *Outlines of Sociology*, p. 122.
16. Chugerman, *Lester Ward*, p. 192.
17. Ward, *Outlines of Sociology*, p. 263.
18. Lester F. Ward, "Plutocracy and Paternalism," in *Lester*

Ward and the Welfare State, ed. Henry Steele Commager (Indianapolis: Bobbs-Merrill, 1967), pp. 189–90.

19. Chugerman, *Lester Ward*, pp. 326–27.
20. Ward, *Outlines of Sociology*, pp. 292–93.
21. Commager, *Lester Ward and the Welfare State*, p. xxxvi.
22. Lester F. Ward, "Psychic Factors of Civilization," in ibid., p. 173.
23. Chugerman, *Lester Ward*, pp. 322–23.
24. Harris E. Starr, *William Graham Sumner* (New York: Henry Holt and Co., 1925), pp. 169–70.
25. William Graham Sumner and Albert G. Keller, *The Science of Society*, vol. 1 (New Haven: Yale University Press, 1927), p. 11.
26. Ibid., p. 20.
27. Starr, *Sumner*, p. 386.
28. William Graham Sumner, *Folkways* (New York: Mentor Books, 1960), p. 520.
29. Ibid., pp. 521–22.
30. Ibid., p. 522.
31. Ibid., p. 523.
32. Ibid., p. 33.
33. Ibid., p. 46.
34. Ibid., pp. 61–62.
35. Loewenberg, *Darwinism*, pp. 14–15.
36. William Graham Sumner, "The Forgotten Man," in *William Graham Sumner: Social Darwinism*, ed. Stow Persons (Englewood Cliffs, N.J.: Prentice-Hall, 1963), p. 119.
37. Ibid., pp. 119–20.
38. Ibid., pp. 116–17.
39. William Graham Sumner, "The Conquest of the United States by Spain," in *William Graham Sumner: The Conquest of the United States by Spain and Other Essays*, ed. Murray Polner (Chicago: Henry Regnery, n.d.), p. 165.
40. Sumner's position here is parallel to that of the eighteenth-century English philosopher Edmund Burke. As Crane Brinton has interpreted Burke's point of view, "Ordinary men if left to the promptings of their desires, their passions, will, according to Burke, always *tend* to run amuck, to cheat, seduce, violate, to make beasts of themselves. Yet in daily life most of them do none of these things, and the criminal exceptions can always be coped with in a sound society. Civil society presents the striking spectacle of potentially, "nat-

urally," bad men behaving like good ones, or at least quiet ones. We must conclude that just the opposite of what Rousseau said is true: Man is saved, not ruined, by his membership in society, by his obedience to convention, tradition, prejudices, law, and the like." Crane Brinton, *The Shaping of Modern Thought* (Englewood Cliffs, N.J.: Prentice-Hall, 1950), p. 177.

41. Edward C. Jandy, *Charles Horton Cooley: His Life and His Social Theory* (New York: Dryden Press, 1942), p. 230.

Chapter Four: The Social-Psychological Perspective

1. Edward Alsworth Ross, *Social Psychology* (New York: Macmillan Co., 1911), p. 5.
2. Quoted by Fay Berger Karpf in her *American Social Psychology* (New York: McGraw-Hill Book Co., 1932), p. 281.
3. Charles Horton Cooley, *Social Organization* (New York: Schocken Books, 1962), p. 3.
4. Ibid., p. 30.
5. Charles Horton Colley, *Human Nature and the Social Order* (New York: Charles Scribner's Sons, 1902), pp. 121–22.
6. Ibid., p. 120.
7. Ibid., pp. 183–84.
8. Charles Horton Cooley, *Sociological Theory and Social Research* (New York: Henry Holt and Co., 1930), p. 307.
9. Quoted by Richard Dewey, "Charles Horton Cooley: Pioneer in Psychosociology," in *An Introduction to the History of Sociology*, ed. Harry Elmer Barnes (Chicago: University of Chicago Press, 1948), chap. 43, p. 844.
10. Ibid.
11. Cooley, *Social Organization*, p. 23.
12. Philip Rieff, in Introduction to Cooley's *Social Organization*, p. xvi.
13. Robert Cooley Angell, "Charles H. Cooley" in *The International Encyclopedia of the Social Sciences*, vol. 3, ed. David L. Sills (New York: Macmillan Co. and Free Press, 1968), p. 381.
14. Edward C. Jandy, *Charles Horton Cooley: His Life and His Social Theory* (New York: Dryden Press, 1942), p. 96.
15. Tamotsu Shibutani, "George Herbert Mead" in *The International Encyclopedia of the Social Sciences*, vol. 10, p. 84.
16. Angell, "Cooley," p. 381.

17. George H. Mead, *Mind, Self and Society,* ed. Charles W. Morris (Chicago: University of Chicago Press, 1934), p. 7.
18. Ibid., p. 7.
19. Ibid., pp. 7–8.
20. Sheldon Stryker, "The Interactional and Situational Approaches," in *Handbook of Marriage and the Family,* ed. Harold T. Christensen (Chicago: Rand McNally & Co., 1964), p. 132.
21. In Andrew J. Reck, Jr., ed., *George Herbert Mead: Selected Writings* (Indianapolis: Bobbs-Merrill Co., 1964), p. 109.
22. Mead, *Mind, Self and Society,* p. 47.
23. Ibid., p. 138.
24. Ibid., p. 135.
25. Ibid., p. 150.
26. Ibid., p. 154.
27. Mead, *Mind, Self and Society,* p. xvi.
28. Reck, *George Herbert Mead,* p. 3.
29. Morris Janowitz, ed., *W. I. Thomas on Social Organization and Social Personality* (Chicago: University of Chicago Press, 1966), p. xxv.
30. W. I. Thomas and Florian Znaniecki, *The Polish Peasant in Europe and America,* vol. 1 (New York: Alfred A. Knopf, 1927), p. 21.
31. Ibid., p. 21.
32. Ibid., p. 22.
33. Ibid., p. 22.
34. Ibid., pp. 32–33.
35. Ibid., p. 36.
36. Ibid., p. 73.
37. Ibid., p. 44.
38. Edmund H. Volkart, ed., *Social Behavior and Personality: Contributions of W. I. Thomas to Theory and Social Research* (New York: Social Science Research Council, 1951), pp. 7–8.
39. Herbert Blumer, *An Appraisal of Thomas and Znaniecki's The Polish Peasant in Europe and America* (New York: Social Science Research Council, 1939), p. 26.
40. Ibid., p. 83.
41. Thomas had compiled cross-cultural materials in his *Source Book for Social Origins* (Boston: Richard G. Badger, 1909).
42. As Volkart has written: "In retrospect, Thomas looms as more than a historical figure of importance. Directly and in-

directly he has influenced the course of social science development, and his basic conceptions can be discerned in much of contemporary theory and research. If today it is difficult to appreciate his originality and authority, it is because so much of his work has been accepted into the body of social science. The study of adjustive behavior in situations, the use of control groups in research, the close interplay of fact and theory, the importance of life history material revealing subjective experience, the mutual interdependence of the social sciences, the recognition that all science is ultimately practical —all this has become common knowledge except to the most provincial." Volkart, *Social Behavior and Personality*, p. 31.

43. Robert M. MacIver, *Social Causation* (New York: Harper & Row, 1964), pp. 296–97.
44. Ibid., pp. 304–5.
45. Ibid., pp. 299–300.
46. George A. Lundberg, *Foundations of Sociology* (New York: David McKay Co., 1964), p. 5.
47. Ibid., p. 5.
48. Ibid., pp. 8–9.
49. Ibid., p. 103.
50. Ibid., p. 106.
51. Ibid., p. 121.
52. Ibid., p. 121.
53. William R. Catton, Jr., *From Animistic to Naturalistic Sociology* (New York: McGraw-Hill Book Co., 1966), p. xii.
54. Ibid., p. 57.
55. Ibid., p. 5.
56. Ibid., p. 114.
57. As Edward Z. Dager has noted, as simple as the assumption of a quest for order may sound, ". . . one cannot escape the conclusion that man's interaction with man is dependent upon the predictable ordering of his physical and social universe." See his "Socialization and Personality Development in the Child," in Christensen, *Handbook*, esp. pp. 745–46. Interactionists such as Dager do not assume that the quest for order is to be accounted for by reference to man's instinctual or biological predispositions. On the contrary, man's attempt to put order in his life is mostly viewed as a defensive reaction necessitated by the absence of instinctive adaptive directions.
58. Stryker, "Interactional and Situational Approaches," p. 135.
59. Ibid., p. 134.

Chapter Five: From Social Action to Social System:
The Parsonian Perspective and Its Critics

1. Reinhard Bendix, *Max Weber: An Intellectual Portrait* (New York: Doubleday Anchor Books, 1960), p. 493.
2. Max Weber, *The Theory of Social and Economic Organization,* trans. A. M. Henderson and Talcott Parsons (New York: Free Press, 1964), p. 88.
3. Ibid., p. 88.
4. Ibid., p. 90.
5. Ibid., p. 90.
6. George Simpson, *Man in Society* (Garden City, N.Y.: Doubleday & Co., 1954), p. 52.
7. Ibid., p. 52.
8. Julien Freund, *The Sociology of Max Weber* (New York: Vintage Books, 1969), pp. 77–78.
9. Weber, *Theory of Social and Economic Organization,* p. 115.
10. Don Martindale, *The Nature and Types of Sociological Theory* (Boston: Houghton Mifflin Co., 1960), p. 388.
11. Weber, *Theory of Social and Economic Organization,* pp. 102–3.
12. Ibid., p. 99.
13. Ibid., p. 328.
14. Max Weber, *The Protestant Ethic and the Spirit of Capitalism* (New York: Charles Scribner's Sons, 1958), p. 51.
15. Ibid., p. 85.
16. Ibid., p. 115.
17. Ibid., p. 183.
18. Freund, *Max Weber,* p. 101.
19. Martindale, *Sociological Theory,* p. 393.
20. Edward C. Devereux, Jr., "Parsons' Sociological Theory," in *The Social Theories of Talcott Parsons,* ed. Max Black (Englewood Cliffs, N.J.: Prentice-Hall, 1961), pp. 20–21.
21. Ibid., p. 39.
22. Talcott Parsons, *The Social System* (New York, Free Press, 1951), p. 152.
23. Talcott Parsons, "The Present Position and Prospects of Systematic Theory in Sociology," in *Essays in Sociological Theory,* ed. Talcott Parsons (New York: Free Press, 1964), chap. 11, p. 217.
24. Talcott Parsons and Edward A. Shils, eds., *Toward a General Theory of Action* (New York: Harper & Row, 1962), p. 58.

25. Ibid., p. 59.
26. Ibid., p. 60.
27. Parsons, "Present Position and Prospects of Systematic Theory in Sociology," p. 212.
28. Ibid., p. 228.
29. Ibid., p. 218.
30. William Morris, ed., *The American Heritage Dictionary of the English Language* (New York: American Heritage Publishing Co. and Houghton Mifflin Co., 1969), p. 1323.
31. Devereux, "Parsons," pp. 26–27.
32. Robert Dubin suggested that self-collectivity is more properly treated as an object category rather than an orientation problem. See his "Parsons' Actor," *American Sociological Review* 25 (1960): 461.
33. Parsons, "Present Position and Prospects of Systematic Theory in Sociology," p. 218.
34. Robert K. Merton, *Social Theory and Social Structure* (New York: Free Press, 1949), p. 45.
35. Ibid., p. 104.
36. Robert K. Merton, *On Theoretical Sociology: Five Essays, Old and New* (New York: Free Press, 1967), p. 45.
37. Wsevolod W. Isajiw, *Causation and Functionalism in Sociology* (New York: Schocken Books, 1968), p. 79.
38. Merton, *Social Theory*, p. 70.
39. Talcott Parsons, "The Prospects of Sociological Theory," in Parsons, *Essays in Sociological Theory*, p. 352.
40. Talcott Parsons, "The Point of View of the Author," in Black, *Social Theories*, p. 336.
41. Lewis A. Coser, *The Functions of Social Conflict* (New York: Free Press, 1956), p. 22.
42. Andrew Hacker, "Sociology and Ideology," in Black, *Social Theories*, p. 291.
43. Devereux, "Parsons," pp. 33–34.
44. Parsons, "Point of View of the Author," pp. 337–38.
45. C. Wright Mills, *The Sociological Imagination* (New York: Oxford University Press, 1959), p. 21.
45. Ibid., p. 9.
47. Ralf Dahrendorf, *Class and Class Conflict in Industrial Society* (Stanford: Stanford University Press, 1959), pp. 161 and 162.
48. There seems to be some conceptual or terminological confusion here as there is nothing to indicate that men resent

legitimate authority. The question is: when do men come to define authority as nonlegitimate?

49. Dahrendorf, *Class*, p. 159.
50. Ibid., p. 164.
51. Coser, *Functions*, esp. pp. 72–80.
52. Pierre L. van den Berghe, "Dialectic and Functionalism," *American Sociological Review* 28 (1963): 704.
53. George C. Homans, "Bringing Men Back In," *American Sociological Review* 29 (1964): 809.
54. Ibid., p. 811.
55. Ibid., p. 818.
56. Isajiw, *Causation*, p. 53.
57. Ibid., pp. 53–54.
58. Ibid., p. 106.
59. Ibid., p. 106.
60. Ibid., p. 106.
61. Ibid., p. 111.
62. Ibid., p. 117.
63. Ibid., p. 117.
64. Ralf Dahrendorf, "Out of Utopia: Toward a Reorientation of Sociological Analysis," *American Journal of Sociology* 64 (1958): 121–22.
65. Parsons, *Social System*, p. 489.
66. Ibid.. p. 486.
67. Ibid., p. 535.

Chapter Six: Exchange Theory and Field Theory: From Social Interaction to Variables in Interaction

1. George C. Homans, *Social Behavior: Its Elementary Forms* (New York: Harcourt, Brace and World, 1961), p. 2.
2. George C. Homans, "Social Behavior as Exchange," *American Journal of Sociology* 62 (1958): 598.
3. Ibid., p. 598.
4. Homans, *Social Behavior*, p. 33.
5. Ibid., p. 34.
6. Ibid., p. 38.
7. Ibid., p. 53.
8. Ibid., p. 54.
9. Ibid., p. 55.
10. Ibid., p. 55.

11. Ibid., p. 75.
12. Homans, "Social Behavior as Exchange," p. 606.
13. Alvin W. Gouldner, "The Norm of Reciprocity," *American Sociological Review* 25 (1960): 169.
14. Ibid., p. 170.
15. Ibid., p. 172.
16. Ibid., p. 172.
17. Ibid., p. 175.
18. Ibid., p. 175.
19. Ibid., p. 174.
20. Peter M. Blau, *Exchange and Power in Social Life* (New York: John Wiley and Sons, 1964), p. 2.
21. Ibid., p. 4.
22. Ibid., p. 5.
23. Peter M. Blau, "Interaction: Social Exchange," in *The International Encyclopedia of the Social Sciences*, vol. 7, ed. David L. Sills (New York: Macmillan Co. and Free Press, 1968), p. 454.
24. Ibid., p. 454.
25. Ibid., p. 454.
26. Blau, *Exchange and Power in Social Life*, p. 28.
27. Ibid., p. 29.
28. Ibid., p. 30.
29. George C. Homans, "Bringing Men Back In," *American Sociological Review* 29 (1964): 818.
30. Blau, *Exchange and Power in Social Life*, p. 123.
31. Ibid., p. 123.
32. Ibid., p. 123.
33. Ibid., pp. 123–24.
34. Peter M. Blau, "A Theory of Social Integration," *American Journal of Sociology* 65 (1960): 555.
35. Blau, *Exchange and Power in Social Life*, p. 43.
36. Ibid., p. 48.
37. Blau, "A Theory of Social Integration," pp. 555–56.
38. A. C. Higgins, "A Review of Homans' *Social Behavior: Its Elementary Forms*," *Social Forces* 40 (1941): 181.
39. Blau, *Exchange and Power in Social Life*, p. 3.
40. Quoted by Fritz Heider in his *The Psychology of Interpersonal Relations* (New York: John Wiley and Sons, 1958), p. 4.
41. Kurt Lewin, "Defining the 'Field at a Given Time,'" in *Field Theory in Social Science: Selected Theoretical Papers*

ed. Dorwin Cartwright (New York: Harper & Row, 1964), chap. 3, p. 45.

42. Ann McGovern, *Aesop's Fables* (New York: Scholastic Book Services, 1963), p. 67.

43. Kurt Lewin, "Field Theory and Learning," in Cartwright, *Field Theory*, p. 60.

44. Ibid., p. 61.

45. Ibid., p. 62.

46. Calvin S. Hall and Gardner Lindzey, *Theories of Personality* (New York: John Wiley and Sons, 1957), p. 210.

47. J. Milton Yinger, *Toward a Field Theory of Behavior* (New York, McGraw-Hill Book Co., 1965), p. 47.

48. Lewin, "Field Theory and Learning," p. 61.

49. Yinger, *Field Theory*, p. 47.

50. Lewin, "Field Theory and Learning," p. 63.

51. Ibid., pp. 63–64.

52. Morton Deutsch, "Field Theory," in *The International Encyclopedia of the Social Sciences*, vol. 5, ed. David L. Sills (New York: Macmillan Co. and Free Press, 1968), p. 406.

53. Kurt Lewin, "Experiments in Social Space," in *Resolving Social Conflicts: Selected Papers on Group Dynamics*, ed. Gertrud Weiss Lewin (New York, Harper & Bros., 1948), p. 72.

54. Ibid., p. 71.

55. Ibid., p. 80.

56. Ibid., p. 82.

57. See Deutsch, "Field Theory," esp. pp. 414–16.

58. Yinger, *Field Theory*, p. 7.

59. Ibid., p. 5.

Chapter Seven: Philosophical Problems and Issues in Contemporary Sociology

1. Peter M. Blau, "Objectives of Sociology," in A *Design for Sociology: Scope, Objectives, and Methods* (Philadelphia: American Academy of Political and Social Science, Monograph 9, April 1969), p. 44.

2. Ibid., p. 52.

3. David Lockwood, "Some Remarks on 'The Social System'," *British Journal of Sociology* 7 (1956): 137.

4. Herbert Blumer, "Society as Symbolic Interaction," in *Symbolic Interaction: A Reader in Social Psychology*, ed. Jerome

G. Manis and Bernard N. Meltzer (Boston: Allyn and Bacon, 1967), pp. 145–46.

5. The investigative practices of financial concerns such as credit agencies have also contributed to the current suspicion regarding the technique of door-to-door interviewing. In this regard, see Myron Brenton, *The Privacy Invaders* (New York: Coward-McCann, 1964).

6. George A. Lundberg, *Foundations of Sociology* (New York: David McKay Co., 1964), pp. 15–16.

7. Gunnar Myrdal, *Objectivity in Social Research* (New York: Pantheon Books, 1969), pp. 61–62.

8. During the recent stir at Yale University over the trial of Black Panthers in New Haven, protesting students developed a series of demands on the University among which was the following: "the abolition of a proposed social-science center on the ground that Yale social scientists treat blacks as experimental research objects." See Robert Brustein, "When the Panther Came to Yale," *New York Times Magazine*, 21 June 1970, p. 55.

9. Myrdal, *Objectivity*, pp. 41–42.

10. William R. Catton, Jr., *From Animistic to Naturalistic Sociology* (New York: McGraw-Hill Book Co., 1966), p. 5.

11. Philip M. Stern, *The Oppenheimer Case: Security on Trial* (New York: Harper & Row, 1969), pp. 81–82.

12. Irving Louis Horowitz, ed., *The Rise and Fall of Project Camelot* (Cambridge, Mass.: MIT Press, 1967), pp. 47–48.

13. Gideon Sjoberg, ed., *Ethics, Politics, and Social Research* (Cambridge, Mass.: Schenkman Publishing Co., 1968), pp. 142–43.

14. Robert Boguslaw, "Ethics and the Social Scientist," in Horowitz, *Camelot*, p. 116.

15. Alvin W. Gouldner, "The Sociologist as Partisan: Sociology and the Welfare State," *The American Sociologist* 3 (May 1968): 106.

16. Ibid., pp. 106–7.

17. Sjoberg, *Ethics*, pp. 157–58.

18. Herbert Blumer, "Threats from Agency-Determined Research: The Case of Camelot," in Horowitz, *Camelot*, p. 169.

19. *Horowitz*, p. 353.

20. Ralph L. Beals, *Politics of Social Research* (Chicago: Aldine Publishing Co., 1969), pp. 3–4.

21. Blumer, in Horowitz, *Camelot*, pp. 163–64.
22. Ibid., p. 168.
23. Boguslaw, "Ethics and the Social Scientist," p. 111.
24. Beals, *Politics*, p. 2.
25. George A. Lundberg, *Can Science Save Us?* (New York: David McKay Co., 1961), p. 33.
26. Boguslaw, "Ethics and the Social Scientist," pp. 117–18.
27. Robert S. Lynd, *Knowledge for What?* (Princeton, N.J.: Princeton University Press, 1939), p. 250.
28. Herbert C. Kelman, *A Time to Speak: On Human Values and Social Research* (San Francisco: Jossey-Bass, 1968), p. 4.
29. Ibid., p. 8–9.
30. Ibid., pp. 9–10.
31. Jean Rostand as quoted by Gordon Rattray Taylor, *The Biological Time Bomb* (New York: Signet Books, 1969), p. 225.
32. Ibid., p. 226.

Bibliography

Charles Horton Cooley

Angell, Robert Cooley. "Charles Horton Cooley." In *The International Encyclopedia of the Social Sciences*, vol. 3, edited by David L. Sills, pp. 378–83. New York: Macmillan Co. and Free Press, 1968.

Cooley, Charles H. *Social Organization*. New York: Schocken Books, 1962.

———. *Human Nature and the Social Order*. New York: Charles Scribner's Sons, 1902.

———. *Social Process*. New York: Charles Scribner's Sons, 1918.

———. *Sociological Theory and Social Research*. New York: Henry Holt and Co., 1930.

Jandy, Edward C. *Charles Horton Cooley: His Life and His Social Theory*. New York: Dryden Press, 1942.

Emile Durkheim

Alpert, Harry. *Emile Durkheim and His Sociology*. New York: Columbia University Press, 1939.

Bierstedt, Robert. *Emile Durkheim*. New York: Dell Publishing Co., 1966.

Durkheim, Emile. *The Elementary Forms of the Religious Life*. New York: Collier Books, 1961.

———. *The Rules of Sociological Method*. New York: Free Press, 1938.

———. *Socialism*. New York: Collier Books, 1962.

———. *Suicide*. Glencoe, Ill.: Free Press, 1961.

233

Gehlke, Charles E. *Emile Durkheim's Contributions to Sociological Theory*. New York: Columbia University Press, 1915.

Johnson, Barclay D. "Durkheim's One Cause of Suicide," *American Sociological Review* 30 (1965): 875–86.

Nisbet, Robert A. *Emile Durkheim*. Englewood Cliffs, N.J.: Prentice-Hall, 1965.

Wolff. Kurt H., ed. *Essays on Sociology & Philosophy by Emile Durkheim et al.* New York: Harper Torchbooks, 1960.

George A. Lundberg

Lundberg, George A. "The Natural Science Trend in Sociology," *American Journal of Sociology* 61 (1955): 191–202.

———. "Science, Scientists, and Values," *Social Forces* 30 (1952): 373–79.

———. "The Thoughtways of Contemporary Sociology," *American Sociological Review* 1 (1936): 703–23.

———. *Can Science Save Us?* New York: David McKay Co., 1961.

———. *Foundations of Sociology*. New York: Macmillan Co., 1939.

Robert M. MacIver

MacIver, Robert M. *Community: A Sociological Study*. London: Macmillan Co., 1917.

———. *Society: A Textbook of Sociology*. New York: Farrar & Rinehart, 1937.

———. *Social Causation*. Boston: Ginn and Co., 1942.

Karl Marx

Bottomore, T. B. "Marxist Sociology." In *The International Encyclopedia of the Social Sciences*, vol. 10, edited by David L. Sills, pp. 46–53. New York: Macmillan Co. and Free Press, 1968.

Caute, David. *Essential Writings of Karl Marx*. New York: Macmillan Co., 1967.

Cornforth, Maurice. *Historical Materialism*. New York: International Publishers, 1954.

Freedman, Robert. *Marxist Social Thought*. New York: Harcourt, Brace and World, 1968.

Lenin, V. I. *State and Revolution*. New York: International Publishers, 1932.

Stalin, Joseph. *Dialectical and Historical Materialism*. New York: International Publishers, 1940.

Wilson, Edmund. *To the Finland Station*. New York: Doubleday Anchor Books, 1953.

Zeitlin, Irving M. *Ideology and the Development of Sociological Theory*. Part 3, *The Marxian Watershed*, pp. 83–108. Englewood Cliffs, N.J.: Prentice-Hall, 1968.

George Herbert Mead

Morris, Charles D., ed. *George H. Mead, Mind, Self, and Society*. Chicago: University of Chicago Press, 1934.

Pfuetze, Paul E. *The Social Self*. New York: Bookman Associates, 1954.

Reck, Andrew J., Jr., ed. *George Herbert Mead: Selected Writings*. Indianapolis: Bobbs-Merrill Co., 1964.

Strauss, Anselm. *George Herbert Mead on Social Psychology*. Chicago: University of Chicago Press, 1964.

Talcott Parsons and Critics

Black, Max. ed. *The Social Theories of Talcott Parsons*. Englewood Cliffs, N.J.: Prentice-Hall, 1961.

Coser, Lewis A. *The Functions of Social Conflict*. New York: Free Press, 1956.

Homans, George C. "Bringing Men Back In," *American Sociological Review* 29 (1964): 809–18.

Isajiw, Wsevolod W. *Causation and Functionalism in Sociology*. New York: Schocken Books, 1968.

Lockwood, David. "Some Remarks on the Social System," *British Journal of Sociology* 12 (1956): 41–51.

Merton, Robert K. *Social Theory and Social Structure*. Glencoe, Ill.: Free Press, 1949.

Parsons, Talcott. "A Short Account of My Intellectual Development," *Alpha Kappa Delta* (Winter 1959): 3–12.

———. *Structure and Process in Modern Societies*. New York: Free Press, 1960.

———. *Essays in Sociological Theory Pure and Applied*. Glencoe. Ill.: Free Press, 1949.

———. *The Social System*. Glencoe, Ill.: Free Press, 1951.

———. *The Structure of Social Action*. Glencoe, Ill.: Free Press, 1949.

———. *Sociological Theory and Modern Society*. New York: Free Press, 1967.

———. *Social Structure and Personality*. New York: Free Press, 1964.

———, and Shils, Edward A., eds. *Toward a General Theory of Action*. New York: Harper Torchbooks, 1951.

———, et al., eds. *Theories of Society*. New York: Free Press, 1961.

Turk, Austin T. "On the Parsonian Approach to Theory Construction," *The Sociological Quarterly* 8 (1967): 37–50.

William G. Sumner

Keller, Albert G., and Davie, M. R., eds. *Selected Essays of William Graham Sumner*. New Haven: Yale University Press, 1924.

Starr, Harris E. *William Graham Sumner*. New York: Henry Holt and Co., 1925.

Sumner, William Graham. *Folkways*. Boston: Ginn and Co., 1907.

———, and Keller, Albert G. *The Science of Society*. New York: Yale University Press, 1927.

W. I. Thomas

Blumer, Herbert. *An Appraisal of Thomas and Znaniecki's The Polish Peasant in Europe and America*. New York: Social Science Research Council, 1939.

Janowitz, Morris, ed. *W. I. Thomas on Social Organization and Social Personality*. Chicago: University of Chicago Press, 1966.

Thomas, William I. *The Unadjusted Girl*. Boston: Little, Brown and Co., 1923.

———. *Source Book for Social Origins*. Chicago: University of Chicago Press, 109.

———, and Znaniecki, Florian. *The Polish Peasant in Europe and America*. Boston: Richard G. Badger, 1918.

Volkart, Edmund H., ed. *Social Behavior and Personality: Contribution of W. I. Thomas to Theory and Social Research*. New York: Social Science Research Council, 1951.

Lester F. Ward

Chugerman, Samuel. *Lester F. Ward, The American Aristotle*. Durham, N.C.: Duke University Press, 1939.

Gerver, Israel. *Lester Frank Ward*. New York: Thomas Y. Crowell Co., 1963.

Ward, Lester F. *Pure Sociology*. New York: Macmillan Co., 1914.

———. *Dynamic Sociology*, 2 vols. New York: D. Appleton and Co., 1911.

———. *Outlines of Sociology*. New York: Macmillan Co., 1899.

———. *Applied Sociology*. Boston: Ginn and Co., 1906.

Max Weber

Bendix, Reinhard. *Max Weber: An Intellectual Portrait*. New York: Doubleday Anchor Books, 1962.

Freund, Julien. *The Sociology of Max Weber*. New York. Vintage Books, 1969.

Parsons, Talcott. *The Structure of Social Action*. Glencoe, Ill.: Free Press, 1949.

Weber, Max. *The Theory of Social and Economic Organization*, edited with an introduction by Talcott Parsons. New York: Free Press, 1947.

———. *The Methodology of the Social Sciences*. Glencoe, Ill.: Free Press, 1949.

Exchange Theory

Blau, Peter M. *Exchange and Power in Social Life*. New York: John Wiley and Sons, 1964.

———. "A Theory of Social Integration," *American Journal of Sociology* 65 (1960): 545–56.

Buckley, Walter. *Sociology and Modern Systems Theory*. Englewood Cliffs, N.J.: Prentice-Hall, 1967.

Gouldner, Alvin W. "The Norm of Reciprocity," *American Sociological Review* 25 (1960): 161–78.

Homans, George C. *Social Behavior: Its Elementary Forms*. New York: Harcourt, Brace and World, 1961.

———. "Social Behavior as Exchange," *American Journal of Sociology* 63 (1961): 597–606.

Field Theory

Deutsch, Morton. "Field Theory." In *The International Encyclopedia of The Social Sciences*, vol. 5, edited by David L. Sills, pp. 405–17. New York: Macmillan Co. and Free Press, 1968.

Hall, Calvin S., and Lindzey, Gardner. "Lewin's Field Theory." *Theories of Personality*. New York: John Wiley and Sons, 1957.

Heider, Fritz. "On Lewin's Methods and Theory," *Journal of Social Issues*, Supplement Series, No. 13, 1959.

Lewin, Kurt. *Field Theory in Social Science*. Edited by Dorwin Cartwright. New York: Harper Torchbooks, 1951.

Lippitt, Ronald. "Kurt Lewin." In *The International Encyclopedia of the Social Sciences*, vol. 9, edited by David L. Sills, pp. 266–71. New York: Macmillan Co. and Free Press, 1968.

Yinger, J. Milton. *Toward a Field Theory of Behavior*. New York: McGraw-Hill Book Co., 1965.

General Reference

Abel, Theodore. "The Present Status of Social Theory," *American Sociological Review* 17 (1952): 156–64.

Aron, Raymond. *Main Currents in Sociological Thought*, vol. 1. New York: Basic Books, 1965.

———. *Main Currents in Sociological Thought*, vol. 2. New York: Basic Books, 1967.

Barnes, Harry Elmer, ed. *An Introduction to the History of Sociology*. Chicago: University of Chicago Press, 1948.

———, and Becker, Howard. *Contemporary Social Theory*. New York: D. Appleton-Century Co., 1940.

Becker, Howard, and Boskoff, Alvin, eds. *Modern Sociological Theory in Continuity and Change*. New York: Holt, Rinehart and Winston, 1957.

Berger, Peter L., and Luckman, Thomas. *The Social Construction of Reality*. New York: Doubleday Anchor Books, 1966.

Bierstedt, Robert, ed. *A Design for Sociology: Scope, Objectives, and Methods*. Philadelphia: American Academy of Political and Social Science, 1969.

Bogardus, Emory S. *The Development of Social Thought*. New York: Longmans, Green and Co., 1955.

Bolton, Charles D. "Is Sociology a Behavioral Science?" *The Pacific Sociological Review* 6 (1963): 3–9.

Brinton, Crane. *The Shaping of Modern Thought*. Englewood Cliffs, N.J.: Prentice-Hall, 1950.

Brown, Roger. *Social Psychology*. New York: Free Press, 1965.

Catton, William R., Jr. *From Animistic to Naturalistic Sociology*. New York: McGraw-Hill Book Co., 1966.

———. "The Functions and Dysfunctions of Ethnocentrism: A Theory," *Social Problems* 8 (1961): 201–11.

Cohen, Percy S. *Modern Social Theory*. New York: Basic Books, 1968.

Coser, Lewis A., and Rosenberg, Bernard, eds. *Sociological Theory: A Book of Readings*. New York: Macmillan Co., 1969.

Dahrendorf, Ralf. *Essays in the Theory of Society*. Stanford: Stanford University Press, 1968.

Edwards, Paul, ed. *The Encyclopedia of Philosophy*. New York: Macmillan Co. and Free Press, 1967.

Encyclopaedia of the Social Sciences. New York: Macmillan Co., 1930.

Faris, Robert E. L., ed. *Handbook of Modern Sociology*. Chicago: Rand McNally & Co., 1964.

Goffman, Erving. *The Presentation of Self in Everyday Life*. New York: Doubleday Anchor Books, 1959.

Gould, Julius, and Kolb, William L. *A Dictionary of the Social Sciences*. New York: Free Press, 1964.

Greenway, John. *The Inevitable Americans*. New York: Alfred A. Knopf, 1964.

Himes, Joseph S. *The Study of Sociology*. Glenview, Ill.: Scott, Foresman and Co., 1968.

Hinkle, Roscoe C., Jr. and Hinkle, Gisela. *The Development of Modern Society: Its Nature and Growth in the United States*. Garden City, N.Y.: Doubleday and Co., 1954.

Hirsch, Walter. *Scientists in American Society*. New York: Random House, 1968.

Hofstadter, Richard. *Social Darwinism in American Thought, 1865–1915*. Philadelphia: University of Pennsylvania Press, 1945.

Karpf, Fay Berger. *American Social Psychology: Its Origins, Development, and European Background*. New York: McGraw-Hill Book Co., 1932.

Kelman, Herbert C. *A Time to Speak: On Human Values and Social Research*. San Francisco: Jossey-Bass, 1968.

Lichtenberger, James P. *The Development of Social Theory*. New York: Century Co., 1923.

Loewenberg, Bert James. *Darwinism: Reaction or Reform*. New York: Rinehart & Co., 1957.

Mannheim, Karl. *Ideology and Utopia*. London: Routledge & Kegan Paul, 1936.

Martindale, Don. *The Nature and Types of Sociological Theory*. New York: Houghton Mifflin Co., 1960.

Marx, Melvin H. *Theories in Contemporary Psychology*. New York: Macmillan Co., 1963.

Merton, Robert K., et al., eds. *Sociology Today*. New York: Basic Books, 1959.

Mihanovich, Clement S., et al. *Glossary of Sociological Terms*. Milwaukee: Bruce Publishing Co., 1957.

Mills, C. Wright. *The Sociological Imagination*. New York: Oxford University Press, 1959.

Mitchell, G. Duncan. *A Dictionary of Sociology*. Chicago: Aldine Publishing Co., 1968.

Nicolaus, Martin. "Remarks at ASA Convention," *American Sociologist* 4 (1969): 154–56.

Ross, Edward Alsworth. *Social Psychology*. New York: Macmillan Co., 1911.

Runes, Dagobert D., ed. *Dictionary of Philosophy*. New York: Philosophical Library, 1960.

Schellenberg, James A. "Divisions of General Sociology," *American Sociological Review* 22 (1957): 660–63.

Seligman, Edwin R. A., ed. *The Encyclopaedia of the Social Sciences*. New York: Macmillan Co., 1933.

Shaw, Marvin E., and Costanzo, Phillip R. *Theories of Social Psychology*. New York: McGraw-Hill Book Co., 1970.

Smelser, Neil J. *Essays in Sociological Explanation*. Englewood Cliffs, N.J.: Prentice-Hall, 1968.

Sorokin, Pitirim A. *Fads and Foibles in Modern Sociology and Related Sciences*. Chicago: Henry Regnery Co., 1956.

———. "Sociology of Yesterday, Today, and Tomorrow," *American Sociological Review* 30 (1965): 875–86.

———. *Contemporary Sociological Theories*. New York: Harper & Bros., 1928.

———. *Sociological Theories of Today*. New York: Harper & Row, 1966.

Stein, Maurice, and Vidich, Arthur. *Sociology on Trial*. Englewood Cliffs, N.J.: Prentice-Hall, 1963.

Timasheff, Nicholas. *Sociological Theory*. New York: Random House, 1967.

Tiryakian, Edward. "Existential Phenomenology and Sociology," *American Sociological Review* 30 (1965): 674–88.

Wallace, Walter L. *Sociological Theory*. Chicago. Aldine Publishing Co., 1969.

White, Leslie A. *The Science of Culture*. New York: Grove Press, 1949.

Wrong, Dennis H. "The Oversocialized Conception of Man," *American Sociological Review* 26 (1961): 183–93.

Zeitlin, Irving M. *Ideology and the Development of Sociological Theory*. Englewood Cliffs, N.J.: Prentice-Hall, 1968.

Goals, Values, Ethics, Control

Beals, Ralph L. *Politics of Social Research*. Chicago: Aldine Publishing Co., 1969.

Blau, Peter M. *Objectives of Sociology. A Design for Sociology: Scope, Objectives, and Methods*. Philadelphia: American Academy of Political and Social Science, Monograph 9, 1969.

Gouldner, Alvin W. "The Sociologist as Partisan: Sociology and the Welfare State," *The American Sociologist* 3 (1968): 103–16.

Horowitz, Irving Louis. *The Rise and Fall of Project Camelot*. Cambridge, Mass.: MIT Press, 1967.

Kelman, Herbert C. *A Time to Speak: On Human Values and Social Research*. San Francisco: Jossey-Bass, 1968.

Lundberg, George A. *Can Science Sace Us?* New York: David McKay Co., 1961.

Lynd, Robert S. *Knowledge for What?* Princeton, N.J.: Princeton University Press, 1939.

Myrdal, Gunnar. *An American Dilemma*, vol. 2, Appendix 2, "A Methodological Note on Facts and Valuations in Social Science," pp. 1035–64. New York: Harper & Row, 1944.

———. *Objectivity in Social Research*. New York: Pantheon Books, 1969.

Sjoberg, Gideon. *Ethics, Politics, and Social Research*. Cambridge, Mass.: Schenkman Publishing Co., 1967.

Stern, Philip M. *The Oppenheimer Case: Security on Trial*. New York: Harper & Row, 1969.

Taylor, Gordon Rattray. *The Biological Time Bomb*. New York: Signet Books, 1968.

Ziman, John. *Public Knowledge: An Essay Concerning the Social*

Dimension of Science. Cambridge, England: Cambridge University Press, 1968.

The Structure of Theory

Allport, Gordon W. *The Nature of Prejudice*. New York: Doubleday and Co., 1958.

Bendix, Reinhard. "Concepts and Generalizations in Contemporary Sociological Studies," *American Sociological Review* 28 (1963): 532–39.

———. "The Image of Man in the Social Sciences: The Basic Assumptions of Present-day Research," *Commentary* 11 (1951): 187–92.

———, and Bennett Berger. "Images of Society and Problems of Concept Formation in Sociology." In *Symposium on Sociological Theory*, edited by L. Gross. New York: Row, Peterson and Co., 1959.

Braithwaite, R. B. *Scientific Explanation*. New York: Harper Torchbooks, 1960.

Brodbeck, May, ed. *Readings in the Philosophy of the Social Sciences*, New York: Macmillan Co., 1968.

Campbell, Norman. *What Is Science?* New York: Dover Publications, 1952.

Chinoy, Ely. *Sociological Perspective: Basic Concepts and Their Application*. New York: Random House, 1954.

Costner, Herbert L., and Leik, Robert K. 1964. "Deductions from 'Axiomatic Theory,'" *American Sociological Review* 29 (1964): 819–35.

Direnzo, Gordon J. *Concepts, Theory, and Explanation in the Behavioral Sciences*. New York: Random House, 1966.

Dubin, Robert. *Theory Building: A Practical Guide to the Construction and Testing of Theoretical Models*. New York: Free Press, 1969.

Einstein, Albert. *Essays on Science*. New York: Philosophical Library, 1934.

Glaser, Barney G., and Strauss, Anselm L. *The Discovery of Grounded Theory: Strategies for Qualitative Research*. Chicago: Aldine Publishing Co., 1967.

Goode, William J., and Hatt, Paul K. *Methods in Social Research*. New York: McGraw-Hill Book Co., 1952.

Gould, Leroy, and Schrag, Clarence. "Theory Construction and

Prediction in Juvenile Delinquency," *Proceedings of the American Statistical Association* (1962): 68–73.

Gross, Llewellyn, ed. *Sociological Theory: Inquiries and Paradigms.* New York: Harper & Row, 1967.

Kuhn, Thomas S. *The Structure of Scientific Revolutions.* Chicago: University of Chicago Press, 1952.

Lazarsfeld, Paul F., and Rosenberg, Morris, eds. *The Language of Social Research.* New York: Free Press, 1955.

MacIver, Robert M. *Social Causation.* New York: Harper Torchbooks, 1942.

McKinney, John C. *Constructive Typology and Social Theory.* New York: Appleton-Century-Crofts, 1966.

Mill, John Stuart. *Philosophy of Scientific Method.* New York: Hafner Publishing Co., 1950.

Myrdal, Gunnar, *An American Dilemma.* New York: McGraw-Hill Book Co., 1964.

Nordberg, Robert B., "Modus Model—Some Problems about the New Jargon, *The American Behavioral Scientist* 9 (1965): 12–14.

Polanyi, Michael. *The Tacit Dimension.* New York: Doubleday Anchor Books, 1966.

Reichenbach, Hans. *The Rise of Scientific Philosophy.* Berkeley and Los Angeles: University of California Press, 1962.

Rudner, Richard S. *Philosophy of Science.* Englewood Cliffs, N.J.: Prentice-Hall, 1966.

Schwirian, Kent P., and Prehn, John. "An Axiomatic Theory of Urbanization," *American Sociological Review* 27 (1962): 812–25.

Stinchcombe, Arthur L. *Constructing Social Theories.* New York: Harcourt, Brace and World, 1968.

Watson, James D. *The Double Helix.* New York: Signet Books, 1969.

Whewell, William. *The Philosophy of the Inductive Sciences.* London: John W. Parker, 1843.

Zetterberg, Hans L. *On Theory and Verification in Sociology.* Totowa, N.J.: Bedminster Press, 1965.

Glossary

Actor: One who performs a social activity whether in or without the presence of others.

ad hoc: That which is done for the particulars at hand and without concern for general relevance or wider application.

Alienation: In Marxian terminology, the condition of one who is involuntarily deprived of a sense of oneness both with himself and his fellows.

Anomie: The condition of a society whose normative structure has been so attenuated that its members are not provided with sufficient information as to what their social obligations should be.

Anthropocentric: The practice of interpreting reality exclusively on the basis of human attitudes, feelings, and values.

a priori: That which is done before or without investigation.

Axiom: In general, a postulate or an accepted principle; in particular, a proposition of demonstrated empirical validity useful as a major premise in a deductive scheme.

Axiomatic Theory: Theory which takes the form of a syllogism; or a method of deductive reasoning consisting of a major premise, a minor premise, and a conclusion.

Behaviorism: That doctrine which holds that scientific knowledge derives from objectively observable activity of organisms and which emphasizes the determining influence of environment in the activity of humans and animals.

244

Bourgeoisie: In general, the capitalistic class, or those who engage in economic activity solely for the purpose of realizing a profit; in particular, and in Marxian terminology, the minority owners of the means of production whose particular interests place them in opposition to the general interests of the majority as represented by the proletariat.

Cathexis: The concentration of emotional energy upon some object or idea.

Charisma: A term used by Max Weber to describe one of seemingly divine, unique, and magnetic personal qualities of leadership.

Concept: A general term used to classify ideas and observable phenomena.

Conceptual Scheme: A set of concepts used to interpret a restricted segment of reality.

Construct: A term used to organize, classify, and interpret common properties among observables.

Constructed Type: A heuristic device, or an abstraction which combines or classifies certain objects and processes in order to aid in the identification and understanding of the relationships among selected variables.

Deduction: Proceeding from the general to the particular.

Definition of the Situation: The manner in which an individual orients himself or decides what to do under perceived conditions.

Dependent Variable: A quantity capable of assuming a set of values depending upon how it is influenced by antecedent or independent qualities.

Determinism: The doctrine that every event, act, or decision is the inevitable result of specific antecedents.

Dialectical Materialism: In the terminology of Karl Marx, the frame of reference based on the view that matter is the fundamental source of change and that all change is the product of conflict between opposing forces which derives from the contradiction inherent in all things.

Emergence: The unpredicted appearance of new characteristics or phenomena in the course of natural evolution.

Empiricism: The doctrine which holds that experience is the only basis of scientific knowledge.

Epistemology: That branch of philosophy which studies the nature and origin of knowledge.

ex post facto: That which is done retroactively.

Exchange Theory: That frame of reference used to study the manner of interaction that occurs between individuals who possess limited but complementary resources and needs.

Field Theory: That frame of reference concerned with identifying the influence of all possible types of variables on individual and social behavior in a given context and at a particular point in time.

Folkways: The least imperative norms operative in a given group.

Forces of Production: In Marxian terminology, the combined effect of people applying the technological means of economic production.

Frame of Reference: The manner in which one observes or focuses attention on a restricted range of objects, conditions, and/or events.

Generalized Other: In the terminology of G. H. Mead, that stage of personality development wherein the individual comes to understand the relationship between particular roles and group performance, and thereby acquires the ability to anticipate appropriate social behavior.

Group: Two or more individuals with an established and continuing relationship.

Heuristic: That which guides or furthers investigation.

Hunch: A strong intuitive impression about something or that something will happen.

Hypothesis: A tentative theory, or a supposition adopted to explain certain events and/or to guide the investigation of others.

Ideal Type: An heuristic device which is a perfect example, that is, a calculated exaggeration, of something that exists.

Idealism: The doctrine that the human mind is a determining and independent source in the acquisition of knowledge and understanding.

Ideology: The body of ideas reflecting the social needs and aspirations of an individual, group, class, or culture.

Independent Variable: A quantity capable of assuming a set of values and which is the influencing agent behind the particular values assumed by another or other quantities.

Induction: Proceeding from the particular to the general.

Instruments of Production: The tools and technology necessary to effect economic production.

Interest Group: In the neo-Marxiam scheme of Ralf Dahrendorf an interest group is a number of individuals whose identical latent authority interests have become manifest; it is an organized conflict group.

Intervening Variable: A quanitity capable of assuming a set of values which may be found to enter into the relationship between other quantities.

Isomorphism: A one-to-one correspondence between two objects.

Lacunae: Blank spots or gaps in knowledge.

Materialism: The doctrine that physical matter is primary and that everything in the universe can be explained in terms of physical laws.

Means of Production: All the ingredients required to effect economic production.

Mode of Production: The economic system, or the manner in which people produce, distribute, and consume the means necessary to sustain physical life.

Model: An exact or scaled replica of something that exists.

Mores: The most imperative norms operative in a given group.

Operationalism: A doctrine based on the notion that something has meaning only to the extent that it can be located in space by means of empirically verifiable operations or procedures.

Paradigm: A universally recognized scientific achievement which for a time provides model problems, theories, and methods for a group of scientists.

Pattern-Variables: A set of dichotomous terms introduced by Talcott Parsons in order to identify the range of criteria used by any actor in deciding how to conduct himself in any situation.

Postulate: An interpretation or statement about something that is assumed without proof in order to develop a line of thought.

Proletariat: In Marxian terminology, the industrial working class.

Proposition: A statement presented for consideration concerning the relationship of variables.

Quasi Group: In the neo-Marxiam scheme of Ralf Dahrendorf a quasi group is a number of individuals who share identical but unrecognized authority interests; it is a potential conflict group.

Reductionism: The doctrine based on the notion that explanations of events and behavior can and should be traced to an originating source.

Reification: The practice of attributing abstractions with material form or physical existence.

Role: The cluster of norms attached to a position within a social group.

Scientific Law: A generalization, that is, a statement describing an order or a pattern in nature based on repeated observations that are invariable under given conditions.

Scientific Theory: A set of logically interrelated propositions of empirical reference.

Social Action: That type of behavior which entails that element of decision-making, or the application of judgment as to what to do in any given set of circumstances and how to do it.

Social Class: In Marxian terminology, a group whose members recognize their commonality as having originated in their occupying or having occupied the same relative position in the economic division of labor.

Social Fact: To Emile Durkheim, all the ways of acting, thinking, and feeling which are "external" to the individual as indicated by their coercive and constraining effects.

Social Interaction: Mutually influencing contact between socialized individuals.

Social Norm: An expected pattern of behavior appropriate in a given situation.

Social Reciprocity: Complementary forms of give-and-take between two or more individuals.

Social System: Two or more individuals who have developed a set of mutual obligations and expectations as part of an on-going and complex relationship.

Social Values: Those shared ideas as to what is important, what should be done, and how to do it.

Status: The position one occupies in a social group.

Stereotype: A preconceived categorical interpretation of an individual, group, object, or event that is fundamentally an unquestioned judgment as opposed to a hypothesis to be tested.

sui generis: That which is unique in and of itself.

Symbolic Interaction: Interpersonal contact between individuals who relate to one another as objects and representations.

Tautology: Redundant reasoning, or the needless interpretation of the same thing in different words.

Teleology: The study of the purpose of natural occurrences.

Theorem: A proposition which can be demonstrated in terms of other more basic propositions.

Variable: A quantity capable of assuming a range of values depending upon its capacity to influence and/or be influenced by other quantities.

Working Hypothesis: A preliminary assumption based on few, uncertain and obscure elements which is used provisionally as a guiding basis in the investigation of something.

Index